Automatic Model Driven Analytical Information Systems

Yvette Teiken

Bibliografische Information der Deutschen Nationalbibliothek

Die Deutsche Nationalbibliothek verzeichnet diese Publikation in der
Deutschen Nationalbibliografie; detaillierte bibliografische Daten sind
im Internet über http://dnb.d-nb.de abrufbar.

ISBN 978-3-8325-3215-4

Logos Verlag Berlin GmbH
Comeniushof, Gubener Str. 47,
10243 Berlin
Tel.: +49 (0)30 42 85 10 90
Fax: +49 (0)30 42 85 10 92
INTERNET: http://www.logos-verlag.de

Danksagung

An dieser Stelle möchte ich den Menschen danken, die mich beim Gelingen dieser Arbeit unterstützt haben.

Zunächst geht mein Dank an meinen Doktorvater Prof. Dr. Andreas Winter für die inhaltlichen Diskussionen und Betreuung recht herzlich bedanken. Weiterhin möchte ich mich bei Prof. Dr. Dr. h.c. Hans-Jürgen Appelrath für die Übernahme des Zweitgutachtens, sowie die Unterstützung, vor allem auf den letzten Metern, bedanken.

Weiterer Dank geht an OFFIS, insbesondere an meinen Bereichsleiter Dr. Wilfried Thoben und meinen Gruppenleiter Martin Rohde, die es mir in interessanten Projekten ermöglicht haben, meine Fähigkeiten und Kompetenzen zu erweitern. Ebenfalls bedanken möchte ich mich für die Gewährung des nötigen Freiraums für die Arbeit an meiner Dissertation.

Meinen Kollegen in der Gruppe Datenmanagement und -analyse möchte ich danken, die mir in den verschiedenen Phasen meiner Dissertation für fachliche Diskussionen und Rat zur Verfügung standen. Dank geht ebenfalls an die Studenten, die im Rahmen von Bachelor-und Diplomarbeiten, oder als wissenschaftliche Hilfskräfte zur Arbeit beigetragen haben. Namentlich sind dies Christian Burmeister, Volker Janz, Torsten Piotraschke und Kai Maschke.

Leslie und Terry danke ich fürs Korrekturlesen.

Und schließlich möchte ich meiner Familie danken. Ich danke meiner Mutter und meinem verstorbenen Vater für die Ermöglichung des Studiums und die Unterstützung in der Promotionszeit. Des Weiteren möchte ich meinem Verlobten Hilmar Bunjes ganz lieb danken, der mich während der ganzen Promotionszeit motiviert und unterstützt hat.

Zusammenfassung

Analytische Informationssysteme dienen der Entscheidungsunterstützung in Organisationen. Sie ermöglichen komplexe Analysen auf integrierten Datenbeständen aus inhaltlich und technisch unterschiedlichen Systemen. Verwendet werden Analytische Informationssysteme von Entscheidern einer Organisation, die auf Basis von Analysen dieser Datenbestände ihre Entscheidungen treffen.

Analytische Informationssysteme sind komplexe Software-Systeme, bei deren Aufbau unterschiedliche technische Aspekte, wie beispielsweise die Anbindung und Transformation von heterogenen Datenquellen oder die Bereitstellung von Analysesichten, beachtet werden müssen. Insbesondere sind am initialen Aufbau und der Weiterentwicklung mehrere Akteure mit unterschiedlichen Sichten auf das Analytische Informationssystem beteiligt. Dies erfordert verschiedene Abstraktionsniveaus. In derzeitigen Lösungen zum Aufbau dieser Systeme werden diese Aspekte nur isoliert betrachtet. Dies führt dazu, dass eine integrierte Konzeption solcher Systeme nur sehr aufwendig möglich ist und damit in der Praxis häufig unterbleibt. Die Isolation der unterschiedlichen Aspekte führt dazu, dass Ergebnisse nicht übertragbar sind und somit der Anteil an schematischer Arbeit in der Realisierung hoch ist. Weiterhin ist die Validierung über verschiedene Aspekte hinweg schwierig. So kann beispielsweise nicht ohne weiteres sicher gestellt werden, dass eine in der Analyseschicht geforderte Kennzahl von den Datenquellen bereitgestellt wird. Zusammengefasst führt dies dazu, dass die Erstellung Analytischer Informationssysteme zeitaufwendig und kostenintensiv ist.

Der zentrale Beitrag dieser Dissertation ist es, durch autoMAIS (Automatische Modellgetriebene Analytische Informationssysteme) den Prozess des initialen Aufbaus und Weiterentwicklung Analytischer Informationssysteme zu vereinfachen. Hierzu werden modellgetriebene Techniken verwendet, um eine integrierte Sicht auf die Erstellung Analytischer Informationssysteme zu ermöglichen. Analytische Informationssysteme werden hierzu in Aspekte auf unterschiedlichen Abstraktionsebenen, wie der Analysebeschreibung oder Datentransformation, zerlegt. Jeder dieser Aspekte wird mit einer eigenen domänenspezifischen Sprache beschrieben. Für die Entwicklung der Sprachen werden entweder bestehende grafische oder textuelle Sprachen adaptiert oder - falls notwendig - komplett neu entwickelt. Zu diesen Sprachen gehören unter anderem Sprachen zur Beschreibung von Kennzahlen, Analyse-Schemata und Integrationsaspekte. Die einzelnen Aspekte bzw. deren Sprachen werden in ein gemeinsames Metamodell integriert, über welches auch die Validierung erfolgen kann. Inhaltlich werden die Aspekte über ein iteratives Prozessmodell integriert.

Die Vorteile eines solchen Vorhabens sind, dass einzelne Aspekte adäquat in einer Notation für die jeweils relevanten Akteure beschrieben werden und trotzdem, aufgrund der integrierten Metamodellierung, globale Aussagen über das zu realisierende System getroffen werden können. Somit kann ebenfalls die Verifikation verbessert werden. AutoMAIS bietet hierzu eine integrierte Sicht auf Design und Konzeption des resultierenden Systems. Weiterhin kann auf Basis des integrierten Metamodells der Großteil des resultierenden Analytischen Informationssystems generiert werden. Ebenfalls verbessert ein solcher Ansatz die Dokumentation von Analytischen Informationssystemen. Hierdurch können Analytische Informationssysteme effizienter und schneller bereitgestellt werden.

Das Vorhaben wurde prototypisch in der im OFFIS entwickelten Analyse-Plattform MUSTANG umgesetzt. In der Evaluation wird dieser Prototyp an zwei Projekten eingesetzt. Hierfür wurden Teile eines bereits realisierten Projekts mit autoMAIS realisiert und mit der traditionellen Umsetzung verglichen. Weiterhin ist autoMAIS in einem realen Projekt eingesetzt worden. Es konnte gezeigt werden, dass mit autoMAIS die Erstellung Analytischer Informationssysteme verbessert werden kann.

Abstract

Analytical Information Systems (AIS) support decision making within organizations. They allow complex analysis based on integrated datasets. These integrated datasets are based on systems with different technologies and content. AIS are complex software systems. During their build-up, many technical aspects, such as connection and data transformation for the involved data sources, or the definition of analysis schemas, have to be considered. During AIS creation projects, different roles with different levels of abstraction are involved. In state-of-the-art approaches, these different aspects are treated individually. Therefore, an integrated creation of these systems is difficult. So, a lot of schematic work is needed to build-up an AIS. Verification of AIS, built-up this way, is also difficult. For instance, it cannot be assured that for a particular computation an analysis exists. For these reasons and others, AIS creation projects are costly.

The key contribution of this thesis is the autoMAIS (Automatic Model-Driven Analytical Information Systems) approach which improves the AIS creation process. Within this approach, techniques of model-driven software development are used to create an integrated view on the AIS creation process. To do so, the AIS creation process is split up into different aspects, such as measures, analysis schema, and data transformation. Each identified aspect is described with a domain-specific language. For language development, already existing textual or graphical languages are used or adapted. In some cases, completely new languages have been developed. The developed languages are integrated into one single meta model which describes the complete resulting AIS. Based on this integrated meta model, transformations can be defined and executed. The transformations enable the generation of the bigger part of an AIS. The creation of the language instances and the generation of the AIS is guided by a process model.

One advantage of the autoMAIS approach is that each aspect is described by an appropriate language which can be understood by the language user. With the integrated meta model, these language instances are connected to each other and, therefore, the complete resulting AIS can be used for making decisions. With this approach, verification is improved and schematic work can be reduced. Additional creation of up-to-date documentation is also possible. These improvements led to a more efficient and faster AIS creation.

The autoMAIS approach has been implemented as a prototype within the MUSTANG analysis platform. In the evaluation, this prototype is used in two different projects. In one project, autoMAIS is used to rebuild parts of an existing AIS to compare the development effort to the traditional approach. After that, autoMAIS is used in a real customer project. It was shown that autoMAIS improves the build of Analytical Information Systems compared to the traditional approaches.

Contents

1 Introduction

Many organizations are using Analytical Informations Systems (AIS) to support management needs [GGD08]. Management supports decision making. This support is done by providing analysis in the form of tables and diagrams in reports or dashboards [KBM10]. The analysis contains up-to-date data about current issues within the organization and consists of measures that express relevant information for decision support. This information is expressed in a compact way so that the relevant information is easy to gather and to understand. Another advantage of an AIS is that information from a variety of sources can be combined with each other. This helps to find correlation which might otherwise not have been considered. An example in the field of health reporting is if immunization has an impact on the disease number. There should be an impact, as shown in medical research, but how will disease numbers change when changing something in immunization politics, such as forcing small children to be immunized for certain diseases. These kinds of questions can be answered by an AIS. Based on these analysis results, managers can make decisions and then see the impact afterward.

Technically, AIS are complex software systems. These systems gather data from different data sources within the organization and unify them. This unification is also called integration. Integrated data is the foundation for all kinds of analysis. It enables the relation of different data from different data sources. The initial build-up of an AIS is a complex task. During the initial build-up, the following analyzing and design steps have to be performed:

- **Define information demand:** Define what information should be provided by the resulting AIS. This can be simple figures or complex computations.

- **Define analysis data model:** Define how fact data can be described and grouped together to enable comfortable analysis for the user of the AIS. Here, the definition of the unification schema takes places, also called an integrated dataset.

- **Analysis of organizational data sources:** To find data that can be used in the resulting AIS, existing data sources within or outside the organization have to be analyzed. This analysis includes the content, format, and accessibility of the data. This kind of data is called fact data. In an AIS, this fact data is extracted and integrated into the so-called data warehouse.

- **Data source transformation:** Fact data has to be transformed into the data format of the integrated dataset. Therefore, for every data source, a transformation has to be designed that translates data into the format of the schema and stores it there.

- **Ensure data quality:** Based on AIS, analysis decisions are made. As a result, it is important to define data quality standards and how to identify invalid data.

To perform these steps, no standardized methodologies exist. The reason is that an AIS is more of a concept than software. When building up an AIS, the technical realization of this system is chosen based on the resulting AIS demands [Ban10]. This demand is, for instance, the update rate of source data. In some AIS, for example, in public health reporting, new data is integrated only once in a few months [TRM10]. Other target domains need more frequent, in some cases nearly real-time, updates on their data [MNSV09]. For example, an electric power company needs real time information and analysis about the current energy spent to determine the network load. In the retail sector, daily updates are necessary. There, the data is used for purchasing or marketing planning. Another example of a demand is the size of data that should be integrated in the AIS. In some special AIS solutions, like hospital market analysis [TRK+10], the integrated dataset consists only of a few megabytes, while in some cases, such as the retail sector, terabytes of data [Sch04] have to be stored in an AIS.

The following questions also have to be considered: What kind of analysis should be performed with the resulting AIS? What amount of data has to be stored and analyzed? Here also, a great variety is possible between standardized reports and complex statistical and mathematical analysis. So it is obvious that there are no technical standards, and technical decisions differ from project to project. In addition, there is not only one technical system, like a database, to choose, but several. In each AIS creation project which software systems to use also has to be determined. These systems have different levels of abstraction and different interfaces. During a project, these systems have to be connected and configured. Therefore, only general guidance, like design patterns and best practices, exist on AIS creation.

AIS creation is more of a concept than a technical system, but the design of an AIS separates it from the sources, so that these are completely different systems. This leads to the following challenges in AIS creation.

1.1 Motivation

Based on the the existing technical diversity, creation of an AIS is a complex task. There are different technical tasks to fulfill, which can be grouped together in the following three challenges.

- **Schematic work:** Because in an AIS different data sources are unified into one integrated dataset with one schema, this integration work has to be repeated in a similar, but not the same, way. Because all data sources have the same target format, the transformations are quite similar but never the same. This kind of work is called schematic work, and can also be found when defining the integrated schema. There, not one big schema, but many small schemas with common elements, have to be defined.

This kind of work can be found in nearly every aspect of AIS creation. Schematic work can be error-prone because it is tedious and, therefore, it leads to more errors. And, as different technical systems with different levels of abstraction exist, there is even more schematic work to be done because of the separation of the technical systems. There, the same information has to be persistent in different systems.

- **Verification:** Based on analysis performed with the resulting AIS, decisions are made. Therefore, it is important to provide correct analysis results. However, finding and fixing verification errors is a challenging task because, in an analysis, all different technical systems have to be passed through to compute the analysis result. In the case of an error, all of the different systems have to be checked to determine which particular system caused the error. This is a time-consuming task because they are specific to the software systems used. Also, technical characteristics of these systems have to be considered.

- **Documentation:** Documentation of an AIS and its creation process represents the current state of the AIS. It describes the defined analysis and realized mathematical procedures. It also shows what kind of data sources are included in the AIS. Documentation consists of a large number of documents that have been created manually. But, as the AIS changes, the documentation usually becomes outdated. Up-to-date documentation is important because the AIS user must be able to trust the analysis results. To do so, some kind of traceability is needed. It is also difficult to make decisions based on non-documented analysis.

These three items have been defined as important challenges during AIS creation, and make the AIS creation process more complex than it is already, because these aspects are not included completely in the principle parts of AIS creation. The principle tasks to enable analysis are integration and unification of data sources. Of course, the analysis results must be correct and they must be documented. Further, the amount of schematic work to do must not be an issue. So, these three aspects are side effects of AIS creation that play an important role, and therefore these challenges are addressed in this thesis.

1.2 Objective of the Work

The goal of this thesis is to improve the AIS creation process by improving the three introduced challenges in the AIS creation process, which are:

- Reduce of schematic work

- Improve verification

- Enable up-to data documentation

These aspects will therefore, improve the AIS creation. The developed approach is called **autoMAIS**, which stands for **AUTOM**atic Analytical Information Systems.

The general concepts and design decisions for an AIS are independent from their type and target domain. During an AIS creation process, the five steps, analysis of organizational data, definition of information demand, data source transformations, data model, and data quality definition must always be performed. But the technical foundations differ from project to project, so during an AIS creation process, many technical decisions have to be made. To improve the AIS creation process, all possible technical decisions should be considered. Because of the huge number of technical alternatives, this is nearly impossible. Therefore, the developed approach should be abstract from the technical aspects and focus instead on conceptual design, because in the conceptual design, all functionality of the resulting AIS is included. The technical aspect deals with transforming these conceptual designs to a technical representation. When focusing on the conceptual design, it is not important to know the technical details. They can be put aside. In this case, the concept modeling documentation can be up-to-date because the general design does not change very much, therefore, verification can be improved because the conceptual design is not hidden in technical aspects. Also, if there is an abstraction from technical representation, automation can be done to reduce schematic work.

The objective of this work is to heighten the level of abstraction in the AIS creation process to have a concrete distinction between conceptual design and technical representation. Still, the conceptual design and the technical aspects have to have relations because it must be assured that the conceptual design is transformed to the needed technical representation. Model-Driven Software Development (MDSD) enables this higher level of abstraction. In MDSD, models are used to describe the application model. And, based on these model instances, concrete software is generated.

In this thesis, the application model is the conceptual design of the AIS. With the help of transformation in MDSD applications, models are transformed to concrete technical systems. These transformations can be adapted to technical circumstances. So a MDSD approach provides dependent technical realization based on a corresponding conceptual model. Only if the technical realization is based on the model, statements made on the models will affect the realization. This is true when using an MDSD approach.

Therefore, the goal of this thesis is to develop an MDSD approach for the AIS creation process that solves some of the named problems. For this, not only the modeling and transformations have to developed, but also other artifacts. The following elements are the contributions of the autoMAIS approach:

- **Languages:** In MDSD, languages are used to describe the domain model of applications. As an AIS can be divided into different aspects with different levels of abstraction, multiple languages will be developed. These languages describe the complete

AIS creation process in an appropriate way for the description of measures, analyses, hierarchies, data sources, data quality, and data transformation.

- **Integrated meta model:** To be able to treat the different languages like an AIS creation model, the different languages are integrated in a common meta model. This meta model describes the complete resulting AIS. This integrated meta model can also be used to enable verification and transformation.

- **Process model:** In this approach, languages, integrated models, and tools will be defined. The AIS creation process is a complex process in which the developed artifacts must be integrated. Therefore, a process model is developed to fulfill this task.

- **Generation:** The goal of an MDSD approach is to generate the schematic part of an application. This thesis will provide transformations to generate a large part of the AIS creation project.

With these developed artifacts it is possible to solve the described problems above, as will be shown in the evaluation of this approach.

1.3 Structure of the Work

This thesis is structured as follows. After this introduction, the foundations to understand this thesis are introduced in chapter 2. This includes foundations in AIS creation and in model-driven software development. In chapter 3, the state of the art in AIS creation is introduced. This chapter includes two aspects. Firstly, two real world AIS creation projects are introduced and analyzed in section 3.1. The analysis results will point out general AIS creation problems in practice. These examples show how schematic work, verification, and documentation influences the AIS creation process. It will also be shown how the missing consideration of these aspects influences an AIS creation project. And therefore, it will show that the aspects covered in this thesis are relevant. Secondly, related work in the field of AIS creation using MDSD is introduced. This provides an overview on current research issues in this field. Here, it will be shown how research deals with current challenges in AIS creation.

The main chapter is chapter 4. Here, the approach itself is introduced. In this chapter, first the requirements and aspects are introduced. This is the foundation for the conceptual modeling of AIS. Then, the different languages for each aspect are defined. Each aspect is introduced in depth to show that the defined language is able to describe the particular aspect appropriately. After this, in section 4.5, the integrated meta model is described. This shows how the different languages can be integrated into each other. With this integrated model, it is possible to make statements on the resulting AIS, including verification. In section 4.6, some remarks on transformations are made. Transformations in this thesis are specific for the chosen technologies, therefore only general guidance is provided in this chapter.

In chapter 5, the evaluation of the approach is presented. For this, some remarks on the prototype implementation are given. In this evaluation, first the application is shown. This shows how the autoMAIS approach can be used to create an AIS. After that, the developed process and the artifacts are compared with a traditional AIS creation project. To do so, the GQM approach is used. This also emphasizes how the autoMAIS approach considers or, better said, improves the three AIS creation challenges of documentation, verification, and schematic work. The thesis ends in chapter 6 with a summary and outlook.

2 Foundations

2.1 Analytical Information Systems

As the focus of this thesis is on AIS creation, this section is used to introduce them. First, the tasks and goals of an AIS and its related terms will be introduced to describe the general usage of an AIS and its role within an organization. After this, technical details on AIS creation are presented. The general AIS architecture is introduced to show the general parts of an AIS. Next, a more detailed view of AIS architecture is presented to provide a more in-depth look at the components and data flow within an AIS. In the following sections, further details about certain parts of an AIS are provided, including technical circumstances and languages for certain aspects.

2.1.1 Tasks and Goals

An Analytical Information System (AIS), as defined by Chamoni and Gluchowski in [CG09], is a term that includes the different technologies: data warehouse, data mining, and Online Analytical Processing (OLAP).

A data warehouse, as defined by Inmon [Inm96], is a subject-oriented, integrated, time-variant, and nonvolatile collection of data to support business decisions and management needs. This means that data in the data warehouse is selected for a specific goal or task. Integrated, in terms of a data warehouse, means that data contains common elements that make it comparable. In most cases, the data stored have a time reference so data can be ordered by time. Nonvolatile data never changes and will never be deleted. This leads to data that can be decades old and, therefore, enables long-term analysis. This also means that data is copied from the sources into the data warehouse to assure that data is not deleted or changed afterwards.

OLAP is an analysis paradigm for AIS. It enables navigation through data without explicit querying. In literature, the terms AIS and data warehouse are used sometimes synonymously. However, in this thesis, data warehouse and AIS have different meanings. Here, a **data warehouse**[1] is the technical integrated dataset.

Data mining is the search of patterns in an integrated dataset with the help of mathematical and statistical procedures.

The goal of an AIS is to support management needs by answering questions about the data in the AIS. The general categories for AIS analysis are reporting, querying, and data mining. In reporting, predefined queries are executed and the results are visualized. Such a predefined query could be, '*How many cases of measles have been recorded this week in Lower Saxony?*'. Depending on the current date, the results would have changed from week to week. This kind of analysis does not provide much flexibility,

---
[1] In this thesis every term in bold print indicates that this term is defined here.

but can be used without much of a learning curve. More flexibility for AIS analysis is provided by querying. For this, there are query languages [EN10] or MDX [SHW+06] that can be used to query the AIS. This approach is more flexible because the queries are not restricted to certain analyses. The question for the measles cases could be also be answered by using queries, but additional parameters and restrictions, like different time periods or ages, can be made. Queries can also have different natures. For example they could be used for comparison, analysis or to search for a correlation. To use this kind of analysis, the query language must be learned. Not all AIS users learn these languages because they are quite complex. One way to perform These types of queries, without knowing the query language, is OLAP which will be introduced in section 2.1.5.

For more complex analysis, a query is not enough; therefore, data mining is used for a question like: *'Is there a correlation between the cases of measles and the immunization rate of children starting school?'*. There is a need for queries combined with statistics. For these kinds of statistics, software like R project [RPr11] or SPSS [IBM11] is used in most cases. Pattern recognition is also achieved by data mining in AIS. AIS analysis results are typically visualized by tables, diagrams, or maps. These visualizations can be combined in applications like dashboards.

In this section, the general goals of AIS and related terms have been introduced. The task of an AIS is to enable decisions support by providing information based on organizational data. The kind of information that the resulting AIS should provide is not always known when creating an AIS. In most cases, more requirements for an AIS are formulated when its powerfulness has been realized by its user. So, when building an AIS, the main challenge is to build up a flexible system that provides the ability to perform all categories of analysis that were introduced here.

2.1.2   Technical AIS Architecture

As introduced in the previous section, AIS are complex software systems which consist of different parts and subsystems. In this section, the basic architecture of an AIS is introduced, which should provide a general understanding of the necessary components and data flow. Based on this architecture, in section 4.2, the needed aspects and languages for describing an AIS with the help of MDSD are derived. In figure 2.1, the base architecture of AIS is shown which is based on [GR09a] and [JW00]. This kind of architecture is also called layer architecture to highlight the physical independence between the data source and the AIS.

The foundation of an AIS consists of different source systems called source layer. These data sources are operational systems or external data. Data from these sources is extracted to be analyzed. In the data staging layer, the data is extracted, transformed, and cleaned. The target of this layer is to convert the heterogeneous systems into one common schema. This layer is also called Extract, Transform, and Load (**ETL**). ETL deals with technical problems like inconsistent data management and incompatible data structures. The data warehouse layer, or more simply, just data warehouse, is one logically-centralized single repository for data. In the application layer, the integrated data is queried to generate reports, statistic analysis, and complex analysis as introduced in the previous section.

2.1.2.1   Reference Architecture

The architecture shown in section 2.1.2 is not detailed enough to build up a general understanding of an AIS architectures, therefore in this section, a more technical view on AIS is given. It is important to understand the parts and aspects of an AIS to understand the overall autoMAIS approach because it deals in depth with all aspects of the AIS architecture and it's data flow.

In figure 2.2, a reference architecture is presented. It is taken from [BG09] and has been translated and modified. The components of the reference architecture are ordered by layer in order to place them relative to the general AIS architecture. Outside, the layers components exist. These are management components that control the AIS and have access to components that are in different layers.

- Source Layer:

  - **Data sources:** These are the sources for the AIS and could be different operational systems or external data. Most often, they are heterogeneous in structure and content. Data sources are not part of the resulting AIS.

- Data Staging: Transforms data from the data source into the unified, integrated schema.

  - **Extraction:** In this component, all techniques that are necessary to extract data from the different sources are grouped. In most cases, according to [LN05], export scripts based on SQL have to be written. The monitored results of data sources are used in this task. For extracting data, [BG09] defines different strategies. The strategy depends on the amount of data and the organizational needs.

    * Periodical: Extractions take place in specific periods. The periods depend on the project's needs.
    * Query-Based: Extraction is started based up on a certain query.
    * Event-Driven: Extraction is based up on a specified event. This event could be a specific database event such as an update. This event could also be an external event, like the change of market-price above a certain value, as [BG09] explains.
    * Directly: Data is extracted immediately after it has been generated.

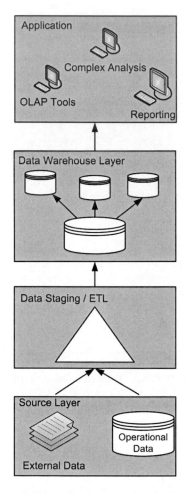

Figure 2.1: General AIS architecture (based on [GR09a] and [JW00])

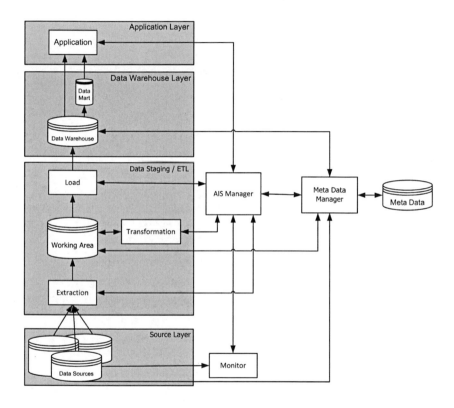

Figure 2.2: Reference architecture for AIS taken from [BG09], translated and modified

- **Working Area**: This component is a temporary database. It contains the data from the source that is not yet integrated into the data warehouse. Transformation is also done in this database because it is more performant.

- **Transformation:** This component executes the transformation from the source to fit the format of the data warehouse. Some general problems handled in this component are different source systems and formats that can lead to conflicts. Another task of this component is **data cleansing**, where attempts are made to eliminate incorrect or poor quality data. The types of problems that occur in this component are particular to the data sources that are integrated.

- **Load:** The transformed data from the working area is loaded into the data warehouse. This intermediate step is needed if data should not be integrated immediately, but, rather, on certain events or at specific times, for example, every night. Otherwise, inconsistent data analysis could occur. The source and target of the transformation is the staging area. This is technically the integration of the data.

- Data Warehouse Layer: The physical integrated data set.

  - **Data Warehouse:** The integrated database that is used for analysis.

  - **Data Mart:** A subset of the data warehouse to enable restricted analysis. The restriction can be done for a particular domain, such as costumer relations.

- Analysis:

  - **Application:** Tools are used for analysis of the integrated database, as introduced in the goal section on page 7.

- Management Components: These components control the overall data and control flow of the AIS.

  - **Monitor:** This component monitors changes in the data sources and reports them to the AIS Manager.

  - **AIS Manager**: This is the central component of the AIS. It manages the initialization, control, monitoring, and analysis of AIS processes. One of its central tasks is data collection, which can be processed by time periods, on change, and on demand.

  - **Meta Data Manager:** In this area, all types of meta data of the AIS are managed, including technical, functional, process, or source meta data.

  - **Meta Data:** A storage of the meta data itself. This meta data describes not only the data warehouse, but all layers of the AIS.

This introduced reference architecture is the foundation for all kinds of AIS. In concrete AIS, not all introduced components may be used, however, the overall architecture will remain. For instance, an additional load component will not always be used because transformed data could be immediately stored in the data warehouse. In other cases, more components will be introduced into an AIS architecture. For example, several physical working areas could exist, but, in general, these components are needed to build up every AIS.

2.1.2.2   Example of a Concrete AIS Architecture

In this section, an example is provided how a concrete AIS architecture can look like and how the different components are used. The provided example describes an AIS that is based on the current version of the MUSTANG platform. **MUSTANG** stands for Multidimensional Statistical Data Analysis Engine and is a data analysis platform developed at OFFIS [TRM10]. It consists of an application for analysis, called CARESS, and some components for definition of computations and data warehouse. AIS that are based on MUSTANG are often used in the target domain of health reporting and population-based cancer registries.

The usage of the components of the AIS reference architecture from figure 2.2 for a particular AIS instance, based on MUSTANG, will be shown here. The described structure was realized for project called CARESS@RKI. In this project, an AIS for a population-based cancer registry was realized. The realized AIS will be described in-depth in section 5.2.3.

For the source layer, databases based on Microsoft SQL Server are used. These data sources are provided by the customer. The data staging layer is realized completely with SQL scripts as there are scripts for extracting data from the sources. The working area is realized by using temporary tables of the database management system. The transformations are realized by writing scalar functions particular for the sources and the data warehouse. The data warehouse was realized as ROLAP. For this, Microsoft SQL Server together with the Microsoft Analysis Services as OLAP server was used. The ROLAP schema was realized as snowflake schema. In general, a snowflake schema is described with SQL scripts which includes DDL and DML. The configuration for the OLAP server is describes with a XMLA file. In the case of the MUSTANG platform this is done differently. Here, C# code is written that describes the multidimensional structure of the data warehouse. The executed C# code generates the SQL scripts for describing the ROLAP schema and the OLAP server configuration. This approach has the advantage that the OLAP server configuration is always valid with the ROLAP schema. For the computation, SQL scripts in conjunction with R packages are used. For the application layer, the analysis software CARESS is used.

The management components do not exists as separate software components. The tasks of these components are done by the administrators of the resulting AIS, because the data within the resulting AIS is not updated often and, therefore, these components are not required.

2.1.2.3   Repository Styles for AIS

In the previous section, a reference architecture for creating AIS was introduced, and it was also noted that this architecture can be adapted to its own needs. In this section, some architectural examples for the data warehouse layer are introduced. These alternatives have been observed by [WA05] and have been found in real world AIS. The different alternatives are visualized in figure 2.3.

To describe an architecture at runtime, [CBB+10] introduced the **component-and-connector style**. Each AIS can be treated as an instance of a **shared-data style**, as also introduced in [CBB+10]. A shared-data style consists of three elements: repository component, data accessor components, and reading and writing connectors. In an AIS, the repository component is the data warehouse. Data accessor components are the data source components because they are used to write data into the repository and the analysis components that reads data from the repository.

The *classical AIS*[2] style is based on the Inmon definition [Inm96]. In this definition, an AIS consists of one central data warehouse and subsets of this data warehouse can be found in the data marts. This style can be seen in figure 2.3.(a)

The *central AIS* does not have data marts, but consists only of the central data warehouse, see 2.3.(b).

A little different in its style is the AIS definition by Kimball [KR02] which is displayed in 2.3.(c). In his definition there is no central database – only data marts exist. The different data marts are integrated via common dimensions. In most cases, this kind of architecture is used when different departments have built up data marts independently within an organization. The integration of data marts will not take place completely, as is the case in a centralized data warehouse, but only parts are integrated. Consequently, only a common analysis can be performed using this style. In this style, neither independent data marts, a central database, nor common dimension elements exist. The data marts exist independently, see 2.3.(d).

In a virtual AIS, the integration is not done physically in a central database, but virtually. This style can be seen in figure 2.3.(e).

These different architectures can be found in real world projects, so it is imaginable that those alternatives need different software components and technical knowledge. In autoMAIS, this is not needed because this technical knowledge persists in the transformations. In this thesis, focus is on the central data warehouse alternative, but, in general, all alternatives are possible because the described variations depend on the organization's needs. For the autoMAIS approach this means that it should be able to deal with all technical alternatives.

---

[2] Technical terms in this thesis are printed in italics. These terms include elements of UML diagrams as well as architectural components and figure elements.

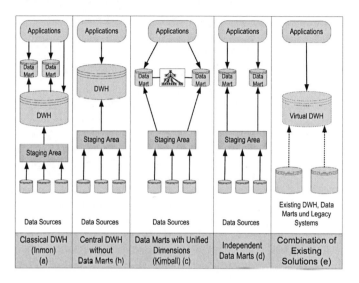

Figure 2.3: AIS architecture alternatives

2.1.3 Developing Methodologies for AIS

There are three different methodologies for developing AIS. An AIS developing methodology describes in which order the different layers and components from the reference architecture shown in figure 2.2 are created. The order depends on the AIS project needs. A good overview of these aspects is given by [LBMS02] and [Gol09]. The general approaches can be distinguished in the following three ways:

- **Data-Driven** This is a bottom-up technique that starts with the analysis of the data sources. Based on the results, the unification schema is defined and the data warehouse is created. From this, the analysis is defined. In this approach, [Gol09] describes three conditions which have to be met. First, detailed knowledge on the sources must be available.

  Second, the source schemas are normalized, which means that the schemas have a well-defined format so that it is easy to gather the business information within the sources.

  Third, the source systems must not be very complex, otherwise it would be difficult to get information about the business value. The resulting analysis cannot fit the user's requirements in the opinion of [Gol09] and [LBMS02], because it deals only with the data that exists within the organization. It does not consider the kind of information that is needed by the management for decision support. Therefore, this approach might be risky but, in the opinion of [Gol09], it can be inexpensive because the costs depend only up on the designer's skills. The original definition of the data warehouse by Inmon was meant to be a data-driven approach, as said by [LBMS02]. [Gol09] also calls the data-driven approach supply-driven. One advantage of this approach is that the data availability is ensured.

- **Goal-Driven** is a top-down approach which integrates the top management of an organization. The resulting AIS is tailored to the management needs and fits to the organization's strategy. Based on their requirements, measures are defined. Based on these measures, the multidimensional model is developed. The challenge in this approach, as said by [Gol09], is transforming the management statements into measures and it cannot be assured that for all measures data exists.

- **User-Driven** is also a top-down approach, but this approach focuses more on the business user than on the top management. The information, as described in [Gol09], is gathered from different users and then transformed into a common multidimensional schema. Challenging in this approach is that users do not always have a clear understanding of the business goals and processes. [Gol09] claims that good moderation skills are needed to apply this approach, but [LBMS02] does not see this problem; they claim that all business users must conform to the organization's strategy. This might not always be true because business users deal with a greater level of details than the top management.

As is done in [GTTY06], these three basic approaches can be mixed based up on the project's needs. In general, it can be said that there are two main approaches: top-down and bottom-up. The AIS creation approach developed in this thesis should be able to cover all three approaches, because otherwise, it could not be used for all kinds of AIS creation projects.

2.1.4   Data Warehouse Layer

Now that the general AIS concepts have been introduced the data warehouse layer can be introduced more deeply. The data warehouse level is a central aspect of every AIS because it represents the integrated data set. Therefore, it will be covered in the autoMAIS and, to do so, here, some aspects are introduced, including the storage format and its use. As autoMAIS wants to use languages for the description of aspects, some existing language for the data warehouse layer is introduced.

2.1.4.1   The Multidimensional Model

In the data warehouse, data is stored in uniform way. A common and widespread way of storage in a data warehouse is the multidimensional schema. The multidimensional model describes how data can be stored in an AIS. When data is stored in the multidimensional schema, data can be analyzed by using OLAP. It allow a flexible analysis of

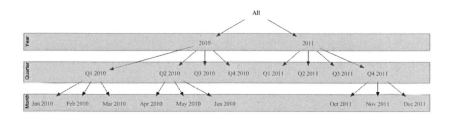

Figure 2.4: Example of a time dimension

data within the warehouse and many analysis tools depend on this schema. Some, like [GR09a], say that the only way to store data in an AIS is using the multidimensional model. For others, like [Zeh03] and [Leh03], the multidimensional model is not essential, but they all agree that this model is important and useful for AIS storage. Therefore, this model will be used in section 4.4.2 to describe analysis, and the autoMAIS approach will use this method of storage. In the following section, this data structure is introduced in detail.

The two main concepts in a multidimensional model are dimensions and cubes. A dimension structures or classifies elements. Examples of dimensions are time, region, and age. The data structure of a dimension is a tree, and the root of the tree represents/includes the whole dimension. It represents all elements in a dimension (e.g., all ages). Going down the tree details the dimension. The most detailed elements can be found at the leaves of the tree. In figure 2.4, a time dimension is displayed. It shows nodes with different levels of details: year, quarter, and month. A path from the root node to one of the leaves is called an aggregation path. In the multidimensional model, this grouping is called a **level**. A level groups elements with the same level of detail together. It is more abstract than the concrete nodes in the tree. In figure 2.4, the levels are shaded gray. The definition of levels and their hierarchy is called a **conceptual model**. The complete dimension tree view with all the elements within the levels is called a **logical model**. The nodes in the tree are called **categories**. An example of a region level hierarchy, and that will be used in this thesis, is federal state → district → county.

A dimension can consist of different sub-trees. These sub-trees are called hierarchies. A time dimension, for example, can have a calendar week hierarchy and a month hierarchy. In figure 2.5, the conceptual model of this hierarchy is shown. The day level in this figure is represented twice. Although this doubling is conceptually correct, it is not logical. The resulting AIS will have only one category for each day. In multidimensional models, there are no categories with the same name. Therefore, three types of hierarchies can be defined, as shown in figure 2.6:

- Linear hierarchy: Every level contains only one parent and one child.

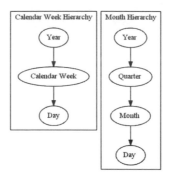

Figure 2.5: An example of a time hierarchy

- Derived hierarchy: Every level has one parent but more than one child.

- Diamond hierarchy: Every level has more than one parent and one child.

The other important element of the multidimensional model is the **cube**. A cube describes the data structure that actually stores the data. The edges of a cube are described by dimensions. In the following examples, the cubes are limited to three dimensions, however, the multidimensional model is not limited to this number. Conceptually, it can have any number of dimensions, but to explain the general concepts, this example uses three dimensions. A cube consists of **cells**. The number of cells is the product of all categories for all cube dimensions. Each cell has a coordinate, and for each dimension, there is one category. Each cell has a value, in most cases a numerical one. This value is called a measure. Each cube can have one or more measures. In figure 2.7, a diagnoses cube and one cell in the cube is also shown. The measure *count diagnoses cases* has the value 46 when the time category is *Q3 2010*, the age category is *40-44*, and the region category is *Oldenburg*. Only values for the most detailed level are stored in this cube. This is called the **data level**. In the diagnoses cube this would show values for quarters, age groups, and counties. The values for the higher cell values (e.g. years) are computed. The kind of computation is defined by the **aggregation function**. Common aggregation functions are sum, count or average. The information described within a cube is also called a **fact**. It describes non-computed values within the resulting AIS. So, the introduced diagnoses cube is one fact within the resulting AIS. This fact has a multidimensional structure and therefore it has attributes that describes the fact in more detail. The facts are directly integrated from the sources.

An AIS consists of a large number of cubes. To enable an integration, as described in section 2.1.2.3, the categories must build an nonempty intersection on different cubes. If there is a nonempty intersection, analysis and integration is done. For a single AIS instance, only one dimension of a kind can exist, otherwise an integration is not possible.

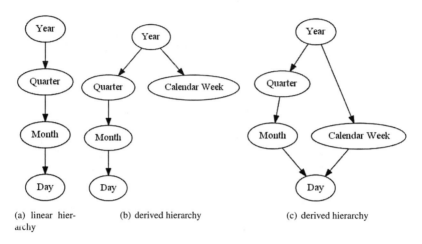

Figure 2.6: Different hierarchy types

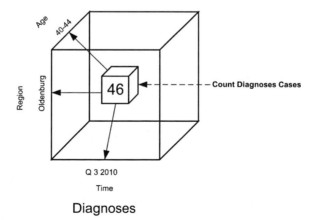

Figure 2.7: Example of a cell value

For example, there can only be one time dimension. This dimension can have different hierarchies that contain all levels and categories. This is called a **global dimension**. A single cube cannot always deliver data on a dimension leaf, for example, if the data level for the time dimension in the diagnoses cubes is *quarters* and the global time dimension defines *days* on its leaves. The reason for this might be that other cubes contain daily data. They still refer to the same dimension, but not to the same data level. However, these cubes still have common elements. Common elements are all categories in and above the *quarter level*. The diagnoses cubes only refer to part of the global dimension, which is called **local dimension**.

The multidimensional schema is a well-established data storage method for AIS. In this thesis, the multidimensional schema will be used to describe the integrated data that is stored in the data warehouse, therefore autoMAIS must be able to deal with all introduced elements of the multidimensional model because they are essential.

2.1.4.2   Technical Alternatives for the Multidimensional Schema

In the previous section, the multidimensional model was introduced. This is only a concept for storage. To apply this concept, it has to be realized and there exists different technical alternatives to do so. In this thesis, there will be a focus on ROLAP, but the other alternatives are also possible with autoMAIS. This will be shown later in this thesis. In this section, the technical realization of these models is introduced. There are three different alternatives available to realize OLAP: ROLAP, MOLAP, and HOLAP. The appropriate technique depends on the requirements of the resulting AIS.

ROLAP stands for relational **OLAP**. In this, alternative cubes and dimensions are stored in a relational database. ROLAP is a wide spread concept because relational databases are an established technology. Most organizations that issue an AIS already have at least one Relational Database Management System (RDBMS). When using RO-LAP, the standard query language, SQL, can be used to access the integrated dataset. When building a ROLAP-based AIS, the multidimensional data model has to be mapped to the relational elements. Wide spread concepts are the **snowflake** and **star schema**. Another schema is the **MADEIRA** schema which has been developed at OFFIS by [Wie00]. These schemas differ in how they map dimension and cubes to relational tables.

MOLAP stands for multidimensional **OLAP**. In this alternative, cubes and dimensions are stored directly as multidimensional entities on the hard drive. This mostly leads to storage in arrays. Dimensions as well as cubes are represented as arrays. A challenge in MOLAP is cube storage, because cubes can have very large cell counts; however, these large numbers of cells do not always have cell values. In most cases, there are more empty cells than filled cells. In a ROLAP representation, this is not a problem because the number of cells is the number of entries in the fact table. This is different than in MOLAP because when the implementation is done by arrays, the full array has to exist. In MOLAP, there are tools that deal with this problem by using indices or statistical methods as described in [GDCZ10]. There are no standardized languages to query MOLAP systems. MOLAP enables fast data access, but the amount of stored data is limited to primary storage. A commercial product that only uses MOLAP is Palo [Jed11], which offers an API for querying.

HOLAP stands for **hybrid OLAP**. It is a combination of ROLAP and MOLAP. In HOLAP, the data is stored relationally as well as directly. Depending on the technical realization, the data can be stored on a hard drive or in memory. In most cases, large and detailed data is stored relationally. Aggregated and frequently queried data is stored in memory. Bigger systems like Microsoft Analysis Services offer this functionality. The challenge when using HOLAP is to deal with both technologies.

In practice, all of these technical alternatives can be found, and it cannot be said which one is the best. For each AIS project, the storage format has to be decided. When using ROLAP, an established technology can be used and an enormous amount of data can be stored. But this would most likely be used in a complex architecture, because in most cases, next to RDBMS, an OLAP Server has to be deployed and maintained. A lightweight alternative is MOLAP, but this alternative can not store as much data as the ROLAP alternative. However, MOLAP is faster in data access because of its data structure.

The storage format is one of the technical details which has to be decided during an AIS creation projects. AutoMAIS can handle all three alternatives because the realization will be put into the transformations. The decision has to be made that technical realization is done by the transformation. In this thesis, the focus is laid on ROLAP.

2.1.4.3 Languages for AIS Description

In this thesis, languages are used to describe the conceptual design of the data warehouse layer because they can be used to abstract from a concrete technical realization. These languages and models have to be developed, but in the field of AIS creation, some languages have already been developed. Some of them could be used in the autoMAIS approach, and some of them are introduced here. As noted in section 2.1.4.1, in this thesis, the data in the data warehouse will be stored using the multidimensional model, therefore languages are introduced here that deal with this schema. All introduced languages are used to define the general concepts of analysis and visualize the multidimensional model. this shows what dimensions are referred to in a concrete analysis. Thus, these languages will be used in autoMAIS to describe the integrated schema of the resulting AIS.

Well-known multidimensional modeling languages are *Multidimensional Entity-Relationship-Model* (MERM) by [SBHD99], *Dimensional Fact Modeling* (DFM) by [GMR98] and *Application Design for Analytical Processing Technologies* (ADAPT) by [Bul96].

To compare the different languages, the same example will be used. It is taken from one of the example projects that will be introduced in section 3.1. The provided example

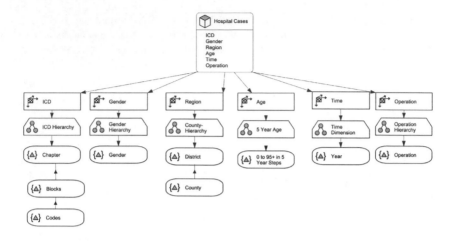

Figure 2.8: Example of the ADAPT notation

is taken from the target domain of health reporting, and the hospital cases describe the kind of diseases that occur in hospitals. The description of hospital cases contains data about the region, the diagnoses (ICD), whether a medical surgery has been performed during the stay (*Operation*), the age of the patient, and how many cases occurred. The different languages now display the hospital cases in their multidimensional model.

ADAPT stands for **A**pplication **D**esign for **A**nalytical **P**rocessing **T**echnologies and was introduced in [Bul96]. It has a large number of elements, with more modeling elements than the other introduced languages, even if the number of elements has been reduced [BF06]. The main elements are hypercubes and dimensions. ADAPT enables the modeling of complex dimensional structures. For example, it provides a special element for hierarchy modeling. Levels can be strictly or loosely connected. Also, categories within a level can be modeled. However, ADAPT is better suited for modeling only a small number of categories; otherwise, the model can get confusing. It is also possible to model attributes. In figure 2.8, an ADAPT instance for hospital cases is provided. An example of what a domain-specific language based on ADAPT can look like, can be seen in [Bur08], which has been formed during this thesis.

MERM stands for **M**ultidimensional **E**ntity-**R**elationship **M**odel and was developed by [SBHD99]. It is based on Entity Relationship Modeling (ER) by [Che76]. The reason ER was selected as a base for MERM was that people who are developing an AIS should be familiar with the modeling of ER diagrams. Their goal was to develop a language that utilizes a minimal set of language elements, to make it easier to learn the language. In figure 2.9, an instance of the MERM language is shown which displays the hospital cases from section 3.1.1.1. As can be seen in this figure, the language only consists

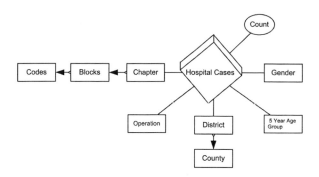

Figure 2.9: MERM instance for the hospital cases from section 3.1.1.1

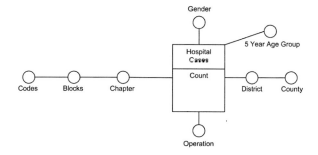

Figure 2.10: Hospital cases with DFM

of four elements. Dimensions and hierarchies are not part of the language; they are implicitly modeled by the aggregation path. Measures and attributes can be modeled and, if needed, ER elements like relationships can be integrated into the language.

DFM stands for **D**imensional **F**act **M**odeling, and is a multidimensional modeling language developed by [GMR98]. Like MERM, it has only three language elements: levels, cubes, and attributes. Measures are modeled within the cube. DFM assumes that all of a dimension's aggregation functions are added once. If not, this has to be modeled by an attribute. As in MERM, dimensions and hierarchies are not modeled implicitly. In figure 2.10, an instance of the MERM language is shown which displays the hospital cases from section 3.1.1.1.

In section 4.4.2, one of these languages will be chosen to describe the integrated data warehouse schema, there also the discussion on the different languages will take place.

In this section, the data warehouse layer was introduced in depth. A common data format for data warehouses is the multidimensional schema, which will be used in autoMAIS to describe the integrated warehouse schema. Instances of this schema have to be developed when describing the data warehouse. How this description could look was also discussed in this section, because languages for describing this schema were introduced. It was also introduced that the multidimensional schema is only a concept. In AIS creation projects, these model instances have to be transformed into a technical representation. For this, ROLAP and other technologies were introduced here. Therefore, transformations have to exist in autoMAIS that transform these models into their technical representation.

2.1.5 Application Layer

In the previous section, the data warehouse layer was introduced in depth. In this section, the application layer and the OLAP paradigm are introduced. The AIS systems that will be created with autoMAIS enable OLAP, therefore it is introduced here. It is also introduced to show how powerful analysis that is based on the multidimensional schemas are. Technically, it can be said that most analysis tools can be used if an multidimensional schema is present.

The term **OLAP** stands for **O**nline **A**nalytical **P**rocessing and is a usage paradigm for data analysis. It describes how users can interact with massive data. When this paradigm is applied to an AIS, the user does not have to write complex queries on the data, but instead, can use operations to navigate through the data. The OLAP paradigm can be used in different kinds of analysis softwares. To enable OLAP, the data in an AIS must be stored within the multidimensional model.

The OLAP paradigm was defined by Codd when presenting an Essbase Software product. In [CCS93], he defined 12 rules which products have to fulfill to be called an OLAP product. In 1995, he defined an extension to these rules. The rules which Codd defined are very specific to products. Based on this fact, [Pen05] introduced the FASMI term to describe key features of OLAP without any product in mind. The reason for building this term was that they worked on an OLAP market report and, therefore, they needed a specific term. FASMI stands for **F**ast **A**nalysis of **S**hared **M**ultidimensional **I**nformation. The properties of an OLAP system based on FASMI are:

- Fast: The response time on average queries should be less than five seconds. Complex queries should not take longer than 20 seconds. The authors claim that a regular user does not want to wait longer than 30 seconds for an analysis result.

- Analysis: An OLAP system should be able to deal with any kind of business logic or statistical analysis. It should also be possible to define new ad hoc analysis without extending the software. The analysis function should be easy to use.

- Shared: Secure multi-user support should be available. The system should, ideally, be able to provide security based on cells (but the authors claim that most systems perform weakly in this aspect).

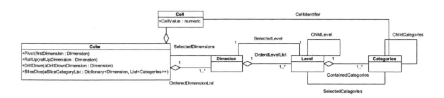

Figure 2.11: OLAP as UML diagram

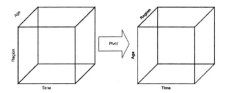

Figure 2.12: Pivot operator

- Multidimensional: Analysis data should be stored multidimensionally.

- Information: In this point, the authors sum up all issues on storage. They do not name certain requirements, but they consider how much data can be handled or stored by the product.

If a software fulfills these rules, it can be called OLAP software. These rules help to understand the OLAP paradigm and it's properties. It describes how data can be accessed and analyzed within an AIS. And this shows that it is useful to build up an AIS in the described way to have these advantages in anylsis application.

To understand the functionality of OLAP, a simplified UML class diagram for this is shown in figure 2.11. In an OLAP representation, not all of the elements of the corresponding cube are displayed, but only a subset. With operators, a user can choose these subsets and perform analysis on these data. An *OlapCube* has *Dimensions*; within an OLAP model only some of them are selected, and the corresponding association is called *SelectedDimension*. Each Dimension has an ordered list of levels which represents the hierarchical structure. Within a level, *Categories* can be selected. These categories are elements within the dimension and identify a cell.

OLAP Operations

To allow for easy analysis, OLAP operations have been defined. These OLAP operations allow easier access to data in the AIS than querying does. A definition of an OLAP operation can be found in a variety of sources, for example, [BG09], [GR09a], or [JVVL10].

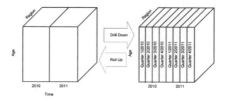

Figure 2.13: Roll Up and Drill Down operators

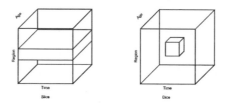

Figure 2.14: Slice and dice operators

The operations are based on the multidimensional model, which was previously introduced. For a better understanding of these operations, a Java-like description of each operator is given. For this example, consider a diagnoses cube that has a time, age, and region dimension.

The first OLAP operator is the Pivot operator, displayed in figure 2.12, which describes the rotation around one of the axes. This operation is used to analyze the data from any perspective. Sometimes changing the perspective helps to get another look at data and identify consequences.

The roll-up and drill-down operations enable navigation through a dimension along the aggregation path. At a roll-up ,the information is compressed. As an example, information on quarters can be compressed to information on years. A drill-down is a complementary operation of a roll-up. These operations are displayed in figure 2.13.

Specific views on data can be issued by using *slice* and *dice*. In this operation, a slice is taken from a cube, for example, a specific year. The other dimensional information stays the same. In a dice, multiple dimensions are selected. This is also called a subcube. These two operations are shown in figure 2.14. In OLAP applications, not only are multiple operators used at a time, but they are also combined. As a result, all information needed can be easily displayed by the combination of these operators.

The introduced operators have only been defined on a single cube. In practice, cubes are combined with each other. This is not part of the OLAP paradigm, nor does there a complete OLAP algebra exist that supports complex combinations. AutoMAIS wants to support this combination of cubes. The way this is done will be shown in the autoMAIS approach itself, in section 4.4.1.

In this section, the application layer was introduced. The goal of this section was to show how analysis on the multidimensional model can be performed. It should illustrate how powerful these kinds of analysis are, and that the effort required to create it is worthwhile. Based on cubes, statistic reports and statistical computations can be made.

For the overall goal of this thesis, it was shown how analysis created with autoMAIS can look, and some basic terms like cell, cell identifiers, and categories were made more concrete.

2.1.6   Data Integration Layer

In this section, the data integration / ETL layer is introduced more deeply and existing languages for describing the ETL process, or parts of it, will be introduced. Also, some basic procedures for data integration are introduced that will be used in this thesis.

2.1.6.1   Existing Languages for the ETL Process

In the field of ETL processes, there are many languages to describe the process or parts of it. In this section, some of these languages are introduced. Based on the existing languages, the concrete syntax of the data transformation language is derived in section 2.1.6.

As ETL is a common task when building an AIS, there are commercial tools that cover the complete ETL process. One example of such a commercial tool is the Microsoft Integration Services [Mic11e] which is part of the Microsoft SQL Server. The services, as described in [GWS07], provide a graphical language to describe single ETL tasks. In these languages, the data flow from the sources to the targets is described. The data flow must be designed by a user. The notes on the graph are tasks that handle the data to be integrated. These tasks have a vast range and include tasks for executing SQL or sending emails. A completely modeled work flow is transformed to a task that can be executed as a part of the SQL Server. Other products have other tools to deal with an ETL task. For example, the Pentaho BI Suite provides Kettle as an ETL tool [CBvD10], and Oracle offers the Data Integration tool. These tools all have more or less the same approach as the described Data Integration Services. These kind of tools cover the complete ETL process.

In the scientific community, there are also different approaches that deal with ETL. The work of Trujillo, which will be introduced more deeply in section 3.2.2, provides two languages for ETL: the Data Mapping Language [LMVT04] and the UML-based language for ETL [TLM03]. Both are graphical languages that are similar to the commercial tools.

A more complex approach is the work of Simitsis. In this PhD, [Sim04] developed an approach for modeling and optimizing ETL processes in AIS. In this work, he covers the conceptual and logical modeling of ETL. The **conceptual modeling** of the ETL describes the mapping and transformation between data sources and targets. The **logical modeling** describes the data flow. The goal of his work was not the modeling, but the optimization of the logical modeling. There, he focuses on algorithms to automate work flow generation [Sim05]. To be able to perform these optimizations, a language for conceptual modeling has been developed [VSG$^+$05]. These languages include graphical and textual language elements. The graphical language is used to describe the mapping. The textual languages describe the transformation. In recent publications, they extended this work to business modeling [WSCD10].

A complete textual modeling approach is introduced in [JD09], which provides a formal method to describe ETL. This strict formalism is needed to cover incremental data integration. An approach for dealing with a large number of ETL tasks based on models is presented in [AN09], but details have not been provided yet.

R$_2$O: A Transformation Language

For data transformation there are different languages like XSLT, R$_2$O, or ATL [JABK08]. The transformation languages that will be used in this thesis is R$_2$O, because it enables the suitable definition of complex transformations on object-oriented structures. More details are be provided in section 4.4.5.

R$_2$O will be used to describe transformations between the data sources and data warehouse schema. The reason for this is that autoMAIS does not want to copy the functionality of existing commercial tools, but rather, to enable a different approach for data integration that includes automation mechanisms. For this approach, which will be introduced in section 4.4.5, the transformation language R$_2$O will be used.

R$_2$O stands for Relational to Ontology. It is a mapping language introduced by [BsCGp04]. The language was developed to map relational databases to ontologies. It is an "extensible, fully declarative language to describe mappings between relational DB schemas and ontologies." [BsCGp04]. The language is based on D2R Map [Biz03]. As the authors of [BsCGp04] claim, this language does not have the ability to express complex transformations and it is not declarative. It is a high-level language which abstracts from an SQL implementation. The focus of the language lies in the definition of conditions and whether a condition applies to the transformation of the elements. The authors of [BsCGp04] provide an EBNF for the syntax of R$_2$O. The statements which are relevant for this thesis, transformed into an Xtext representation, can be found in the appendix. R$_2$O defines different language blocks, one for conditions, one for transformations, and one for mappings. The Xtext definition for these language elements can be found in the appendix from listing A.3 to listing A.5.

In listing 2.1, a concrete instance of the data transformation language is given. It describes how gender attribute instances are transformed for measles cases analysis. In this transformation, the long description for gender (male/female) is transformed to a shorter format (m/f). In lines 1 to 8, this was done for male, and in lines 10 to 18 for female. The defined transformation is a constant (lines 4 and 5). The condition that specifies when this transformation is executed is defined in lines 7 to 9, when the attribute *Gender* in the *measlesCases2010* data source has the value *Male*. The female definition is analog.

```
1    conceptmap-def name 'Men'
2        identified-by  'Men'
3        uri-as
4        constant
5            arg-restriction on-param  'const' has-value string  'm'
6    applies-if
7        equals_str
8          arg-restriction on-param  'string1' has-column  'measlesCases2010.Gender'
9          arg-restriction on-param  'string2' has-value string  'Male'
10   conceptmap-def name  'Woman'
11       identified-by  'Woman'
12       uri-as
13           constant
14               arg-restriction on-param  'const' has-value string  'w'
15       applies-if
16       equals_str
17           arg-restriction on-param  'string1' has-column  'measlesCases2010.Gender
                 '
18           arg-restriction on-param  'string2' has-value string  'Female'
```

Listing 2.1: An example of R2O syntax

2.1.6.2   Relevant Terms in Data Integration

In this section some terms and concepts will be introduced that will be used in the autoMAIS data integration approach.

What is done in the ETL process, generally in the field of databases, is called **information integration**, as introduced by [LN05]. Information integration deals with all aspects of integrating different sources or systems into one integrated, central database. Data integration is not only an issue during AIS creation. Relevant terms for this thesis are schema mapping, correspondence, and schema matching.

If two schemas are supposed to be integrated with each other, the mapping from one schema to the other is called schema mapping. In this process, the elements which belong to each other are identified. When this mapping is done by hand, it is called schema mapping. If this mapping is defined semi-automatically by algorithms, then it is called schema matching. An overview on different schema matching approaches is given in [RB01]. In this thesis, matching will be used during data integration. A languages which used this concepts was developed in [Mas11], which has been formed during this thesis.

Data transformations are important for the AIS creation process. Therefore, concepts for data integration must be part of the autoMAIS approach. To delimit from existing commercial tools matching will be used within the autoMAIS. This will be used to reduce schematic work during data integration.

2.1.7 Conclusion on AIS

In this section the goals and architecture of an AIS was introduced. First, the possibilities of AIS were sketched. A consequence for this thesis is that an AIS has to be built up flexibly to support different kinds of analysis. Also in this section, the technical AIS architecture was introduced. It shows what components have to be covered in the autoMAIS approach. Here also, different methodologies for AIS creation were introduced. To be successful in AIS creation, all of these alternatives should be supported in the autoMAIS approach.

In the data warehouse layer, the multidimensional model and its technical representation were introduced. The multidimensional model is a de facto storage standard for the integrated data warehouse. Therefore, in this thesis, it will be used to describe unification. ROLAP has been selected as the technical representation of this schema. Also in this section, languages for describing the multidimensional model were established. One of these languages will be used to describe analysis.

For the application layer, the OLAP paradigm was introduced to show the capabilities of the multidimensional-based analysis and, therefore, the capabilities of an AIS created with the approach described in this thesis.

For the data integration layer, the transformation language R_2O, that will be used in this thesis, has been introduced. As autoMAIS aims to support a different approach of data integration, relevant terms for this were introduced in the last part of this section.

2.2 Model-Driven Software Development

In this section, the relevant foundations in the field of software engineering are introduced. First, the general Model-Driven Software Development (MDSD) concepts are introduced. An Model-Driven Software Development approach raises the level of abstraction in software development. It helps to model applications in its problem domain and hides the technical realization away from the model as noted in [KT08a]. Thus, MDSD is used in this approach to abstract form the different technical alternatives in AIS creation at design time, but enabling these for the resulting AIS by providing transformations for them.

After introducing the general concepts of MDSD, specific terms in MDSD are established. These special terms include MDA, DSL, meta modeling, and transformations.

After this, some technologies for MDSD development, that will be used in this thesis, are introduced.

2.2.1 General Concepts

Model-Driven Software Development is a specific approach in software development. The general idea is to generate a large part of software based on models and their transformations.

A demand for MDSD raises from organizations or project teams that realize the same kind of software several times and want to save time on repeated work steps. An example of such software is an AIS. A project team realized AIS for different costumers in different target domains. In every project they do technically the same things, definition of ETL-processes, definition of the multidimensional model, and their technical representation. The steps described only differ in their target domain. In such cases, it is useful to apply MDSD, because the repeated work can be reduced nearly to zero by using models and their transformations. Another advantage of an MDSD approach is that knowledge is persisted in transformations and models. This enables non-experts to perform tasks within the AIS creation process that, in a traditional approach, only experts can do.

The following description and arguments have been introduced by [SVE07]. In figure 2.15 the general MDSD approach is sketched. The figure is taken from [SVE07] and has been adopted to AIS systems. Every software, therefore also an AIS, consists of three types of elements: schematic, individual and generic code. This is shown on the left side of the figure. Schematic code is always similar but never identical in different projects because it contains the concepts of the target domain. Schematic work describes that type of work during a project that follows a certain template or principle. When writing code, schematic work is: Copy&Paste with adaption to the particular case. This leads to code clones which are badly maintainable. In an AIS creation project, this is, for example, the definition of elements within the multidimensional structure. In this thesis, the process of doing this by hand is called **schematic work**. **Generic code** is that code that is identical for all kind of applications. This code is usually often reused. An example of generic code in AIS creation is querying the data warehouse to get a list of all hierarchies. **Individual code** is specific for the particular project and cannot be reused. In an AIS project this could be for a specific authentification mechanism.

MDSD takes every type of code and treats it differently, this can be seen at the right side of figure 2.15. Schematic code is generated by transformation. These transformations are based on the AIS application models that are described using domain-specific languages (DSL). A DSL describes those parts of an application that cannot be generalized because they are specific for the target domain. In the case of autoMAIS, this is not one DSL, but several. As individual code is specific to the current application it stays the same. In some cases, this code can be empty. Generic code is transferred into a platform. This platform is the foundation for all applications and encapsulates general

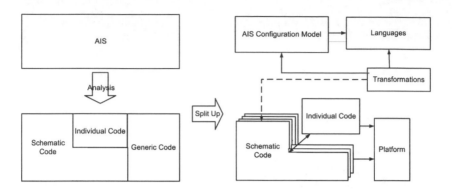

Figure 2.15: Foundations of MDSD adapted for AIS development

functionality. A special aspect of AIS creation is that an AIS is based on a set of standard components and therefore, they are an implicit part of the platform.

With this separation, MDSD provides the following advantages:

- **Separation of concerns:** Technical and target domain development is kept separately. The target domain knowledge is presented with the DSL and the technical knowledge is located in the platform and the transformations.

- **Formalization of development:** The development focus moves from the technical realization to the problem domain.

- **Higher abstraction:** The general level of abstraction during the development process is higher because it has moved from 3GL languages to model languages.

- **Quality:** The usage of MDSD has some advantages in quality, therefore they are introduced one by one.

    - **Persistent expert knowledge:** An expert can conserve his or her technical knowledge into the transformations, languages, and the platform so this knowledge can be kept and referred during AIS creation projects.

    - **Up-to date documentation:** In non-MDSD approaches, software is developed for a particular technical platform. This kind of development has a low level of abstraction. Therefore, the overall concepts of the application have to be documented separately. Under time pressure, this is often left out. In MDSD, the treatment of documentation changes. Also, in MDSD the model instances are the central artifacts of the development process. The models are used to get an overview of the target application and play the role of documentation.

The transformation defines the models semantics. All of this can be used to document the overall application.

– **Code quality:** The quality of the generated code depends on the quality of the transformation that generates code. This quality is always the same, and any found errors can be fixed and are then fixed for all artifacts.

2.2.2   Model Driven Architecture

An important term in the field of MDSD is **Model Driven Architecture (MDA)**. MDA is the implementation of MDSD by the OMG. AutoMAIS does not use MDA, but some of the related work in section 3.2 uses MDA, therefore, it is introduced here.

MDA is an OMG standard [Obj11c] that focuses on certain aspects of MDSD. The models in MDA are based on UML. MDA provides, as introduced by [ZW05], three main models. The Computation Independent Model (**CIM**), Platform-Independent Model (**PIM**), and Platform-Specific Model (**PSM**). The CIM describes the target domain model. It describes all relevant information in the target domain without considering the implementation. The PIM describes the platform-independent model for the resulting software without providing any detail on the specific implementation. The PSM provides the specific technical implementation details that the PIM does not provide. The different models relate to each other. The CIM is transformed to the PIM, and this is transformed to PSM. Based on the PSM, code is generated.

MDSD is a powerful approach for software development because it reduces schematic work and improves documentation. The goal of this thesis is to apply such an approach to the development of AIS, to have these and other benefits.

2.2.3   Domain-Specific Languages

As introduced in section 2.2.1, a **domain-specific language (DSL)** describes the application model. In this thesis, DSLs will be used to describe the different aspects of AIS creation. But, as the term specific indicates, a general language is not used but, rather, a specific language for the target domain [KT08a]. These languages are especially developed for the target domain and therefore they are useless for another target domain. Examples of DSLs that are based on text are SQL and HTML. Examples of graphical DSLs are ER diagrams by [Che76] or UML. Another term for the development of languages in the way of engineering is **Software Language Engineering** (SLE).

A DSL consists of a syntax and a semantic. The syntax can be divided into **concrete syntax** and **abstract syntax**. The concrete syntax describes the symbol and notations the language user works with. The abstract syntax describes the structure and the grammatical rules of the languages. In most cases the abstract syntax is represented by a meta model or a grammar. A meta model describes the internal structure and relation of the models. For the definition of a meta model, a language is needed. Theoretically, a meta model can be defined in every suitable language. In practice, **Meta Object Facility** (**MOF**) [Obj06] is often used for this task. MOF is an OMG standard and is used for meta-meta modeling. As UML is also defined with MOF, concrete instances look the same, which is sometimes confusing.

For the definition of a concrete syntax, two alternatives exists. A concrete syntax can either be graphical or textual. In a **graphical language** or graphical DSL, the language elements are defined graphically. The elements are represented by boxes, shapes, or icons. According to [KP09], it is important to choose symbols and icons that are directly from the problem domain because people can better interact with symbols they are used to than they can with boxes with labels. The relations are visualized by lines. In a **textual language**, all elements are represented by text. The definition of a textual DSL is done with a grammar. According to [Völ11], no general advice can be given on when to choose which alternative.

2.2.4 Transformation Languages

As introduced in section 2.2.1, transformations are used to generate schematic code. Not only code is generated, but other artifacts can also be generated when using an MDSD approach. In MDSD, two kinds of transformations exist: model-to-model, and model-to-text transformations. All transformations are based on the abstract syntax, the meta model. The definition of a transformation is also based on the meta model. Transformations are executed on meta model instances. In a **model-to-model transformation**, the meta model is transformed to another model. In MDA, the PIM to PSM transformation is a model-to-model transformation. These kinds of transformations are used to make models more concrete. In a **model-to-text transformation**, the model is transformed to text. This text can be source code or other text. If this text is compiled and executed, then it is software. In MDSD, sometimes many M2M transformations are executed one after the other, but in the end there is always an M2T transformation that generates the artifacts. These kinds of transformations are used within the autoMAIS approach to generate components, or configuration for components, from the reference architecture in figure 2.2.

The distinction between model-to-model and model-to-text transformations is a little bit artificial because in a model-to-text transformation the generated text, like programming code, also follows a meta model, or better said, a grammar. In some cases, as by report generation, this may not be explicit, but it is always there. But, these different terms have been established in literature, and will therefore be used in this thesis.

2.2.5   Technologies for Applying MDSD

In the previous section, MDSD and their related terms have been introduced shortly. Now in this section, the different technologies for realizing an MDSD approach are introduced. These technologies are used to implement the concepts from chapter 4.

Eclipse Modeling Framework

The **Eclipse Modeling Framework (EMF)** is a modeling framework that is based on Eclipse, which is the core of the Eclipse modeling platform. The model that is used to represent models in EMF is called **Ecore**. Ecore implements essential parts of MOF to enable modeling. With the help of EMF, it is possible to generate Java code to define and query model instances. In this thesis, EMF is used for the definition of meta models of the different languages, and also for the integrated meta model.

Graphical Modeling Framework

The **Graphical Modeling Framework (GMF)** is an Eclipse project for the development of graphical DSL [Gro09]. The developed DSLs are based on EMF, therefore the meta model of the DSL has the same capabilities as an Ecore model. It provides tools for the definition of notation elements and mapping elements to Ecore elements. Based on this, a graphical editor can be generated that enables graphical modeling. In this thesis, GMF is used for the data transformation language.

Domain-Specific Language Tools

The **Domain-Specific Language Tools** is a framework from Microsoft for the definition of graphical DSL within Visual Studio [CJK07]. The meta models are described graphically. The meta model elements can be mapped to notation elements and, based on this, a graphical editor for the language is generated, as shown for instance in [KT08b]. The meta model definition is not as separated as in EMF. The meta model cannot be used on it own, as it can in EMF. The Domain-Specific Language Tools are used for the implementation of the analysis and hierarchy language.

Model-to-Model Transformation Languages

In the surroundings of EMF, two different implementations of model-to-model transformation languages exist: QVT and ATL. They are both supporting Ecore. **ATL** stands for **ATLAS transformation language** and has been developed by ATLAS INRIA and LINA research groups [JABK08]. **QVT** stands for Query/View/Transformation, and provides standard languages for model transformations [Obj11a]. Model-to-model transformations are not needed in this thesis, therefore, these languages will not be used here. However, some of the introduced related work in section 3.2 uses such transformation, and therefore it was introduced here.

Xpand

Xpand is a model-to-text transformation language that uses Ecore [The10]. The generation of artifacts in this thesis is done with Xpand.

Xtext

Xtext is an Eclipse project for the definition of textual DSLs [The11]. The definition of DSL is done with the definition of an EBNF. The concrete syntax of the EBNF is a specific Xtext development. Based on this, EBNF editors and Ecore models are generated. In this thesis, all textual languages are realized using Xtext. These languages are the measure and the data transformation language.

2.3 Conclusion

In this section, the foundation to understand the autoMAIS approach was introduced. This includes a section about AIS, in which the general goals and needs of an AIS were introduced. Also, general AIS components and developing methodologies were introduced. These provide a good overview of which components and methodologies have to be covered when creating a general approach for AIS creation. In the AIS section, the different layers of an AIS were introduced more deeply. Here, some definitions for the autoMAIS approach were made. AutoMAIS will use the multidimensional model to describe the data warehouse. In the prototype implementation, ROLAP will be used to persist the multidimensional model. In the field of data integration some basic terms were introduced. Also, in the AIS section, different languages that will be used in the autoMAIS approach to describe parts of an AIS, were introduced.

Next to AIS, some foundations in the field of software engineering were introduced as well. Here, the software development approach MDSD and related terms were introduced. MDSD is an approach that will be used in this thesis because it addresses the problems of documentation, verification, and schematic work. In this section, terms like languages and transformation, which will all be part of the autoMAIS solution, were described, too.

3 State of the Art of AIS creation

Section 2.1 showed the foundation of AIS based on textbooks and literature. This section gives a different view on AIS creation. First, two real world AIS creation projects are introduced as typical AIS creation projects. This section describes how these kinds of projects are realized. Additionally, general issues of AIS creation are described here. These general issues are mainly management of integration and abstraction. Management of integration means that the different introduced layers of an AIS are not integrated with each other, because they are different kinds of systems. Management of abstraction means that different levels of abstraction must be provided by the resulting AIS. In the second part of this section, in section 3.2, later approaches of AIS creation are reflected. These later approaches are those that deal with MDSD for AIS creation. These approaches differ in what aspects of AIS creation they cover. Based on the example projects and current research, requirements for the autoMAIS approaches are derived.

3.1 Examples of AIS Creation Projects

Two example AIS creation projects, in different target domains, are described in this section. The first one deals with health reporting and the second one, with private equity management. These projects focus on how AIS are created, what the general issues are, and what kinds of problems might occur.

As these two projects are AIS creation projects, all phases for AIS creation projects described in section 2.1.3 have to be performed. These phases cannot be identified clearly because, at times, they are mixed or not named. However, to build an AIS, all phases have to be passed.

3.1.1 AIS for Health Reporting: Gesundheit NRW

Gesundheit NRW is a project that was developed for **LIGA** by OFFIS. LIGA stands for "Landesinstitut für Gesundheit und Arbeit" (Federal Institute for Health and Work) in North Rhine-Westphalia (NRW). The general task of LIGA is to provide health information to the local government and interested citizens. Therefore, it collects health information and analyzes it. It also has to provide data to other organizations, such as the Robert Koch Institute. These reporting policies, as shown in figure 3.1, are taken from [Lan08b] and simplified. This figure has been simplified for this thesis. It visualizes the data flow for health information and shows that reports on certain diseases are reported by hospitals, physicians in private practices, and laboratories to their local public health department. In NRW, there is a public health department for every county. These local health departments collect the reports and perform research and field work. They report their cases and results to LIGA. LIGA collects the data from the different county departments and unifies them. They perform analyses on this data. Based on these analyses,

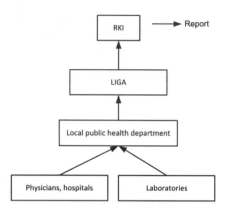

Figure 3.1: Reporting policies at LIGA, taken from [Lan08b] and simplified

they can perform warnings or take other actions. They publish their analysis results, for example, in annual reports such as [Lan08b] or [Lan11]. They also provide information to their stakeholders and, in addition, report their data to the Robert Koch Institute (RKI). The RKI is the German federal institution that, according to [Rob04], is the central federal institution responsible for disease control and prevention. Therefore, it is the central federal reference institution for applied and response-orientated research in public health. They perform some of the LIGA tasks for the whole republic of Germany.

OFFIS has completed many projects with LIGA. The project that is described here is called Gesundheit NRW. In this project, an AIS for public health indicators was built up. These indicators provide general information about public health in NRW and make the different counties of NRW comparable. A subset of these indicators has to be provided by every federal state in Germany, therefore these indicators also enable national comparison.

The size of the resulting project is described in the following. The AIS has 28 dimensions, and the dimension list can be foundin table 3.1. In addition, 38 different data sources have been integrated. Each data source is represented in one analysis, therefore the resulting project consists of 40 multidimensional cubes. For each data source, LIGA had already done the unification for the different local health departments. So, the integration of different source systems was not part of this project. A list of these data sources can be found in table[1] 3.2. Based on these 40 cubes, 466 measures were defined. Examples of these measures for the data source, hospital cases, are crude rates, relative risks, expected cases, and many more. A general measure description will be presented in this section.

---

[1] For readability, these names have been translated into English, as the original definition was in German and can be fond in the appendix.

Dimension Name
ICD
Age
Gender
Time
Region
Nationality
Location of infection
Point of reference
Reporting category
Hospitalization
Epidemiological link
Pathogen-proof
Disease status
Death status
Case definition category
Reference definition (RKI)
Historical time
Type of care
Level of care
Surgery
Type of placement
Period of service
Habitual place of residence
Physician group
Disease
Accommodation provided by carers
Whereabouts prior
Type of performance

Table 3.1: Dimension list for Gesundheit NRW project

Source Name
Population
Infectious diseases
Infectious diseases (Annual Report)
Standard population
Patient-days
Historical infectious diseases
Historical population
Inhabitants (31.12.)
Official median population
Reason of deaths
Deaths
Death by accident at home
Hospital statistics
Rehabilitation cases
Cancer Registry
Assessment of care
Care statistics
Severely disabled
New pensions
Rehabilitation
Active insured
Pension population
Health Insurance Fund members
Cases of inability to work
Days of inability to work
Mental health law type of placement
Mental health law cases in period of service
Mental health law cases by habitual place of residence
Mental health law cases by age and gender
Mental health law cases by physician group
Mental health law cases by disease
Law of Care number of supervised
Law of Care cases by type of placement
Law of Care cases by habitual place of residence
Law of Care cases by age and gender
Number of displays

Table 3.2: Example of data sources

Header Translated	Description	Field Length
Key	Community Identification Number	4
ICD	ICD-10 (blocks)	3
Surgery	1=yes, 2=no	1
Gender	1=m, 2=f	1
Age	0(01), 1-4(05), 5-9(10) ... 90-94(95), 95+(99)	2
Time	year in digits	4
Count	number of cases in this specific group	7

Table 3.3: Data source description of hospital cases, taken from [Lan08a]

For the realization of this project, a user-driven approach was used. The engineering part was realized by using a waterfall process. The technical foundation was the Microsoft SQL Server [Mic11d] which was used for the data warehouse. The technical integration was done with the Integration Services, which are also part of the Microsoft SQL Server. For analyses, the MUSTANG platform was used.

The Gesundheit NRW project was not the first project done in the field of health reporting. Therefore, the target domain of health reporting was not new. The project team was already familiar with the required dimensions and measures. Also, the team was familiar with the target domain of the resulting AIS and the creation of AIS themselves.

3.1.1.1   Example Data

In this section, some example data of hospital cases is introduced. The hospital cases describe what kind of diseases occur in hospitals. In table 3.3, the data source description of the hospital cases is given. The data source is a file with a fixed length for each field. It contains data about the region (*Key*), the diagnoses (*ICD*), whether a medical surgery during the stay has been done (*surgery*), the age of the patient (*Age*), and how many cases occur (*Count*). This data was integrated, which means a cube for this data was created. The multidimensional model for describing this cube, has already been displayed in the foundation section. In the foundations, the different languages for describing the multidimensional models were also introduced. In section 2.1.4.3, the different visualizations for this cube are displayed, so the multidimensional structure can be found there. One task, when creating an AIS, is to create analysis structures in the form of a multidimensional models. This includes the definition of hierarchies and levels.

For the hospital cases from the example, 26 measures are defined, including measures for average, crude rate or simple counts. To give a brief and general overview on health reporting measures, only the most important ones are introduced here. The definitions and descriptions are taken from my work when developing the MUSTANG platform at OFFIS, as well as [Lan05] and [RMK04]. All the described measures and their computations are displayed as single variables. These variables are meant to be single values, but in AIS, these computations have to be applied on cubes. These kinds of computations are not included in the OLAP paradigm, and, additionally, a cube algebra does not exist. How this kind of computation can be applied on cubes will be discussed in section 4.4.1. An understanding of the general measure computation variables is sufficient here, but it has to be kept in mind that the variables, Number of Cases and Population, are cubes with a multidimensional structure in the resulting AIS.

The foundation for all measures are raw number of cases. This is called:

$$NumberOfCases$$

To make geographical regions comparable with each other the **crude rate** is defined. This measure eliminates the amount of population. To enable this computation, population numbers have to be part of the AIS, too.

$$\text{Crude rate} = \frac{\text{Number of Cases}}{\text{Population}} * 100000$$

Not only population, but also differences in the age structures of a region, prohibit the comparability. To deal with this, the **standardized incidence rate** can be defined. In this case, the rate for age is defined. To compute this rate, the **age-specific rate** has to be computed first. The age-specific rate is computed for every age group i. In most cases, these age groups consist of five years each.

$$\text{age-specific rate}_i = \frac{\text{Number of cases in age group i}}{\text{Average population in age group i}}$$

Further, a **standardized population** is needed, when the impact of age distribution should be reduced. A standardized population describes how many persons are normally in the age of 34, for example. This construct is also called study population. A study population can be self-defined or can be provided and must be integrated in the AIS.

$$N_i = \text{Number of persons in a specific age group i in the standardized population}$$

With this last definition, we can now define the age specific rate:

$$\text{Age standardized incidence rate} = \frac{\sum (N_i * \text{age-specific rate}_i)}{\sum N_i}$$

These presented measures are important for health reporting. They are not only used for health indicators, but also for cancer registration [Reg10] and infection epidemiology [Zen08].

3.1.1.2 Schematic Work in the Gesundheit NRW Project

In an AIS project, a lot of schematic work exists. The reason for some parts of the schematic work is the missing integration of different components of the AIS architecture. In this section, some aspects of schematic work in the context of Gesundheit NRW are introduced.

Schematic Work in Multidimensional Schema Creation

The ROLAP realization is based on the MADEIRA schema, which was introduced on page 20. In the MADEIRA representation, as well as in all other ROLAP realizations, the multidimensional model is defined by writing DDL and DML SQL scripts. In listing 3.1, the DML script for the gender dimension is shown. The *gender dimension* is a very simple dimension. It consists of only three categories (male, female, and unknown) and has one data level and one overall level. In the listing, the creation of the categories themselves is defined first (lines 1 to 10).

The identifiers for the categories are defined by hand. Hence, when defining new categories it has to be determined whether this *CATEGORY_ID* was already used. *NAME* and *DESCRIPTION* are values that are displayed during analysis. In the next step, the categories are assigned to a specific level (lines 11 to 20). In the last step, the categories themselves are connected to each other to describe the parent-child relationship (lines 22-25).

Taking only this snippet into account, it is obvious that this kind of work is error-prone. Identifiers can be swapped, which leads to errors during analysis. Category relationships are not correctly described. This way of defining the multidimensional model is not very user-friendly because the overall image is not clear and the level of abstraction is very low.

```
1  --Definition of Categories
2  INSERT INTO CS_DIM_Categories_GENDER ( CATEGORY_ID, DIM_ID, NAME, LATEX_NAME,
       DESCRIPTION, NULLWERT, LU_VALUE ) VALUES (
3  2, 10, 'M', '\male', 'male', 0, 1);
4  INSERT INTO CS_DIM_Categories_GENDER ( CATEGORY_ID, DIM_ID, NAME, LATEX_NAME,
       DESCRIPTION, NULLWERT, LU_VALUE ) VALUES (
5  3, 10, 'W', '\female', 'female', 0, 2);
6  INSERT INTO CS_DIM_Categories_GENDER ( CATEGORY_ID, DIM_ID, NAME, LATEX_NAME,
       DESCRIPTION, NULLWERT, LU_VALUE ) VALUES ( unknown
7  4, 10, 'X', 'unknown', 'unknown', 0, -1);
8  INSERT INTO CS_DIM_Categories_GENDER ( CATEGORY_ID, DIM_ID, NAME, LATEX_NAME,
       DESCRIPTION, NULLWERT, LU_VALUE ) VALUES (
9  5, 10, 'N', 'not recorded', 'not recorded', 0, 0);
10 -- Attach to a specific level (data level)
11 INSERT INTO CS_DIM_NODES ( NODES_ID, DIM_ID, LAYER_REF, KATEGORIE_REF )
12 VALUES ( 1, 10, 1, 1);
13 INSERT INTO CS_DIM_NODES ( NODES_ID, DIM_ID, LAYER_REF, KATEGORIE_REF )
14 VALUES ( 2, 10, 2, 2);
15 INSERT INTO CS_DIM_NODES ( NODES_ID, DIM_ID, LAYER_REF, KATEGORIE_REF )
16 VALUES ( 3, 10, 2, 3);
17 INSERT INTO CS_DIM_NODES ( NODES_ID, DIM_ID, LAYER_REF, KATEGORIE_REF )
18 VALUES ( 4, 10, 2, 4);
```

```
19 INSERT INTO CS_DIM_NODES ( NODES_ID, DIM_ID, LAYER_REF, KATEGORIE_REF )
20 VALUES ( 5, 10, 2, 5);
21 -- Define category based parent child relationship
22 INSERT INTO CS_DIM_NODES_HIERARCHIES ( DIM_ID, FATHER_NODE_ID, SOHN_KNOTEN_ID )
        VALUES ( 10, 1, 2);
23 INSERT INTO CS_DIM_NODES_HIERARCHIES ( DIM_ID, FATHER_NODE_ID, SOHN_KNOTEN_ID )
        VALUES ( 10, 1, 3);
24 INSERT INTO CS_DIM_NODES_HIERARCHIES ( DIM_ID, FATHER_NODE_ID, SOHN_KNOTEN_ID )
        VALUES ( 10, 1, 4);
25 INSERT INTO CS_DIM_NODES_HIERARCHIES ( DIM_ID, FATHER_NODE_ID, SOHN_KNOTEN_ID )
        VALUES ( 10, 1, 5);
```

Listing 3.1: Excerpt from the gender dimension definition in Gesundheit NRW

The needed schematic work can be seen in listing 3.2. This listing is an excerpt of a dimension definition which is called *Operation*. The dimension consists of an overall dimension and a data level which again consists of only two categories. The definition, compared to the gender dimension, also contains a lot of schematic work. The definition of a single category is nearly the same, including unique identifiers. Only the name and *DIM_ID* that refer to the operation dimension are changed. During the level attachment, the IDs have to be changed to the new level identifiers, too. For the definition of the parent-child relationships, the identifiers also have to be changed.

```
1  --Definition of Categories
2  INSERT INTO CS_DIM_KATEGORIEN_NUMERIC ( CATEGORY_ID, DIM_ID, NAME, DESCRIPTION,
       ZEROVALUE, LU_VALUE ) VALUES (
3  3, 61, '0', 'no surgery', 0, 2);
4  INSERT INTO CS_DIM_KATEGORIEN_NUMERIC ( CATEGORY_ID, DIM_ID, NAME, DESCRIPTION,
       ZEROVALUE, LU_VALUE ) VALUES (
5  4, 61, '1', 'surgery', 0, 1);
6  ...
7  -- Attach to a specific level (data level)
8  INSERT INTO CS_DIM_NODES ( NODES_ID, DIM_ID, LAYER_REF, CATEGORY_REF )
9  VALUES ( 2, 61, 2, 2);
10 ...
11 INSERT INTO CS_DIM_NODES ( NODES_ID, DIM_ID, LAYER_REF, CATEGORY_REF )
12 VALUES ( 3, 61, 2, 3);
13 -- Define category based parent child relationship
14 INSERT INTO CS_DIM_NODES_HIERARCHIES ( DIM_ID, FATHER_NODE_ID, SON_CATEGORY_ID )
15 VALUES ( 61, 1, 3);
16 INSERT INTO CS_DIM_NODES_HIERARCHIES ( DIM_ID, FATHER_NODE_ID, SON_CATEGORY_ID )
17 VALUES ( 61, 1, 4);
18 ...
```

Listing 3.2: Excerpt from the operation surgery definition in Gesundheit NRW

It is not surprising that this kind of work is error-prone, because one always has to take care of identifiers. Furthermore, it is not such a complex task that requires much attention. In addition, these kinds of scripts have not only been written for these two dimensions, but also for the other 26 dimensions. These other dimensions are much more complex than the ones shown here. They have more categories and many more levels and, therefore, a lot of parent-child relationships that can result in higher error-proneness.

Data Source Name	Attributes					
Pension cases	gender	age	county	time		
Population	gender	age	county	time	nationality	
Assessment of care	gender	age	county	time	provider	level of care
Cancer cases	gender	age	county	time	ICD	
Severely handicapped	gender	age	county	time		
Rehababilitation cases	gender	age	county	time	ICD	
Pension intake	gender	age	county	time		
Reason of deaths	gender	age	county	time	ICD	
Deaths	gender	age	county	time		

Table 3.4: Data sources and their attributes

Schematic Work During Data Integration

Another field of schematic work in the Gesundheit NRW project is data integration. Most data that has to be integrated is comparable to the data source in figure 3.3, and the target schemas are most comparable to those in figure 2.8. To see that the data sources are very similar, the attributes of the data sources are displayed in table 3.4. It can be seen there that all of the listed data sources share the attributes gender, age, county, and time, so it is obvious that data integration is similar for all of these data sources. It is not the same because the attributes values are, in most cases, differently described. For instance, the attribute representation for the gender female is sometimes f, w, or a number like 1 or 2. So for each data source, this has to be handled with different scripts or statements. This is a challenge during data integration.

3.1.1.3   Verification in the Gesundheit NRW Project

According to [Som10], **verification** is a process to ensure that a software meets its specification. This includes testing.

Finding Integration Errors in the Integrated Dataset

A challenge of this project, as in every other project, is verification. The different aspects of the resulting AIS are not integrated with each other and could, therefore, lead to verification errors. One example of this verification problem and its consequences is introduced here.

To check whether the Gesundheit NRW data was integrated properly, computed results have been provided by LIGA. This verification data contains the results that must be generated by the resulting AIS in the end of the AIS creation process.

In the case of the hospital cases from the example in section 3.1.1.1, this was the number of cases for each county per year. For every single year, a file with the specific data was provided. The integration process was designed and realized with a file from a specific year. After the integration was complete, the verification was performed and all computations were correct. Then the other files were integrated by using the designed process. When performing the verification with the new integrated data, the results were not correct. In some years, the sums differ a little bit with less than 10 cases. Finding the reason for this error required some time. First, a check was made to confirm that the IDs were mapped to the sources correctly. As this was correct, something else during the integration must have gone wrong. The problem was that some files contained the ICD code *AAA*, which is an invalid ICD. Based on the joins performed during the integration, this additional code was not found because it did not exist in the integrated database. It was defined by the orderer that this code should be mapped to the general unknown category. After doing this, the verification was still not correct. So, the error search started again. The mapping of identifiers was still correct, as well as the integrated data, but it was found, that for one particular year, the coding *AAA* was mapped to the *AA* group. Therefore, an exception handling had to be built into the integration process.

To ensure that all computations are correct, all dimensions have to be included in the computation. Next to this, static analysis of dimensions has to be performed.

These errors are quite usual for this type of project, however, finding and solving them is very complicated. The different aspects have to be checked independently, and always right after solving an error. The reason for the *AA* error may have also been a wrongly-mapped identifier, wrongly-mapped level, false model schema, or a false table, and so on. For each verification error, all these steps have to be checked. The low abstraction level makes searching even more difficult because IDs within different SQL scripts are not easy to handle.

3.1.1.4   Documentation in the Gesundheit NRW Project

There is no explicit documentation in the Gesundheit NRW project. During the conceptional design phase, some pencil notes were made but a real conceptual design was not set up. The reason is that this kind of project is similar to those that have been done before, and so work was done as before. The LIGA did not order a manual, so none was produced. Problems occur with this approach when a new developer joins the project. They are not necessarily familiar with the target domain or with the schema, but with general AIS concepts. The documentation is not complete with the pencil notes and, in most cases, these notes are also is outdated. This leads to delay in the realization because the dimensional models are already defined and the integration process must be understood by the developers. Due to the missing documentation, the information needed has to be gathered by writing SQL queries and looking at the integration process to get a complete overview of the project.

So, in general, it can be said, that documentation exists, but in most cases, it is outdated.

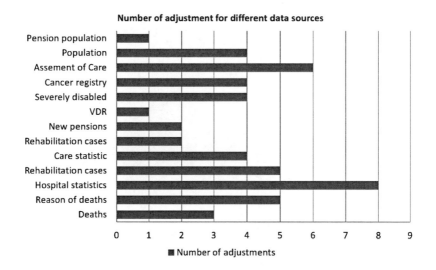

Figure 3.2: Adjustments of data sources in the Gesundheit NRW project

3.1.1.5   Remarks on Iterations in the Engineering Part

As mentioned on page 37, the engineering part of the Gesundheit NRW project was realized as an iterative process. Taking into account the verification issues from section 3.1.1.3, iterations have to be performed, not for the complete project, but to those parts that have been reworked. In figures 3.2 and 3.3, the number of iterations are displayed. These iterations are not iterations in the meaning of agile development, but adjustments based on verification errors. In these cases, the corresponding dimension creation or the integration process had to be reworked.

In figure 3.2, the number of reworkings during the integration process is displayed. Information about the integration adjustments exists for 10 data sources. The average adjustment count is 4.2. Some data sources only had to be touched once, such as pension cases. For these two sources, the originally-claimed waterfall process was performed. The KH Diagnose had a total of nine adjustments. This was due to the AA problem, as introduced on page 45.

In figure 3.3, the adjustments of dimension are displayed. There are not many adjustments, except for in the *Age* and *ICD* dimensions. The reason for this is the rich

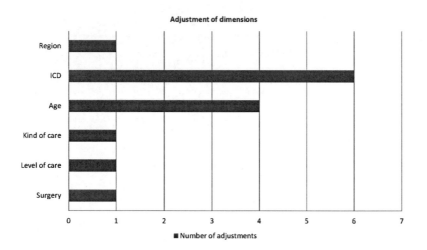

Figure 3.3: Adjustments of dimension

experience with the target domain within the project team. The dimensions needed already existed before the project started. There are two reasons for this. First, a part of the dimensions existed from earlier LIGA projects. Second, the dimensions, as well as the measures, are based on a law for the most part but, nevertheless, for these very well-known subjects, adjustments were also needed.

In summary, even if a project is meant to be a waterfall project, iterations are needed due to verification. In this case, the schematic work increases. In the case of chaining data sources, not only the integration script itself has to be changed, but also, in most cases, the multidimensional schema or the analysis configuration.

3.1.2   AIS for Private Equity: PEIS

The **PEIS** project was an InfoAnalytics project for a family office, with OFFIS as the sub-contractor. A family office is a private company which manages investments and trusts for a single wealthy family. To minimize risks, the investments are widely spread. This includes investments in foreign currency and different assets. In most cases, and also in the PEIS project, a family office has different trustors. These trustors can be private persons or companies. Before the PEIS project, the family office that was a purchaser of the PEIS project, managed its investments in a single Excel spreadsheet. Over time, the number of assets and trustors grew, making the Excel spreadsheet more and more complex and difficult to manage. Another problem with the Excel solution was that only one person was able to edit the spreadsheet at a time. To solve this problem, the PEIS project was issued by the family office. As the family office was used to working with Excel, the resulting AIS was meant to be accessed using this tool also. Another requirement was to develop a lightweight solution. Therefore, Palo for Excel [Jed11] was used for the PEIS project. Palo is a MOLAP server, and the provided front-end was an Excel plug-in.

The resulting PEIS AIS consists of 22 cubes and the project consists of 18 dimensions. These cubes contain cubes for taxes, commitments, repayment, and exchange rates from the European Central Bank (ECB). Based on these cubes, 100 measures were defined. Examples for these measures are book value, balance, current market value, DPI, Net Cash Flow, Total Value to Paid In, and Internal Rate of Return. For example **DPI** stands for Distributions to Paid and describes the relative return from called capital. It is a performance indicator for enhancement in values.

3.1.2.1   Schematic Work in the PEIS Project

In the PEIS project, lots of schematic work was also done. In this section, a few aspects of this schematic work are introduced.

```
1  SummaryAttributeVO summaryDPI = new SummaryAttributeVO() {
2      IsAdhoc = false,
3      ShortName = "DPI",
```

```
 4      LongName = "DPI",
 5      Description = "DPI",
 6      IsVisible = true,
 7      IsBase = false,
 8      DerivedDetails = new MeasureDerivedVO()
 9  };
10  summaryDPI.DerivedDetails.Function = new StatisticalFunctionVO() {
11      ShortName = "DPI",
12      LongName = "DPI",
13      Library = String.Empty,
14      Instructions = new List<String>(),
15      Operands = new List<String>()
16  };
17  summaryDPI.DerivedDetails.Function.Operands.Add("abrufe");
18  summaryDPI.DerivedDetails.Function.Operands.Add("rueckfluesse");
19
20  summaryDPI.DerivedDetails.Function.Instructions.Add("rueckfluesse/abrufe");
```

Listing 3.3: Excerpt from measure definition for DPI in PEIS NRW

The configuration for the 100 measures was done by C# code. This included code for addressing the base cube, the reference of the global dimensions and the specific needed hierarchies, other measures that are included in the computation, and, of course, the computation itself. An excerpt of the definition of DPI is given in listing 3.3.

The definition of the computation itself is only a small part of the measure definition. The configuration of the corresponding part is the larger part. To see the schematic work, the complete definition of the two measures is given in the appendix. The complete DPI definition is quite long and can therefore be found in the appendix in listing A.1. Here also, the complete definition of netto DPI in listing A.2 can be found.

Another example of schematic work was the definition of dimensions. As the OLAP server used is not a relational database, the dimension definition was not done by SQL scripts, but by C# code. Therefore, for each category, level, and hierarchy, code had to be written. A big task was the time dimension, which required categories for each day of the year over the last ten years.

3.1.2.2 Verification in the PEIS Project

A big effort in the PEIS project was the verification of the computed measures. The Palo server offers mechanisms for measure computation, but in the case of PEIS, this was not performant enough at runtime. Therefore, a custom mechanism for measure computation was built. These computations enable precalculation of measures and OLAP operations. As a result, some computations in the PEIS project are not computed at runtime. These precalculations are performed during nights or on demand. An example of this is net asset value (NAV). If the investments are made in foreign currency, the NAV values of each investment changes because the exchange rate of the ECB changes every day. To ensure that the current NAV values are always up-to-date, these precalculations are made.

However, these precalculations lead to temporary verification errors in the development process because the aspects of measure and the multidimensional schema definitions are not integrated. The missing integration, errors or incorrect results occur during measure computation at runtime in the resulting AIS. The elements of the multidimensional model, such as level, categories, and dimensions are only referred by strings in the measure definition. So, if the multidimensional model changes, for instance, if a level is renamed but not in the corresponding measure definition, this leads to errors at runtime. In addition, if you consider that there are more than 100 measures, it is easy to forget one reference. Still, these kinds of errors can be found more easily than errors in computation results. More often than renaming, reassignment is done in the multidimensional model. This can mean that the corresponding categories for a level change quite often. This change can lead to false calculations because the performed aggregations are different. To avoid this error, the rearranged levels in every computation definition have to be checked or the change can lead to wrong results. This was only a problem at development time, however, not at runtime.

In the PEIS project, the team tried to look at these changes carefully, but they still occurred often. Therefore, unit tests based on legacy data to validate the computations were written. These tests were written manually, as obviously only a few cases could be tested automatically. As a result, a lot of manual verifications had to be made.

3.1.2.3 Documentation in the PEIS Project

One special thing in the PEIS project was that the project team was not as familiar with the target domain as it was with health reporting. Therefore, more effort on documentation was made than in Gesundheit NRW. The conceptual design for the project consists, more or less, of the multidimensional models. This modeling was done in a Microsoft Word document and the aggregation structures were visualized by item lists. The huge role of the Word document decreased during the project because more focus was laid on the realization part later. However, attempts were made to keep the document up-to-date. The updating of the documentation is a general problem in software development.

There is also a user manual that describes the main user functions of the software.

3.1.2.4 Remarks on Iterations in the Engineering Part

For the realization of this project, a user-driven approach was used. The engineering part was realized by using Agile Project Management (APM) [OW07] based on Scrum. The iterations in this project lasted between four and six weeks, depending on the customer's time planning. At the end of each iteration, a review meeting with the customer was held. In this review meeting, the requirements for the next iteration were gathered based on the user's feedback. As a goal for each iteration, as is usual in Scrum projects, a working prototype was presented. These working prototypes consist of several cubes with a fully-defined multidimensional model and some measure definitions.

For defining the multidimensional model, many more iterations were needed than in the Gesundheit NRW project. One reason for this was that this project was developed for a new customer, in contrast to the Gesundheit NRW project, which was issued by a well-known customer. The difference here is that the needs of a new customer are not known in the beginning and therefore the needs of organizational and data structures have to be identified. With a known customer, this knowledge exists and therefore less iterations are needed. Another reason for this was that there are no standard classifications like ICD in public health projects, so the dimensions must be completely self-defined. An example of such a self-defined hierarchy is assets. This hierarchy consists of many different shares and funds, as well as their classifications. For this hierarchy, many changes have been made. The reason was not only due to the new target domain, but also that the orderer himself had new ideas during the review meetings. The structure was such that implicit knowledge in the orderer's head had to be externalized. To support this process, the iterations were necessary and helpful.

3.1.3   Conclusion on Example Projects: Main Challenges for AIS Creation

In the example projects presented, it was observed that there are two main challenges during AIS creation: management of integration and management of abstraction.

One main challenge of AIS creation is management of abstraction. In an analysis or report, aggregated and calculated data is needed. At the sources, single data records are important. These results may even be a single boolean answer as was described in the immunization rate example from section 2.1. To perform this kind of aggregation, it is obvious that elements within the different layers must be alike to enable this kind of aggregation, therefore, schematic work within these aspects is also needed here.

Another main challenge in AIS creation is the missing integration of aspects, which means that the systems in the different AIS layers are not integrated with each other. The reason for this is that the resulting AIS is not limited to one technical system. In practice, many different technical systems are involved to fit the needs of the resulting AIS. The introduced projects have been realized by the same project team and, even in this case, different technical solutions have been chosen based on the AIS's needs. Another reason for the missing integration is, considering the original definition of an AIS, that integration was not part of the definition. The goal was to not disturb the operational systems with analysis tasks. This missing integration leads to challenges in AIS creation. In the resulting AIS, the different layers have to be connected with each other because otherwise, the analysis could not be performed. The same information must therefore be created in the different technical systems and then mapped to common elements. The mapping between common elements must be done manually, which leads to schematic work. This kind of mapping is error-prone and impedes verification. Another verification challenge is that statements about the whole resulting AIS cannot

| | Name of Example Project | |
	Gesundheit NRW	**PEIS**
Analysis	• Definition of measures	• Definition of measures
		• Mapping of measures to cubes
DWH layer	• Definition of dimension, hierarchies, and categories	• Definition of dimension, hierarchies, and categories
	• Definition of cubes	• Definition of cubes
Data staging	• Source analysis	• Mapping from source sheet to cubes
	• Data cleaning	
	• Mapping sources to cubes	

Table 3.5: Schematic work in the example projects for AIS creation

be made. To document the whole resulting AIS, all the different technical systems have to be documented. This is a lot of work and therefore will not often be done, and, as a result, outdated documentation often exists.

This results in the three points that sould be addressed in this thesis: schematic work, verification and documentation. In the example projects, the three points have been observed.

3.1.3.1 Schematic Work

With the description of the example projects, it was shown that a lot of schematic work is done in the AIS creation process. One reason for this is the missing integration of aspects. As seen in section 3.1.2.1, this was the main reason for schematic work in the PEIS project. As seen in section 3.1.1.2, schematic work can be found in every AIS creation project. It is quite obvious that schematic work has to be done, as the goal of an AIS is to make different data sources comparable to each other, and, to enable this, similarities are necessary. These similarities can rapidly lead to schematic work. An unpleasant aspect of schematic work is the increase in errors, as shown in the example projects. The reason for this might be that less attention is paid to this work as it consists of many repetitions.

A list of the overall performed schematic work is displayed in table 3.5. Each row represents one layer of the AIS architecture from section 2.1.2. In the columns, the schematic task for a particular project and layer is displayed. The definition of measures was not explained in this text. To mention it briefly, it consists of a program code for the computation itself and database entries to address the computation for certain cubes. It can be seen that the schematic tasks are more or less the same on an abstract level, but the realization differs from project to project. For the multidimensional model definition in Gesundheit NRW, SQL statements were used. In PEIS a Palo API was used. In both projects, all elements and relations of the multidimensional model, as they were introduced in section 2.1.4.1, had to be defined.

For a better overview on schematic work, the different schematic tasks are displayed in table 3.5. So, one goal for this thesis must be to reduce or better support the common schematic tasks to improve integration of the different aspects and management of abstraction.

3.1.3.2   Verification

Validation errors occur often because of the missing integration of the components of the reference architecture. This leads to schematic work and, therefore, to schematic errors. These errors are not easy to handle, as described in this section. A main reason for this is the low level of abstraction. So, another goal of this thesis must be to improve the verification. As verification is a general problem, a focus should be to improve verification at the integration of the different aspects, because this could solve the described problems on an higher level of abstraction.

3.1.3.3   Documentation

Outdated documentation was an issue in the different projects. This leads to problems, at least when new members join the project. Therefore, documentation should be addressed in this thesis.

To conclude this section, in order to have a practical impact on real AIS creation projects, autoMAIS has the following requirements:

- Reducing schematic work for common schematic tasks.

- Improving verification.

- Providing documentation and keeping documentation up-to-date.

These aspects can be addressed when using an MDSD-based approach because MDSD addresses some of the requirements.

3.2 Related Work

In section 2.1, the state of AIS creation was presented. This state of the art was based on literature, such as standard books and textbooks on AIS. Furthermore, experience from real world projects were presented as well in section 3.1. At least in the example projects, it was made clear that challenges still exist in the field of AIS creation. In this section, new approaches on AIS creation are introduced. This related work focuses on MDSD and SLE approaches. MDSD is an approach for software creation based on models, and SLE deals with the development of software languages. These concepts and their advantages have been introduced in section 2.2.1 and section 2.2.3. These approaches will help to solve the problems in AIS creation projects as introduced in section 3.1. The relevant related work has been identified by scanning the relevant conferences like ACM International Conference on Conceptual Modeling (ER), ACM International Workshop On Data Warehousing and OLAP (DOLAP), Multikonferenz Wirtschaftsinformatik (MKWI), International Conference on Data Warehousing and Knowledge Discovery (DaWAK), and the Very Large Data Bases (VLDB) Conference. The reason for this is that the autoMAIS approach uses the concept of MDSD and SLE, and therefore, these conferences were scanned for similar approaches. Other approaches or techniques, like multidimensional modeling or schema matching, are introduced in the specific chapters of the concept in chapter 4, or have been introduced in the foundations in chapter 2.

To be able to classify the different approaches, criteria are needed. These criteria are based on challenges in AIS creation which have been identified in the previous section. One issue is the reduction of schematic work. One way to eliminate schematic work is to use MDSD to generate software, because MDSD uses models to describe domain concepts and, based on this, artifacts are generated, which reduces schematic work. Therefore, the use of software generation is one aspect for comparison. Another source for schematic work is the missing integration of the different aspects of AIS creation, because then tasks have to be repeated. Also, the use of a process model is important because the different approaches have to fit into the existing project surroundings. Because AIS creation is a complex task, the developed models must fit into the already-existing AIS creation process. Therefore, it is important to know if there exists a particular process model for the approach.

Another issue in AIS creation processes is outdated or missing documentation. When using the MDSD approach, models are the central artifacts of the software development process and can serve as documentation, according to [VS06]. Therefore, the models and their properties are part of the comparison. These properties include facts about whether languages are used, or have been developed, in the specific approach. As introduced in section 2, there exist languages within the field of AIS creation, so the use of these languages is also considered. In most cases, using an existing, well-engineered language is better than developing a new one because these languages are already established, have been tested, and are in use. Also, the kind of language (textual or graphical) is considered. Textual languages are faster to write, but more complex to understand, while graphical notations are good for representing relations and provide a clear, graphical notation.

Another consideration is what aspects of AIS creation are covered by the particular approach. The first criteria is which layer from the AIS base architecture, as shown in figure 2.1, is covered by the specific approach. Based on this base architecture, these aspects are the source layer and, therefore, the data sources, data transformation within the data staging layer, the analysis schema, and the analysis. Given the different approaches and applications, analysis as a single aspect would not be enough here. As seen in the case study in section 3.1, computations are an important aspect in real world projects, and therefore, should be part of the classification. Also, data quality is an important aspect in AIS creation, so it, too, is part of the classification. The complete classification matrix can be found in figure 3.6.

3.2.1   Common Warehouse Metamodel Specification

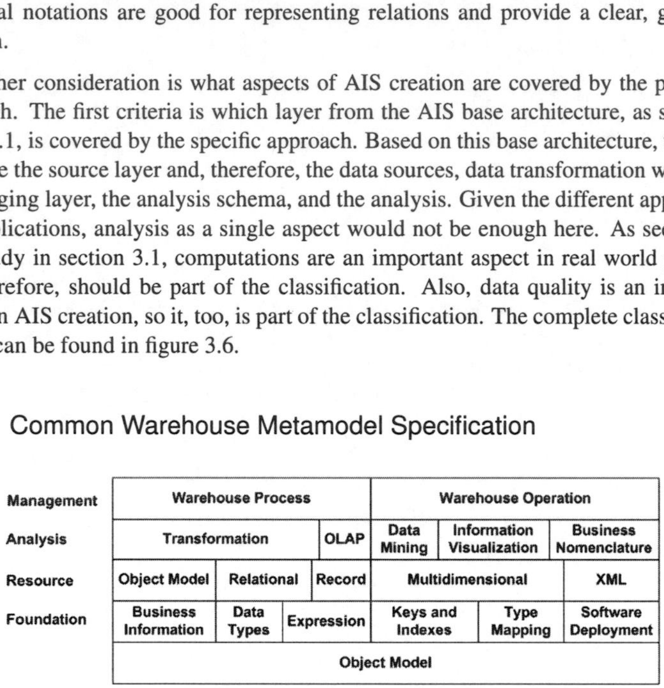

Management	Warehouse Process			Warehouse Operation		
Analysis	Transformation		OLAP	Data Mining	Information Visualization	Business Nomenclature
Resource	Object Model	Relational	Record	Multidimensional		XML
Foundation	Business Information	Data Types	Expression	Keys and Indexes	Type Mapping	Software Deployment
	Object Model					

Figure 3.4: Package structure of CWM, taken from [Obj03]

The **Common Warehouse Metamodel (CWM)** [Obj03] is a standard defined by the OMG. The main purpose of CWM is to enable the interchange of warehouse meta data. What the OMG called a warehouse, is referred to as an AIS in this thesis. The CWM standard is defined on the basis of the following three OMG standards:

- UML - Unified Modeling Language [Obj00]

- MOF - Meta Object Facility [Obj04]

- XMI - XML Metadata Interchange [2]

The CWM provides meta models for different aspects of AIS creation. The OMG describes warehouse meta data as the conjunction of all kind of data and information that is used for building, maintaining, managing, and using the data warehouse, except the data itself. The reason why the CWM focuses on meta data interchange and not meta data

---
[2] Specification used is version 1.1. For newer version, see http://www.omg.org/spec/XMI/

itself is because every specific data management tool needs its own models and meta models, therefore, it would be impossible to develop one meta model for all kinds of data management applications. To be able to share information between different data management applications, the CWM was developed. The CWM is organized into five different areas and packages, as can be seen in figure 3.4. The five main areas describe different architectural layers of a data warehouse.

3.2.1.1 Elements of the CWM

Object Model

The object model provides basic constructs for creating and describing meta model classes in all other packages. The object model is a UML subset which only contains those constructs that are necessary to describe the CWM. It consists of four different meta models: core, behavioral, relationships, and instance.

Foundation

The foundation area contains different fundamental meta models that are used by a group of other packages. They only describe certain aspects and not complete concepts. These concepts are described in other packages, but the concept of the foundation packages can be used and extended.

Resource

The resource area provides meta models that represent object-oriented, relational, record, multidimensional, and XML data resources. In the case of object-oriented data resources, CWM reuses the base object model. The relational package describes relational structures based on the SQL standard. The data record package describes traditional data records. The multidimensional package describes meta models for multidimensional storage. The XML packages contain elements to describe XML structures.

Analysis

This area includes meta models that represent data transformations, OLAP, data mining, information visualization, and business nomenclature. Data transformation covers transformation for different kinds of data sources, targets, and formats. Black box and white box transformations can be described. The transformations can be grouped into logical units. The OLAP package contains elements to describe multidimensional structures likes cubes and dimensions. In the data mining package, mining models like clustering and classification are described. The information visualization package consists of meta data for information publishing and visualization. The model is very generic and abstract and provides only container-like meta models. The reason for that is that visualization is a huge problem domain, so more specific models are difficult to define. The Business Nomenclature package describes business meta data with the help of taxonomy and glossary classes that can build up the business semantics.

Management

These packages includes meta models for representing warehouse processes and results of warehouse operations. The warehouse process describes flows for executing transformations, and includes triggers and other events. The warehouse operation package consists of elements to describe day-to-day operations of the warehouse processes. Aspects covered are transformation execution, like monitoring recently-executed transformations, measurements, and change requests.

If the provided constructs do not fulfill the application's requirements, the CWM can be extended, as said in [MSH03]. The extension mechanism was a proposal but it is not included in the standard. This proposal contains extensions for creating tagged values, stereotypes, and subclasses. Although the extension proposal is not part of the standard, extension of the CWM can be made. This is a very important aspect because extensions are necessary to use the CWM in practice. The provided meta models are not concrete enough to be used in practice. One example already described is visualization, which is just a container. Some relevant aspects for visualization will be discussed in section 4.4.1.2. Another example of the abstraction is the business nomenclature package. It just contains elements to build up a vocabulary, but not any specific business modeling. Even the multidimensional modeling is too generic, as claimed in [MT02]. For instance, the CWM does not model levels and their relationships in detail.

3.2.1.2   Classification

Because of the higher abstraction, CWM cannot be used, as it is for a certain specific application in general. It has to be extended to meet specific needs.

A big advantage of CWM is that it covers all relevant aspects of data warehousing. The OMG uses the power of UML and MOF to develop the CWM so that the resulting models are very compact. Another advantage of the CWM is that many warehouse tool makers, such as Oracle Corporation, Hyperion Solutions Corporation, SAS Institute Inc., and others were involved in the development, so the CWM has a big foundation in the industry. This includes tool support and knowledge about the relevant aspects. Nevertheless, the CWM has not succeeded in industry and the scientific community as expected. The last version of this standard is from 2003, and this was only the second version of the standard.

The CWM also uses an old UML standard (1.3) and has never been updated to a later version. There are only few tools that support CWM. One reason for this might be the abstract modeling of the CWM, so that it cannot be used without extensions.

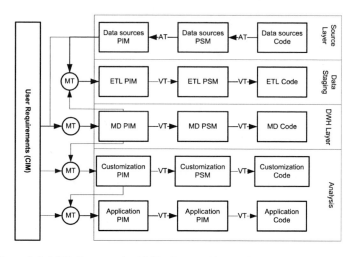

Figure 3.5: MDA Framework of [MT08], turned by 90 degrees and layers added

The CWM addresses the aspect of integration of the different AIS layers, as introduced in section 2.1.2. This aspect is useful for this thesis because it shows how the different levels of abstraction can be integrated with each other. The CWM can act as a foundation for meta models in this thesis. Because the CWM only consists of meta models, the aspect of languages is missing, so it does not show how a user interaction with this meta model can take place. But this aspect is important because meta models must be instantiated by a user because he provides the domain knowledge. If this knowledge is contained in the models, autoMAIS can generate software. AutoMAIS should therefore provide meta models based on the CWM because it shows how meta models can be integrated with each other. The CWM only provides a foundation for modeling, so more concrete meta models have to developed in autoMAIS. However, in this thesis, languages based on the developed meta models should also be provided to enable user interaction.

3.2.2   Trujillo et al.

Trujillo and his working group have published many papers on the subject of applying MDA on data warehousing. In this section, relevant selected papers of this group are introduced. A good overview of the Trujillo approach is given in [MT08]. In this paper, the authors give a general overview on their MDA approach and their transformations. This approach is shown in figure 3.5. This approach covers the complete AIS architecture as introduced in section 2.1.2 and covers the layers: source layer, data staging layer, DWH layer, and application layer. For every one of these introduced layers, the authors provide PIMs, PSMs, and code. The CIM consists of one single model only. For this CIM, no specific model is given; it is just said that this model covers the requirements for the resulting DWH. The PIM level describes the resulting DWH from a conceptual viewpoint. This viewpoint contains DWH properties without including technology details. The PSM level describes certain platform-specific views like a ROLAP implementation. To integrate the different models, they use different types of transformations, including vertical (VT), horizontal (AT), and merging (MT) transformations. The VTs are model-to-model transformations that transform models into another level of abstraction. ATs transform models into other models on the same level of abstraction. And, finally, the MT unites different models into one model. They do not provide deep information on how these different transformations work and how they are synchronized.

3.2.2.1   Developed Languages for PIM and PSM Level

Many languages for the different warehouse layers have been introduced by Trujillo and his group. In this section, an overview of these languages is given. These languages have in common that they describe a PIM or a PSM. The languages are based on UML profiles.

In [TLM03], a language for modeling UML processes has been introduced. The domain of the language is the conceptual modeling of ETL. Ten ETL operations (stereotypes) are introduced. These mechanisms describe common ETL tasks, as introduced in section 2.1.2.1. [TLM03] provides operations like aggregation, conversion, log, and load. The data sources are described with UML classes and can be connected with the ETL operations.

In this paper, they only describe the operations and provide some examples of them. It is not said how they are integrated or used within a real AIS project. The provided languages are very similar to tools, like Pentaho Data Integration [CBvD10] or Microsoft Integration Service [Mic11e] that perform ETL tasks, but the provided languages do not have as many capabilities as these tools. The provided languages are just described and not executable.

In [LMVT04], another language for describing ETL processes is introduced. This language focuses on mapping data sources and targets on different levels of granularity. In this language, different levels of mappings are described. For the different levels, the authors provide different views that are based on UML class diagrams. For the more abstract levels, the authors do not provide specific profiles. They define them on the table and attribute level. The table level can be used to describe the data flow between the sources via temporary tables to the targets tables. Based on this data flow diagram, concrete mappings between attributes, the next level, can be defined. For this level another diagram has to be created. This level defines the concrete mappings between attributes. If a transformation which cannot be aimed at by the temporary tables has to be performed, the transformations are defined in a UML comment element. With this language, it is possible to model the ETL process conceptually as data flow. For the concrete transformations, no modeling concepts are provided.

In [MTSP05], [PMT08], [LMTS02a], [LMTS02b], and [MT08], a language for the multidimensional model is described. An instance of this language is provided in figure 3.6. In this figure, a sale cube with the five dimensions Salesperson, Auto, Dealership, Time, and Customer is modeled. Dimension hierarchies are also modeled. Levels are models with a '"B" notation and the aggregation paths are modeled by associations. Attributes can also be modeled. In figure 3.6, the customer dimension is modeled with the levels state, region, city, and customer. The city layer has two attributes: name and population. It is not possible to provide types for attributes.

In [MT08], it is also said that there are PIMs for customization and application, but no cite if provided. Others by this group, like [PT08], focus on repositories. In this paper, it is described how models can be reused. Another aspect this group considers is physical modeling [LMT06]. In this work, they use UML component models to describe the deployment of sources, hard disks, and servers.

3.2.2.2   Transformations

In [MT08] and [MTSP05], model transformations are introduced. They only provide these transformations for one of their aspects: the multidimensional model. For this model, they provide model-to-model and model-to-code transformations. The transformations are described with QVT [Obj11a] .

With the transformation, a ROLAP storage of the multidimensional schema is created. They transform the multidimensional PIM into an relational PSM. This PSM contains model elements for tables, key-constraints, and so on. The PSM is based on a CWM relational model. Based on this model, transformations into SQL-DDL scripts are generated. With these scripts, it is possible to describe a complete multidimensional model in a relational representation. No other transformations are given.

3.2.2.3   Classification

The work of Trujillo and his working group covers many aspects of AIS creation. Their developed languages are all based on UML profiles and there is no automation support for generating model instances, as will be done in autoMAIS. How this is done in this thesis will be introduced in section 4.4.4. In the data mapping language, for instance, the data sources and the targets must be defined by hand as class diagrams. This kind of modeling is redundant. Their languages focus only on graphical languages. They do not use any existing language, except UML, to describe an AIS, although there are many of them. The language design is not appropriate. For example, in a multidimensional modeling language the multidimensional structures must be clear. In their work, this aspect is a little hidden. Another example is the data mapping language. In this language,

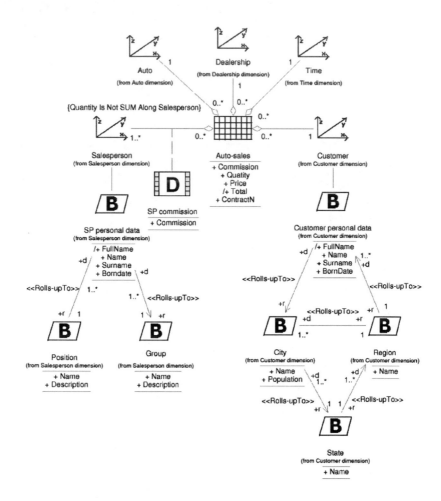

Figure 3.6: Instance of the multidimensional modeling language as introduced by Trujillo, taken from [MT08]

the different levels lead to a situation where it is not clear which sources belong together and which attributes or tables have been mapped.

In figure 3.5, the integration of the languages is sketched. Actually, how these integrations take place is not described. In their other publications, Trujillo and his working group do not refer to a kind of integration, so it can be assumed that the integration does not take place; although they claim that integration is important for a MDA DWH approach. In recent publications like [CMPT10] and [GMT10], they move their focus to other aspects of DWH like applying OCL to certain models, or spatial aspects of DWH, so they may not lay focus on the MDA and the integration approach any longer. As they only provide transformations for the multidimensional model and not for the other aspects, they show that it is possible to generate parts of the AIS.

Summing it up, the group has developed languages for many aspects of the AIS. This includes models for the source, data staging, data warehouse, and the application layer. These languages are graphical, custom-developed languages which could be used as a foundation for the languages developed in this thesis. Because this working group shows a useful classification of aspects and models for AIS creation, it will be the foundation for identifying the models that will be developed within autoMAIS.

For some aspects, they have developed transformations to enable software integration. This shows that it is possible to generate parts of an AIS. They say that the integration of the different DWH aspects is important, but they do not provide integration mechanisms in depth. They also do not show how their process model fits into existing development processes by providing a process model. However, a process model would be useful to show how the different models interact with each other. They also do not show the benefits of integration for the reduction of schematic work and verification, but this will be shown in this thesis. It will also be shown that integration enables automatic verification that is not possible without the integration. Further, in the evaluation in section 5, it will be shown that an integrated approach reduces schematic work.

3.2.3 CAWE

3.2.3.1 Introducing CAWE

CAWE stands for **C**omputer **A**ided **W**arehouse **E**ngineering and is an approach which combines MDA and Architecture-Driven Modernization (ADM by [Ulr07]) for data warehousing. The goal of this work, as said in [Kur11], is the creation of a model driven framework that enables model-driven forward-, reverse- and re-engineering for AIS. CAWE is based on the work of [MT08] which was introduced in section 3.2.2. In [KG10b], he claims that, in the work of Trujillo et al., they have shown that applying MDA on AIS is possible, but they did not give many details on the implementation. In his work, Kurze, as well as Trujillo, focus on the multidimensional model. As a research approach, he uses a design science approach. Kurze develops a graphical language for the multidimensional model that is based on ADAPT. His CIM is based on the CWM (see section 3.2.1). When using the CWM, he found that the CWM was too abstract to use it completely. Therefore, Kurze used a CIM that is based on the one from Trujillo, but he suggests that further research should include well-founded literature research to be able to develop a good multidimensional CIM. In [KG10b], he describes the complete transformation chain for the multidimensional model. Next to the graphical language meta model, he develops two intermediate models: the multidimensional CIM and a snowflake meta model. The snowflake model represents the relational structure of the modeled multidimensional data. Based on his graphical language meta model, he develops a model-to-model transformation to the multidimensional CIM and, from there, a model-to-model transformation to the snowflake model. From the snowflake model, a model-to-text transformation to a SQL snowflake DDL script is given. The graphical language is explained in detail in [GKS09]. For this language, he uses all elements of ADAPT. Kurze's language is limited to the conceptual modeling of dimensions. He does not say anything about the logical model.

3.2.3.2   Classification

Kurze also deals with organizational aspects of AIS, and the result of this is presented in [KG10a], together with Gluchowski. In this work, Kurze focuses on the different AIS creation methodologies which have been introduced in section 2.1.3. He uses this method to enable the different engineering approaches. To enable all introduced methodologies, Kurze modifies and extends the Trujillo framework. This extension is only conceptually done by rearranging the arrows and introducing new architecture elements like end-users. This work can be a basis for further development of MDA approaches and process modeling. In his work, as said in [Kur11], he focuses on the multidimensional model and the storage, and not with the other aspects of an AIS system. He presents two case studies to evaluate his approach. In the second case study, he shows the re-engineering capabilities of this approach: he uses an existing AIS and generates ADAPT models from the existing warehouse and creates MediaWiki [Wik07] pages for them.

To conclude the section about the CAWE, it can be said that CAWE provides an MDSD approach for AIS creation which is based on existing languages. This shows that such an approach is possible because it provides a complete vertical prototype for his work, and shows how MDSD models can be used as documentation for the AIS creation process. They also introduce some kind of process model to show how different languages in the AIS creation process can interact with each other, but they only provide concrete models for the data warehouse layer. The usage of the ADAPT language seems to be a good approach, and this language will also be used in this thesis. CAWE, however, only deals with analysis and the multidimensional model. As there are no other aspects covered in this approach, there is no integration or verification, as it will be done in this thesis. AutoMAIS covers the complete AIS creation process and not only the multidimensional model.

3.2.4 Rizzi et al.

3.2.4.1 Introducing the Work

The work of the group around Stefano Rizzi covers a large field in data warehousing and MDSD. The working group does not deal with the whole AIS creation process, but only with the aspects of analysis and application. They lay a slight focus on analysis. They recently provided a book on AIS design ([GR09a]). In this section, selected work of this group is presented.

Like Trujillo and Kurze, this group also works with the multidimensional model. They have developed a custom language for the conceptual modeling of the multidimensional schema called DFM [GMR98]. This language was introduced in section 2.1.4.3. However, Rizzi and his working group do not use this in their current research. It is not clear why they do not use it, because it provides the same elements and functionality as in their current work, and it would be no problem to realize this as a DSL. In their current research, they used YAM [Abe02] and the multidimensional model based on the work of Trujillo. All of these approaches, though, are based more or less on the same meta model. Only the concrete syntax differs a little. These models are based on UML. Based on this work, Rizzi and his working group presented an approach for automated detection of multidimensional models in relational data sources in [CMR10]. The goal of this work is to support users by identifying candidates for facts and dimensions during the AIS creation process.

To achieve this, they use a model-driven approach which is based on parts of the relational CWM. First, Rizzi generates a model for all database elements. Then they use a heuristic approach to identify candidates for the multidimensional model. Based on the candidates, they have defined transformations that generate parts of their multidimensional model. For these transformations they use QVT. In [CMR10], they only show the application of this approach and do not provide specific numbers of the success of the identifying algorithms. Nevertheless, this approach is interesting because it shows how model-driven techniques can be used to support management of the complexity of AIS creation.

Regarding analysis, their work on what-if analysis [GR08] and expressing OLAP preferences [GR09b] is more specific. In their work on the OLAP preferences, Rizzi and his working group introduce an algebra to describe OLAP queries based on user requirements. They say that it is difficult to find the needed information in an OLAP database, like the preference on a specific month in a certain professional group. Therefore, they have defined a number of operators to describe these preferences, which can be applied on facts and dimensional elements. An example of a preference is $BETWEEN(AvgIncome, MINIC, 1000)$. This preference describes that the values in $AvgIncome$ which are lower than 1000 are preferred. Different operations can be combined. With this algebra, the user can express what kind of data they are looking for and do not have to search for it. In this paper, they only describe the different opera-

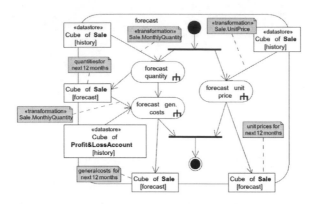

Figure 3.7: Example of a What-If Analysis, taken from [GR08]

tions, but not a complete language. They also do not show how these preferences can be realized in a concrete system nor do they say anything about the usability of these preferences. The definitions are very formal and algebraic, so they might not be easy to use. This is because they are not based on existing languages that the user might know and, further, they provide a large number of elements. These two aspects might make using this language more difficult. Most of the introduced concepts can also be expressed by using MDX which is, of course, not always present in an AIS systems.

In the paper on what-if analysis, [GR08] work on simulation. In [GR08] they develop a UML-based approach to model certain scenarios, such as a specific "pay 2 take 3" promotion. An example of this is given in figure 3.7. To achieve this, they extend the UML activity diagram to describe certain simulation criteria. This includes the description of involved cubes, measures, used statistical methods, and the flow of how the simulation data should be derived. This model is used to communicate between users within an organization that want to work with the simulation results, and the developers that implement these scenarios. They were able to provide a semi-formal model to describe certain scenarios. This can help to provide traceability to the users because they know how the simulation results are computed. However, it is not formal enough to enable any automatic generation or validation. For the modeled actions, the realization might be slightly complex. In their provided example in figure 3.7, they modeled an action node called *regression*. A regression, depending on the underlaying data, is a complex mathematical task, even if only a linear approach is used. Even here, many aspects, as described in [Sta08], have to be considered, making complete automation impossible. The presented models can only be used for communication among stakeholders.

3.2.4.2 Classification

The provided examples show how MDSD and SLE can be applied to support the AIS creation process, especially in the application area. They show how models can be used for documentation. They do not cover the complete AIS creation process. Instead, they deal only with applications and analysis, like Kurze or Trujillo do. Rizzi and his working group do not say that they are up to this. Nevertheless, they provide good ideas on how these techniques can be used in different fields of AIS creation and shows that building of complex languages is possible. This work can be used as the basis for the creation of custom languages.

AutoMAIS aims to build up complex languages for the description of AIS, but it covers the complete AIS creation process, and not only the analysis. AutoMAIS also connects the different aspects of AIS creation with a process model.

3.2.5 Conclusion

In the last section, different approaches for combining SLE and MDSD for AIS creation have been introduced. Now in this section, these different approaches are classified and rated against each other. The result of this classification is shown in table 3.6. First, the classification criteria have been defined at the beginning of this section.

In some works, these different aspects are treated independently; in others, they are not. For the generation of an AIS instance, this aspect is important. Therefore, it is part of the classification matrix. Also, the item process model is added because it is interesting to see how they deal with it in the context of MDSD and SLE. Some approaches generate software artifacts while others only define languages. Therefore, the generation of software is added. All introduced approaches use or develop languages, so languages and their design is an important aspect, so the language design of the related work is included in the classification matrix. This aspect is subdivided into three different categories. These are the development of languages, meaning whether they define languages with a concrete syntax or they only define a meta model. In the field of AIS, many different languages have been developed. Some of them have already been introduced in section 2.1, and others will be introduced in chapter 4. The good design of a language is expensive, therefore, whether existing languages were used in the different approaches should be considered. Using an appropriate language is often better than developing a new one from scratch. Another aspect of language design is if a language is textual or graphical.

The introduced classification matrix is only limited to those newer approaches that use MDSD and SLE. In table 3.6, the classification results are displayed. A ✓ indicates that an entry is presented in the approach.

A process model is only supported by Trujillo, and as Kurze is based on his work, he also covers this aspect. They define a process model only implicitly when they define

	CWM	Trujillo	Rizzi	CAWE
Integration				
Process Model		✓		✓
Integrated Meta model				
Software Generation		✓	✓	✓
Languages Properties				
Language Development		✓	✓	✓
Usage of Existing Languages				✓
Textual Language	✓		✓	
Graphical Language		✓	✓	✓
Aspects				
Application		✓	✓	✓
Computation				
Multidimensional Model	✓	✓	✓	✓
Data Sources	✓	✓		
Data Quality				
Data Transformation	✓	✓		

Table 3.6: Classification of related work

their integration architecture. Kurze lays a bigger focus on the process model. He works with the different AIS design methodologies from section 2.1.3 to define the different engineering methods, but his process model does not contain explicit activities and roles, as introduced in section 4.3. Further, the process models introduced here do not show how they fit into existing software creation projects.

An integrated meta model is only supported by the CWM. They have defined a complex UML model with inheritance and composition to make this integration possible. Trujillo has defined an integrated approach where the integration of the different models is performed by transformations, but in their different publications, they do not introduce their transformations in detail or describe how the different models interact, and what the concrete consequences from these interactions are. As Kurze focuses only on the multidimensional integration, there is nothing to integrate.

Software generation for parts of an AIS is described by Trujillo, Rizzi, and Kurze. Trujillo and Kurze describe the software generation for data storage in the multidimensional model as ROLAP. Additionally, Kurze describes transformations that generate documentation. Trujillo does not generate AIS components, but transformations for identifying multidimensional structures.

All introduced approaches deal with languages except CWM. As CWM only provides meta models, no concrete syntax is included here. Existing AIS languages are only used by Kurze. The others define new languages that are mostly based on UML profiles.

None of them report anything about the user's experience with these languages. Textual languages are used by Rizzi and CWM, as it uses OCL. Rizzi defines his own complex textual languages for certain aspects of AIS creation. Graphical languages are supported by all approaches, except CWM.

All approaches deal with the multidimensional model, as it is a key concept in AIS creation. Trujillo lays the focus of this work on the application aspect. Trujillo also deals with the application aspect, but it is only slightly touched upon by defining an application model. The mathematical computation is not handled by any of the introduced approaches. The reason for this may be that statistics does not play such an important role as in the shown example projects from section 3.1. In practice, computations play an important role because, based on raw data, a lot of computations are made. The aspect of data sources is covered by the CWM and Trujillo. Data quality is not part of the introduced approaches. The transformation of data is handled by the CWM and Trujillo.

To conclude this section, it can be said that in the field of AIS creation, there are good approaches that are based on MDSD and SLE. However, these approaches lack two aspects: usage of existing languages, and integration. There are many well-developed languages for AIS creation but they are, except for one, not used in the introduced approaches. Good language development takes time and, therefore, using an existing language rather than developing something from scratch should be considered because enabling usability will always be more difficult when using a new, custom language. The other aspect is the missing integration. Not all of the approaches integrate the different aspects of AIS creation. An integration on the logical level would enable great benefits, such as better documentation [Kur11]. In [MT08], they provide three benefits of an integrated approach. First, the complete AIS design can be made systematically and well-structured. Second, it can avoid integration problems, and third, an AIS can be generated by transformation.

Taking the real world AIS creation projects from this section into account, it can be added that another important aspect of AIS creation is the huge amount of schematic work. This aspect is not covered in depth in the introduced approaches. Also, verification has not been covered in depth. The introduced related work shows that work in this field will enhance the AIS creation process.

4 The autoMAIS Approach

In this chapter, the autoMAIS approach for integrated description and generation of AIS is introduced. The chapter is structured as follows. First, the requirements based on the example AIS projects and related work are derived in section 4.1. Then, the needed aspects and languages are identified in section 4.2. After that, the autoMAIS process model is introduced in section 4.3, which orders the languages and the AIS creation itself to fit into the creation process. In section 4.4, the different developed languages for the identified aspects are introduced. After the language introduction, the integration of languages is described. Section 4.6 describes the transformations for the generation of an AIS configuration. This chapter ends with a conclusion in section 4.7.

4.1 Requirements for autoMAIS

In this section, the requirements for the autoMAIS approach are derived. The sources for the requirements are the observations in the example AIS projects from section 3.1 and the classification of related work from section 3.2.

One of the main issues of AIS creation is the huge amount of schematic work due to missing integration and different layers of abstraction. According to [SVE07], one way to reduce schematic work is using model-driven software development, as introduced in [Tei09]. In the related work in section 3.2, the model-driven approach is already introduced in the field of AIS creation with two examples given ([GKS09] and [MT08]). In the example projects, the schematic work due to missing integration of aspects and different abstraction layers between those aspects was shown. The aspect of integration has also been considered as important in literature. In the example AIS creation projects it has been observed, too, that this missing integration leads to verification problems and makes AIS creation projects more costly.

Another issue in AIS creation is documentation. In MDSD, models are used as always up-to-date documentation. In the related work section with [GR09b], or [KG10a], approaches were introduced that specify formal models to describe analyses and applications.

Based on these observations, the following overall requirements could be identified:

- **O1. Covered Aspects:** The autoMAIS approach should cover a large, or, if possible, the whole AIS creation process. In the work of [Kur11], only the aspect of analysis has been covered. He comes to the conclusion that covering more than one aspect would have bigger advantages. Another reason to cover a large number of aspects is, that only in that case an integration can take place. The aspects to cover are based on the base architecture in figure 2.1 from section 2.1.2, which describes the essential parts of an AIS. The architecture shows the following aspects to be covered by the autoMAIS approach: data sources, data staging, data warehouse, and analysis.

- **O2. Languages:** For the description of the relevant aspects, languages should be used. For each language, at least one appropriate language should be developed. The introduced related work has successfully devolved or used languages for the description of AIS projects. They have also shown successful applications for languages. However, also outside the SLE and MDSD approaches, languages for AIS descriptions have been introduced, as presented in chapter 2. Developing new languages is a bigger effort, as introduced in [FGLW08]. The work of Trujillo shows, that developing new languages may not always be the best choice. Therefore, an additional requirement for the languages of autoMAIS is to reuse appropriate existing languages, if possible.

- **O3. Integration:** The missing integration of aspects leads, as shown in section 3.1, to schematic work and verification problems. Therefore, in the autoMAIS approach the different aspects should be integrated with each other to reduce verification effort, and schematic work.

- **O4. Process Model:** For building up an AIS, different methodologies, as introduced in section 2.1.3, exist. An approach, such as autoMAIS, that wants to cover the whole AIS creation process, must be able to support all types of methodologies. Otherwise, it could not be used in certain projects and this would indirectly violate requirement O1. Another issue in AIS creation projects is, that it is always a software development project. For the development of software, process models exist. As autoMAIS is a complex process, it should consider, how it fits into software development projects. To fulfill these two issues, a process model is appropriate. The process model should include the different types of activity within the autoMAIS approach. It should also show, how the different activities fit into exisiting process models and methodologies.

- **O5. Generation:** As shown in the related work section, it is possible to generate parts of an AI. As this reduces schematic work, this approach should be used in autoMAIS. Another expected profit of generation is less errors in the generated code than in manually written code.

This are the five requirements for the autoMAIS approach. In the following section it is shown how these requirements are fulfilled.

4.2 Derivation of Relevant Aspects

The AIS creation process is a complex one. In this process, different roles are involved. A minimum number of roles are used by the autoMAIS process model, which is introduced in section 4.3.1.1. Because of the complexity, and for clarity, it is useful to split the AIS creation process into different aspects. For each aspect, an appropriate language will be developed to fulfill requirements O1 and O2. The aspect's language is complete and delivers a certain abstraction. Based on the AIS reference architecture in section

2.1.2.1, related work and my own AIS creation experience, the following six aspects have been identified and have already been published in [Tei10]:

- **Measures:** Next to fact data, an AIS consists of computations on this fact data. These computations are called measures. An AIS uses different kinds of measures based on the target domain. Based on the complexity of a computation external procedures are called. Details on this concepts will be given in section 4.4.1.

- **Analysis:** This describes the kind of analyses that can be performed with the resulting AIS. Because this thesis is based on the OLAP paradigm, the analysis description is a description of the multidimensional model. This consists of the analyses themselves and hierarchies, and will be introduced in section 4.4.2.

- **Hierarchy:** As hierarchies are central aspects of an analysis, because they are part of the multidimensional model and therefore for the resulting AIS, this aspect is treated individually. Another reason for the separation is that there is a difference between conceptual and logical modeling of analysis that only can be handled when this aspect is split. Detailed arguments for the separation will be provided in section 4.4.3.

- **Data sources:** Description of all of the data sources within the organization that issues the AIS. In this aspect, information content, representation, and technical accessibility are described in one place. Only those data sources that are described with this language can be integrated into the resulting AIS. This aspect will be introduced in section 4.4.4.

- **Data source transformations:** This aspects describes how data sources must be transformed to fit into the data format of the resulting AIS. A concept with automatic mapping will be introduced in section 4.4.5.

- **Data quality:** Based on AIS analysis results, decisions are made in organizations. Therefore, it is important to have quality-assured data and this aspect is treated separately. Quality assurance is a broad field during AIS creation, therefore only one approach is introduced in section 4.4.6 to show that the integration of data quality issues is possible.

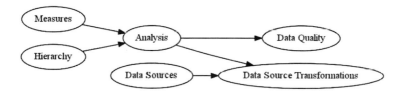

Figure 4.1: AutoMAIS meta model dependency graph

These six aspects and their languages are the central part of this thesis. To fulfill the integration requirement (O3), the different languages, or, better said, their meta models, must be integrated with each other. This means that the different elements within the meta models depend on each other. How these dependencies look is shown in figure 4.1. The reason why these dependencies exist is due to the kind of integration that was used within autoMAIS. This will be introduced in depth in section 4.5. In figure 4.1, it is shown how the different meta models depend on each other. The analysis depends on the hierarchies and measures. This means that, in an integrated meta model, measures are made concrete by defining an analysis for a measure. A measure only describes the general computation, and the analysis based on this measure makes them concrete by defining the multidimensional model for them. To be able to define an analysis, hierarchies must exist. Hierarchies are the global dimensions in the multidimensional model. These are referred to in an analysis. To be able to define data transformations, analysis and data sources must exist; otherwise, the definition of transformation from the sources to the analysis schema would be impossible. Data quality, in this special approach, is based on analysis. Based on these dependencies, a process model can be defined.

4.3 AutoMAIS Process Model

The autoMAIS process model describes the AIS creation process with the help of autoMAIS. It describes what activities have to be performed to generate an AIS with autoMAIS, including the definition of roles and artifacts. This process model also explains how it can be integrated into existing ones. First, the process model itself is introduced in section 4.3.1. Here, the involved roles are introduced first. After that, the process activities are described. These descriptions include the activities, tools used, and aftifacts produced. Then the different general process models for software development are introduced briefly in section 4.3.3 and it describes how they can be used within autoMAIS. Then the same is done in section 4.3.4 for AIS creation methodologies. This section ends with a conclusion in section 4.3.5.

4.3.1 Introducing the autoMAIS Process Model

Now in this section, the autoMAIS process model itself is introduced. The definition of the process model is based on [Bal00]. In this definition, a process model definition consists of the elements, activities, and roles. The roles describes which abilities, experience, and knowledge is needed to perform the activities. First the roles and then the activities themselves are described.

4.3.1.1 Roles

The following roles have been identified to take part in the autoMAIS process. These roles have been identified based on the observations made in the example projects and literature research. Here, similar role definitions can be found.

- **Target domain expert** This person is an expert of the target domain and, in most cases, also the principal of the AIS. The resulting AIS will help them in their daily work. They know about useful analyses and the relevant target domain measures.

- **AIS design expert** This individual is an expert for creating AIS systems. They have already developed different AIS for different target domains and know about hierarchy, cube, and measure modeling. They are used to the autoMAIS approach and its tools and languages.

- **System administrator** This role is a technical expert for the operational systems. This also includes data base administration. They are familiar with the accessibility and know the functional contact person.

- **Transformation developer** This role is a developer for transformations in the sense of MDSD. If needed, they develop new transformation for a concrete component of the reference architecture from section 2.1.2.1. This has to be done if new technical components are introduced into the target architecture.

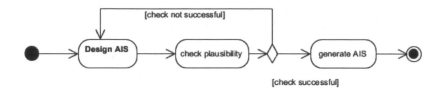

Figure 4.2: Process model overview

These definitions of the different roles have been made simply to clearly mark the responsibility. The target domain expert provides all knowledge about the target domain and also represents the needs of an AIS user. The AIS design experts transforms this domain knowledge into an AIS design and realization. They use the help of the system administrator to access different data sources and their content.

4.3.2   Description of Activities

In this section, the autoMAIS process model is introduced. The process model is shown in figure 4.2 and figure 4.3 as UML activity diagrams. These diagrams shows the activities that have to be performed to generate an AIS that is based on autoMAIS. In figure 4.2, the complete process model is shown in detail and in figure 4.3, the activity *Design AIS* is shown in detail. These activities can be completed once, then a complete AIS is generated at once, or many times in iteration as in agile development. In the case of agile development, the complete process in figure 4.2 would be completed many times. When all the activities within the process model have been completed successfully, an AIS is created. The size of the resulting AIS depends on the number of model instances defined within the different languages.

The needed activities can be divided into two blocks, design and generation activities. The design activities describes the needed aspects from section 4.2 and shown in figure 4.3. These aspects are describes with the help of languages. These languages and their meta models will be introduced in depth from section 4.4.4 to section 4.4.6. To be able to understand the autoMAIS process model, it is not important to have a deep understanding of the language; the goal of the particular activity is described here. The particular languages have been developed to achieve the goal of the activity. The activities, especially the design activities shown in figure 4.2, have to be processed in a particular order. These possible orders are shown in the activity diagrams. The order is needed because some languages depend on each other. For instance, a data transformation from a data source to the integrated schema cannot be described without the description of a data source or the integrated schema. The activity diagram shows possible paths. For a concrete project, a concrete path has to be chosen.

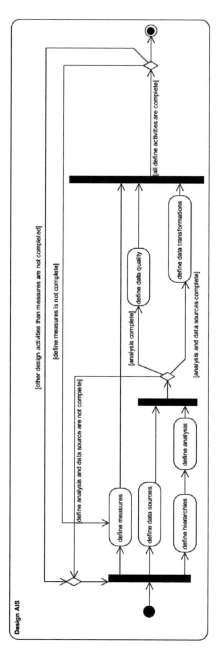

Figure 4.3: AutoMAIS process model

Next to the design activities, there are the generation activities. These are shown in the overall process model in figure 4.3. In the last activity, *generate AIS*, the generation of the AIS is done, which is the overall goal O5 of the autoMAIS process, as said in section 4.1. Before the generation can take place, the activity *check plausibility* must be performed. If this check is not successful, an error or inconsistency within one or more activities has occurred. In this case, it has to be corrected in the design activity. The check can only be successful if all design activities have been completed and at least one language instance has been defined.

In the following, the activities are described more detailed. Based on [Bal00], the following elements are needed to describe the process accurately:

- **Goals of the particular activity:** Describe why the activity is performed and what goal this activity has. In most cases, the goal is the definition of a particular model to describe an aspect, as introduced in section 4.2, for the resulting AIS.

- **Involved roles:** Describe which roles are involved in this activity and what their responsibilities are.

- **Input artifacts:** Describe which artifacts are needed from one of the previous activities.

- **Generated or produced artifacts:** Explain what output is produces in this activity.

- **Used languages and tools:** For each activity, different tools and/or languages have to be used, and these are introduced here.

4.3.2.1   Define Measures

Goals	Define all possible measures for the resulting AIS
Input artifacts	None
Artifacts	Instance of the measure language
Roles	AIS design expert, target domain expert
Language	Measures language

Table 4.1: Activity: Define measures

In this activity, all computations that can be used in the resulting AIS are defined. In the AIS foundation in section 2.1, the aspect of computation was not covered in depth. In section 2.1.4.1, it was introduced that the multidimensional model describes facts in the resulting AIS. But, as it was shown in the example projects in section 3.1 and in some of the related work in section 3.2, computations based on these multidimensional facts are important. Therefore, the measure language fulfills two goals: definition of facts that should exist in the resulting AIS, and the computation on these facts. So, all possible measures that are available in the resulting AIS are defined here. These facts are called base measures and measures in autoMAIS. In the AIS reference architecture in figure 2.2, this activity is part of the application layer because measures and their computations are stored within the data warehouse. By doing so, every kind of analysis software can access the computations and they are not specific for certain kinds of analysis software.

As will be introduced in the measure language section 4.4.1, the measure definition defines the mathematical computation and procedures. This also includes the needed parameters. These defined measures are instantiated for a particular project. The mathematical procedures are given by the target domain expert. The AIS domain experts support him using advice from his experience with former projects and can suggest useful measures. The measures are stored in an instance of the measure language, also introduced in section 4.4.1. This is done by the AIS design expert because he knows the usage.

In the case of Gesundheit NRW, a measure definition would contain the computation rules for the crude or age-specific rates. In the project measure definitions these measures would be instantiated for the hospital cases, so the resulting AIS provides crude or age-specific rates on hospital cases. The hospital cases themselves are a base measure and will be mapped to analysis.

4.3.2.2 Define Hierarchies

Goals	Definition of all hierarchies within the resulting AIS
Input artifacts	None
Artifacts	Instances of hierarchy language for complete resulting AIS
Roles	AIS design expert, target domain expert
Language	Hierarchy language

Table 4.2: Activity: Define hierarchies

As also introduced in section 2.1.4.1, hierarchies consist of the two elements, dimensions and cubes. In autoMAIS, there exist two activities for defining analysis, one for each core part of the multidimensional model. The first activity, definition of hierarchies, is the definition of the global dimensions. In the reference architecture, this is part of the data warehouse layer. To have a distinction from the technical representation of multidimensional models, this dimension is called hierarchy. The hierarchies are defined by the AIS design expert based on the knowledge he or she has gathered from the target domain expert. The target domain expert has to validate the resulting models. For defining these structures, the hierarchy language that will be introduced in section 4.4.3, is used.

In the Gesundheit NRW project, the definition of hierarchies means identifying ICD, surgery, gender, age, and region as dimensions and defines their hierarchy, levels, categories, and their relations for each dimension. The hierarchy language is introduced in section 4.4.3.

4.3.2.3   Define Analysis

Goals	Define multidimensional structure of analysis
Input artifacts	Instances of the hierarchy language
Artifacts	Instances of the analysis language for complete resulting AIS
Roles	AIS design expert, target domain expert
Tools	Analysis language

Table 4.3: Activity: Define analysis

Next to dimensions, which are modeled in the hierarchy language, cubes exist within the multidimensional model. In this activity these cubes are defined. To distinguish the technical representation of a multidimensional cube, this is called analysis within autoMAIS. Also, this activity is part of the data warehouse layer from the reference architecture.

This activity defines what kinds of hierarchies are used in analysis and, therefore, the global dimensions from the hierarchy language are referred. The involved roles are the same then in the *define hierarchies* activity, as the circumstances here are the same. The definition is done with the analysis language which will be introduced in section 4.4.2.

In the Gesundheit NRW project, the definition of analysis would include the reference of age, gender, ICD and time hierarchies. An analysis, like the hospital cases, will be described with the analysis language, and the previously-defined dimensions like time and age are referred.

4.3.2.4   Define Data Sources

Goals	Catalog of possible data sources and their structure for the resulting AIS
Input artifacts	None
Artifacts	Catalog of data source instances
	Data source structure description
Language	Data source language

Table 4.4: Define data sources

The data that is analysed in the resulting AIS comes from the different systems and data sources that exists within the organization that issues the AIS, as introduced in section 2.1.6. The goal of this activity is to catalog all possible data sources for the resulting AIS and describes the source layer from the reference architecture described in section 2.2. All these data sources are possible candidates for integration. If they are not cataloged and described here, they cannot be part of the resulting AIS. The data structure descriptions contains information about the content and the structure of the data sources. The content describes what the data source is about. This information can be used to identify the corresponding analysis. The structure of a data source is used for the tools that extract the the data from the sources. The data sources are described by the AIS design expert with the help of the other roles as support. The structure description is generated automatically by the DQ2MM tool. The language and the tool will be introduced in section 4.4.4.

The involved roles are system administrator, target domain expert and AIS design expert. The administrator is responsible for naming of, and technical access to, data sources. The target domain expert provides the knowledge about what kind of data is described in the source. He also decides if a source might be relevant or not. It might be better to have all possible data sources cataloged, because at this point in the process, it might not be clear if a source is needed or not. This depends on the organization's needs. The description and the source definition and structure are used for data transformation.

In the case of the Gesundheit NRW, the definition of data sources would contain the description of the hospital data source as it was introduced in section 3.1.1.1, and the description of the population data. Then the DQ2MM tool would automatically detect the structure.

4.3.2.5 Define Data Transformations

Goals	Describe transformation to fit the target schema
Input artifacts	Data source and analysis language instances
Artifacts	Mapping and transformation instances
Roles	System Administrator, AIS design expert
Language	Data transformation language

Table 4.5: Define data transformations

The goal of this activity is to define transformation so that the data source instances from the activity *define data sources* fit to the instances of the analysis language from the *define analysis* activity, that was previously defined. This kind of activity was called ETL in section 2.1.6 and, therefore, it covers the data staging/ ETL layer from section 2.2, as well as the monitor components.

To be able to describe a transformation, first it has to be identified which sources can be mapped to which analysis. In most cases, the format of the data source is not the same format as the analysis; therefore, transformations for this have to be defined. For this, a data transformation language, introduced in section 4.4.5, has been created. The activity is performed by the AIS design expert, assisted by the system administrator who provides data access information.

In the case of the Gesundheit NRW project, these activities were performed by the created data integration packages within the Microsoft Integration Services.

4.3.2.6   Define Data Quality

Goals	Define data quality constraints
Input artifacts	Analysis and hierarchy instances
Artifacts	InDaQu instances
Roles	AIS design expert, target domain expert
Language	Data quality language

Table 4.6: Activity: Defining data quality

In the previous activities, the structure of analysis has been defined, so it is now clear how the cells in the multidimensional model must look when they are integrated into the resulting AIS. The cells must be correct. If not, the analysis will provide invalid results. As described in section 4.4.6, data quality is an important factor for AIS, therefore, data quality has to be considered in the autoMAIS process model.

As data quality is a complex task, it is not covered completely here. It only introduces a language defining consistency constraints. This language will be introduced in section 4.4.6. However, this is not enough to ensure data quality. Other provisions like data cleansing have to be performed, but these provisions are specific to the target organization. These tasks are very specific for the particular resulting AIS. Therefore, in each project, decisions on what actions need to be performed must be made.

The target domain experts define the consistency rules because they know the general conditions of the target domain. To define the constraints, the InDaQu language is used. These rules are used during integration to identify invalid tuples.

4.3.2.7   Check Plausibility

Goals	Enable generation of the resulting AIS
Input artifacts	All previous defined model instances
Artifacts	Implemented checks
Roles	Target domain expert, AIS design expert, System administrator

Table 4.7: Activity: Check plausibility

In this activity, different language instances are checked to determine if they fit together, to ensure correct generation of the resulting AIS. This activity is performed automatically. First, the different meta models are integrated. How this is done will be explained in section 4.5. Technical details will be provided in section 2.1.2. In this activity, a check is made to determine if the different instances and aspects all fit together properly. Some examples of those tests will be provided in section 4.5.1, and, to ensure that in the generate code these relations are correct, this is checked in this activitypriot to generation. The results of the global AIS check have to be interpreted. If one of the checks fails, it has to be corrected. Therefore, it has to go back to the particular activity in which the test failed.

In this activity, all roles are involved because they all have to rate the results and fix errors if needed. Only the global AIS checks produce artifacts. These are the test results.

This activity works together with the AIS manager from the reference architecture in figure 2.2. The AIS manager is a dynamic component during runtime, and the check helps to assure that the control flow fits together properly for the AIS manager. At AIS runtime, the extraction and monitoring has to be done by the ETL components; it cannot be provided in this check.

In the case of Gesundheit NRW, this activity was not performed in the same way as it is done in autoMAIS. The verification was done manually as described on page 45.

4.3.2.8   Generate AIS

Goals	Create an AIS instance
Input artifacts	Complete instance of the meta model
Artifacts	AIS instance
Roles	None
Tools	Transformations defined by the transformation developer

Table 4.8: Activity: Create AIS

Here, the resulting AIS is created. It can only be performed if the previous activity *check plausibility* was successful. The generation is done with a set of transformations, which will be described in more detail in section 4.6. This leads to software components of the target architecture, as introduced in section 2.1.2.1. The generation is performed automatically.

In the Gesundheit NRW project, this was done manually, including all activities for writing SQL scripts and DTS components.

4.3.3   Software Engineering Process Models

In chapter 2 and in the example projects, it has been shown that the engineering part is done with different kinds of process models. Therefore, autoMAIS provides a process model to support the engineering part. But, as seen in the example projects, different types of process models are used. An autoMAIS process model should be able to deal with this difference. In this section, it will be shown how the autoMAIS process model fits into other Software Development Process Models. It will be shown that the engineering part can be fulfilled with different process models. For this, it will be shown how the different autoMAIS process activities fits into the particular process.

4.3.3.1 Waterfall Model

The waterfall model, as introduced in [Roy70] is a very strict model. It does not allow looping or going backwards. It consists of five phases: requirements, design, implementation, verification, and maintenance. These phases are completed one after another. The autoMAIS process model, as displayed in figure 4.3, covers only the phases design and implementation. The other phases stay more or less the same, because phases deal with general AIS creation issues that are not covered with autoMAIS. As a result, autoMAIS does not help by gathering requirements for the resulting AIS or maintenance issues directly. AutoMAIS focuses on the design and implementation of an AIS. In the design phase of an AIS, all layers of the AIS architecture are designed. In the implementation phase, these designs are realized.

When using autoMAIS, the design phase has the same goal as without autoMAIS, but autoMAIS provides tool support for this phase by providing languages for the different aspects, as introduced in section 4.2. In the autoMAIS-enabled design phases, different activities have to be performed. The goal of these different activities is to describe the complete resulting AIS, so the design phase might be more strict than in a traditional approach. The autoMAIS-enabled implementation phases, however, offset these extra efforts. The implementation phase is done automatically by the given transformation, to fulfill requirement O5. Then autoMAIS does not require any implementation by hand. This means that the size of the different phases changes when using autoMAIS within a waterfall. The design phase is bigger and the implementation phase is reduced nearly to zero, but the overall effort will also be reduced, as will be shown in chapter 5.

In figure 4.3, the activities that have to be performed in the design phase are all the activities starting with define. But these activities do not look like a waterfall because they contain parallel parts and looping. That said, it is possible to describe a path that includes all activities in the design phase that represents a waterfall. In this case, the order of design activities is fixed. The implementation phase is represented by the activity, generate AIS.

A problem might be the check activity. This activity tests whether the AIS is ready for generation or not. If not, a backward step is necessary. In a strict waterfall process, this would not be possible. So, when applying a strict waterfall, it has to be assured that this check is successful. In this case, this activity is a part of the implementation phase. The verification and maintenance are not part of the autoMAIS process, so they remain the same.

What has been shown here is that it is possible to perform an AIS creation project as a waterfall with autoMAIS. When doing so, the amount of the design phase rises and it is stricter than without autoMAIS because the steps that have to be performed are given, but the amount of the realization phase is reduced. For the design phase, a fixed order of the autoMAIS activities have to be defined, as will be introduced in section 4.3.1.

4.3.3.2   Iterative Model

The iterative process models, like the concrete instances of the spiral model [Boe88], have a focus on risk management. Risk management is not included in autoMAIS. At the end of each iteration, artifacts are produced. These artifacts are used in the next iteration. AutoMAIS can be used to implement – or rather to generate – these artifacts. But to generate a prototype, all activities have to be completed successfully. The model instance within the design phases also have to be complete. As an example, a dimension must contains levels and categories in these levels, but this definition must not include all categories or levels. So there is not much variety for the prototype definition. The only aspect that can be reduced is the number of elements in the model instances. With autoMAIS, it is possible to generate an instance for one base measure, but the definition has to be complete for this measure. If, during the iterations, the focus of the risk management lays on the different measures then the realization of the spiral model will work fine with autoMAIS. However, if focusing on other aspects, the collaboration will not work as well. The autoMAIS process activities can be arranged in an iterative process. The process model, as shown in figure 4.3, describes one necessary iteration to produce an AIS configuration. In the next iteration, all phases from the autoMAIS process model have to be completed again. The already-existing models could be reused and, if needed, changed. It can be said that autoMAIS supports iterative process models.

4.3.3.3   Agile

Agile methods, like those used in the PEIS project described in section 3.1.2, can be compared with the spiral model but the iterations are shorter. Agile methods are based on iterations. These iterations are time-boxed and feature-based. At the end of each iteration, a complete product, which is not necessary an executable product, can be delivered. Agile development includes a deeper customer collaboration than in traditional approaches. Using autoMAIS within agile processes means that to have a working AIS configuration, at least one base measure has to be defined. This is not always needed because model instances are also valid iteration results. For instance, during an iteration, analysis models could have been developed. These models can be discussed with the customer to get feedback for the next iteration. So it is not necessary to perform all activities within the autoMAIS process within one agile iteration, as models are also valid iteration results. To have a usable AIS configuration that can be used for testing, at least one base measure has to be described completely with all of the autoMAIS activities.

Taking into account the fact that the goal is faster development, the complete definition will not be a handicap. With autoMAIS, the engineering part is faster, because realization time is reduced, so the overall goal is achieved. AutoMAIS improves communication with customers because the developed model instances can be used for communication. The customer can validate the results. If something is wrong, the corresponding model will be changed and the generation redone, so no additional implementation is needed. It has been shown in section 3.1.2.4 that an agile approach for AIS creation is useful.

In the PEIS project, they presented at each review meeting at least one base measure. Otherwise, it was not possible to show progress. The focus on base measures or some other measures during an iteration can be compared to the rapid warehousing methodology as suggested by [GR09a]. They suggest to realize one data mart during one iteration because it minimizes the risks. The data mart concept is not considered in depth in this thesis, but a collection of measures can be equalized with a data mart.

4.3.4   AIS Design Methodologies in autoMAIS

An AIS creation is also a software creation process and therefore, in section 4.3.3, it was shown that the autoMAIS process supports different kinds of software development processes. For AIS creation, different methodologies exists. This describes how the different layers and components from the reference architecture in figure 2.2 are created. These methodologies have been introduced in section 2.1.3 and are independent from the chosen development process model. The development process model defines how many times the complete autoMAIS process is completed during one AIS creation process. The chosen methodology shows in which order the design activities within the autoMAIS process are completed.

To be able to show that all kinds of methodologies are possible, it has to be shown that a bottom-up and top-down approach is possible, because all others methodologies are a variation of these two. For a bottom-up process, it has to be shown that the process can start with the description of data sources. This is possible as it can be seen in the activity diagram in figure 4.3. The definition of data sources is possible without precondition. So, a bottom-up process is possible.

A top-down approach would start with the definition of measures independent from any precondition, in particular, without the definition of data sources. In the evaluation in chapter 5, a top-down realization is shown.

The other introduced methodologies are not based on the order of activities, but on how the role of the target domain expert is filled. So, all kind of methodologies are supported by the autoMAIS process.

4.3.5   Conclusion

In this section the autoMAIS process model has been introduced. The involved activities, their order and roles have been introduced. Also the goals of the particular activities were given, indicating which task the languages, introduced in section 4.4.1 to section 4.4.6, fulfill. It has been shown that the introduced process model can be used in all kinds of software development processes and in all kinds of AIS methodologies. So it can be said that overall requirement O4 from section 4.1 is fulfilled. Next to this, the process model helps to identify and order the needed activities to create an AIS with autoMAIS.

4.4   Description of Aspects and Their Languages

Now in this section, the autoMAIS languages are introduced. These languages all together fulfill requirement O2 from section 4.1. The introduced languages cover all aspects of AIS creation. First, in section 4.4.1, measures are introduced that describe computations in the resulting AIS. In section 4.4.2, a languages for describing analysis is introduced. In section 4.4.3, hierarchies, a special part of the multidimensional model, are introduced. Then in section 4.4.4, a language for describing data sources is introduced. After this, in section 4.4.5, a data transformation languages is introduced. The last introduced language is the data quality language in section 4.4.6.

4.4.1   Measures

As described in the requirements in section 4.2, there is a need for describing facts and computations on them. In this thesis, this aspect is called **measure**. It describes what kind of facts and computations are possible with the resulting AIS. This does not include the multidimensional or any other analysis model, but only the general analysis terms. In this section, a language for measures is introduced. First, the requirements for such a language are introduced. Then existing languages for the measure description are presented in section 4.4.1.2. There it is also described what computation power the resulting language should provide. Then in section 4.4.1.3, the abstract syntax, and, after this, in section 4.4.1.4, the concrete syntax is introduced . This section ends in section 4.4.1.5 with a conclusion.

4.4.1.1   General Requirements for a Measures Language

As seen in the example projects section, there are a large number of measures based on a small number of facts. In the Gesundheit NRW project, 466 measures were defined based on 38 cubes. In the PEIS project, there were 100 measures defined based on 22 cubes. The measures are those elements that the user of the resulting AIS interacts with because they describe facts and relations in the target domain. The required computations are the central part of the AIS requirements and therefore the interaction has to be considered. So the following requirements for a measure language can be identified:

- **M1. Distinction between facts and computed values:** In an AIS, there exist facts and computations on facts. The facts are those elements that are not computed and directly integrated in the data warehouse from the data sources. These facts are the foundation of all computations in the resulting AIS. These facts are called **base measures**. A base measure describes one fact in the target domain. In the case of the Gesundheit NRW project, an example of a base measure is hospital statistics data from section 3.1.1.1. A base measure is not a single value, but values with attributes, so in a way, a relational table with two kinds of attributes: describing attributes and numerical attributes. The numerical attributes represent, in the case of hospital cases, how many hospital cases exists. The describing attributes refine the numerical attributes by adding information, like a specific year or gender for a single numeric attribute.

Base measures can be combined by mathematical operations, the result of these combinations is called a **measure**. A measure is not physically present in a data warehouse because it is the result of a computation at runtime. Therefore, it is important to differ between facts and computed values in the measure language.

- **M2. Traceability in the target domain:** As measures can be the results of mathematical operations, these relations have to be described in the language, and the descriptions have to be traceable. This means that the mathematical formulas must be explicitly described. The traceability has to be enabled for different views. First, the target domain expert of the resulting AIS has to understand the relations because, based on this computation, decisions are made within the organization. The target domain expert must know how the measures are combined and how the results are computed. To enable generation of the measure computation, the relation modeling must also be traceable for the transformation.

- **M3. Nesting of measures:** As seen in the example projects, measures depend on each other. For instance, the age-specific rate depends on the crude rate computation. Therefore, the resulting language must support this nesting.

- **M4. Reuse of domain knowledge:** In a particular target domain like health reporting, there are computations or procedures that are particular for the target domain. These procedures are generally valid for the target domain and not for a specific project. In a specific project, these general procedures are instantiated in a project. For example, the crude definition in the example project Gesundheit NRW from page 41 is a specific procedure for health reporting. In the particular project Gesundheit NRW, this procedure was instantiated with the hospital cases and population data provided by LIGA.

The resulting language should distinguish between these aspects because it enables reuse for other projects and helps to differentiate between a computation description and a particular project.

- **M5. Inclusion of external procedures:** The defined computation within an AIS can become very complex. Examples of complex measures are special data mining procedures like clusters or regression, from the related work section 3.2.4. Such complex procedures are frequently realized by mathematicians because they require complex mathematical knowledge. Describing this in measure language would mean to integrate all kind of mathematics in this language. This would be beyond the scope of this language. The resulting language would be too complex and therefore not traceable for the user, therefore, this should not be part of the language. As the

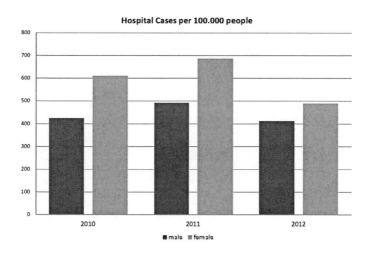

Figure 4.4: Hospital cases as a diagram

resulting AIS should be able to provide those kinds of functionality, the language should support the call of external procedures, like R project [RPr11] packages.

4.4.1.2 Existing Languages

To define a measure language, different possibilities for describing the concrete syntax exists. As the measure aspect is a very general aspect, there do not exist specialized languages for this aspect, such as, for example, in the analysis language in section 4.4.2. Mathematical notations would not be enough, however, because the measure language must contain more than just mathematical computations. A pure mathematical notation would not fulfill all requirements, but it would be possible to adapt some more general languages for the measure domain. These different adaptable languages are introduced now.

Requirement M2 for this language is the traceability for the target domain expert, therefore it could be reasonable to define a concrete syntax based on those elements that are used in the analysis within the resulting AIS later. Common visualization elements are tables and diagrams [Spe06].

An example of this is given in figure 4.4. Here, a diagram is displayed that shows an analysis that should be provided by the resulting AIS. The elements are fictive but defines the requirements for analysis in the resulting AIS. It can be seen, in the title of the diagram, that the hospital cases for 100,000 people should be available. It is not clear whether this should be a base measure or a measure, but it defines possible categories for the analysis: the different years. It also provides the target visualization, a bar chart. With this kind of representation, it is not possible to trace the computations or to define them. However, this provides a good impression of how the resulting AIS analysis should look, even if the numbers are fictive. This kind of visualization is more similar to reporting tools like Crystal Reports [SAP11] than it is to a measure language that enables computation. Therefore, this kind of concrete syntax is not as suitable because of the missing traceability (M2) for computations. If a measure language exists, a diagram or table-like based language could be used as a reporting or visualization language.

```
1  Select Population.Year, (HospitalCases.Numbers / Population.Numbers) * 100000 as
        "'Hospital cases per 100,000 people"'
2  FROM HospitalCases, Population
3  WHERE Population.Year = HospitalCases.Year
```

Listing 4.1: Hospital cases in query language

In a way, the measure language defines queries for the resulting AIS, so a query language like SQL, MDX, or tuple algebra by [Hol02] could be used. Listing 4.1 shows how this could look as SQL using an example of the hospital cases per 100,000 people. In the select clause in line 1, the required levels, here only years, are requested, and the computation is defined. The computation is traceable (M2). This may be different when defining complex measures because then the SQL statements could get very complex. The computation has also a name. In this case, that is the name of the measure. The involved measures for the computation can be identified via the from clause in line 2. With this definition, it is not clear whether the involved measures are measures or base measures, so this concrete syntax does not fulfill requirement M1, but this kind of modeling would enable nesting (M3). A query-based language is thus more suitable than a visualization-based language.

There are two challenges with this approach. First, it cannot be assumed that the target domain expert knows query languages like SQL. In the case of not knowing, traceability would be a little more difficult. The AIS design expert, of course, knows SQL because of his experience with databases, but in his case, there is another challenge. Standard query languages like SQL or MDX are general purpose languages for querying data pools, and so they are very complex and provide a large field of possibilities of how to define queries. A measure language based on a query language must be a domain-specific language, so the power of the chosen query language must be reduced. Not all elements would help in the domain of measure definition. This leads to the problem that when a design expert is used to the power of these languages, the reduction can lead to confusions when defining measures. Another challenge would be the traceability for the transformation. Because of the power, defining transformation would be complex and some subtleties are not easy to consider.

Another possibility for defining measure would be the use of mathematics. The example of hospital cases would look like the following:

$$\text{hospital cases per } 100{,}000 \text{ people} = \frac{\text{Hospital cases}}{\text{Population}} * 100000$$

Here, the computation is traceable. The included elements can be clearly identified. A language based on mathematics would be traceable for both target domain experts and AIS design experts because they are all familiar with mathematics. Also, the traceability for a transformation is given, so M2 is fulfilled, because math is more clear and pure than a query language. A challenge when using this alternative, as in a query-based approach, is that mathematics is also a general language. So the scope of mathematics also has to be reduced when using it. Still, reduced math would be easier to define because of the clear math structures and definitions.

Based on these considerations math is chosen as the base for a concrete syntax for a measure language, because it supports the traceability (M2) for all kinds of views, and the computation can be clearly expressed. Based on this concrete syntax as a foundation, a complete concrete and abstract syntax can be developed.

The goal is to reduce the scope of mathematics so that all requirements from the beginning of the measure section are fulfilled, and it is possible to generate the defined mathematical definition on multidimensional structures. In the resulting AIS, the computation is not done on single values but on multidimensional structures such as cubes. This makes transformation building a little bit complicated, because computations have to be done on cells. To better introduce the power of the measure language, it will be stepwise introduced what elements are used.

```
1  Cube HospitalCases,Population;
2  DerivedCube crudeRate =  (HospitalCases/Population)* 100000
3
4  //computation of measure values
5  foreach(Cell singleCell in HospitalCases.Cells)
6  {
7      Cell newCell = new Cell();
8      newCell.Identifier = singleCell.Identifier;
9      newCell.Value =(HospitalCases.Cell(singleCell.Identifier).Value
10                            /Population.Cell(singleCell.Identifier).
                              Value)
11                            * 100000
12 }
```

Listing 4.2: Programmable example of diagnoses

The most common way of interacting with cubes is to work with them cell-by-cell. This is called **cell-by-cell computation**. When doing a cell-by-cell computation, the cells of the cubes are iterated and the results are computed for each cell. How this computation could look in a programming language is shown in listing 4.2. Here, the computation of the hospital cases for 100,000 people is defined, and is based on the measure definition from page 42. It is assumed that hospital cases and population are base measures. This means that they are mapped to cubes during the autoMAIS process. The program excerpt defines how these two cubes are combined in computation to provide the measure results. The result of the computation of the two cubes is a cube, but this cube is not stored in the resulting AIS, so the resulting cube is called a derived cube. A derived cube has the same properties as a cube, with the storage exception. After the definition of the computation in lines 1 and 2, this is executed in lines 5 to 11. The derived cube has the same cell identifiers as the cubes, so the results can be commutated by iteration.

For the power of the measure language, all computations that can be transformed to a cell-by-cell computation will be included. This is true for all basic arithmetic operations (+,-,*,/), because each can be handled in the same way as introduced above. In the measure language, the basic arithmetic operations are applied to base measures, measures, and numeric values. These numeric values act as factors. The cell-by-cell computation assumes that, in a computation, all dimensions within involved cubes are identical. This cannot always be the case. This is not a problem here though, because there are methods to deal with this problem, according to [Koc01]. So it can be assumed that dimensionality in cell-by-cell computation is not a problem. This method has some consequences for analysis, which will be discussed in section 4.5.1 as it is an integration problem.

```
 1  Cube StandardPopulation, CrudeRate;
 2  Dimension iteratingDimension = Age;
 3  DerivedCube ageStandardizedRate  = (Sum((StandardPopulation * CrudeRate))) /
 4      Sum(StandardPopulation)
 5  AgeSpecficRate.OrderedDimensionList = CrudeRate.OrderedDimensionList - Age;
 6  List<Categories> ids = CrudeRate.Identifiers - Age;
 7  foreach(CellIdentifiers singleId in ids)
 8  {
 9      Cell newCell = new Cell();
10      newCell.CellIdentifier = singleID;
11      foreach(Category cat in Age.Categories)
12      {
13          CellIdentifiers running = singleId+cat;
14          newCell.Value += (CrudeRate.Cell(running).Value
15              * StandardPopulation.Cell(running).Value )
16              / StandardPopulation.Cell(running).Value
17      }
18  }
```

Listing 4.3: Programmable example of age standardized rate

To define the next set of possible operations for the measure language, the examples from section 3.1.1.1 are referenced. For defining an age-specific rate, average sums over categories are needed. In listing 4.3, the computation for an age-specific rate is given. The sums are needed for the different age groups. Therefore, in line 2, Age is marked as an iterating dimension. The computation is defined in line 3. For the sum, the mathematical symbol $\sum$ with indices would be appropriate, but most programming languages do not normally provide this functionality. The goal of an age-standardized rate is to reduce the age impact, therefore, the resulting cubes does not contain this dimension (lines 5,6). The computation is done cell-by-cell in a for each statement

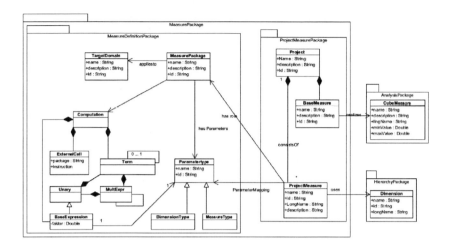

Figure 4.5: Abstract syntax for the measure language

(lines 9-16). For each cell of the resulting cube, a sum over age is defined in lines 11 to 15.

This example shows that more complex mathematics are possible to define within the measure language so that it is traceable for the transformation. This requires additional work, but enables a new set of functionality for the measure language and the generated resulting AIS. Challenging for the measure is to enable more complex computation. In section 3.2.4, a language was introduced that was able to describe complex computation that included regression. When using or defining such a language within in autoMAIS, the requirement would be that those computations, like regression, can be completely described within a language so that a transformation can be defined that enables this defined computation in the resulting AIS. Based on the chosen procedure, this might need a very special language and the transformations. Therefore, these kinds of procedures are not part of the measure language. To be able to still use them, external calls are introduced in the measure language. Complex procedures are done by an external call. In this case, it is assumed that the external component can deal with multidimensional structures.

4.4.1.3 Abstract Syntax

In the last section, it was discussed what kind of mathematical computations can and must be included in a measure language, but this specification only fulfills measure requirement M2, not the other four. To fulfill the other requirements, some concepts have to be introduced. Therefore, in this language, first the abstract syntax is introduced and, after this, the concrete syntax. In figure 4.5 the measure language as UML class diagram is given.

An important requirement is the reuse of domain knowledge (M4). To enable this the measure language is divided into two parts, *MeasureDefinitionPackage* and *Project-MeasuresPackage*, visualized as packages. The *MeasureDefinitionPackage* is used to describe the computations within the target domain as, for example, health reporting. In a concrete project, these measure definitions are imported and instantiated so all computations and procedures are described in this package. For example, a measure definition for the target domain of health reporting is built. In this package, a crude rate definition is included. This inclusion contains the parameter and the computation itself. It says that, for a crude rate definition, cases, population, and a factor are needed, and indicates how these are combined.

In a concrete health reporting project like Gesundheit NRW, the *ProjectMeasures-Package* is used. There, *ProjectMeasures* are defined and the needed parameters are mapped. In this project, 52 measure definitions are introduced and all needed computations within a concrete project can be realized with one of theses definitions. The definitions include, for example, crude rate or expected cases. In detail, the measure package consists of parameters. These parameters can have different *Parametertypes*. These types are *MeasureType* or *DimensionType*. *MeasureType* is used to describe procedures or computations, like cell-by-cell computation, based on multidimensional structures. There is no distinction between base measures and measures because, for the definition of a computation, this is not needed. With this construct, nesting is also included and, therefore, requirement M3 is fulfilled. *DimensionType* is used to describe operations on dimensions, like the introduced summation. The *MeasureDefinition* itself is used to describe a single computation. It uses the defined parameter for describing the computation. For the computation description, two alternatives exists: a *Term* or an *ExternalCall*. An external call describes the call of an external math component. This call has to be precise to that it can be automatically generated by the transformation. With this construct, requirement M5 is fulfilled. A *Term*, together with *MultExpr* and *Unary*, describes the computation. In *Term*, elements of addition and subtraction are stored. In *MultExpr*, elements of multiplication and division are stored. In *Unary*, parentheses and negation are stored. The *BaseExpression* stores a factor or associates a *Parameter*. So, it is possible to describe elementary arithmetic operations.

Within the *ProjectMeasurePackage*, all concrete measures instances for a single project like PEIS or Gesundheit NRW are described. In the case of the Gesundheit NRW project, the 466 measures would have been defined in this package. An instance of this package imports measure definitions. These describes the computations. A single project can import multiple definitions, because a project might not be limited to a concrete target domain. A *Project* consists of *ProjectMeasures*. Each project measure has a *MeasureDefinition* type. This is a concrete measure and defines how the values are computed.

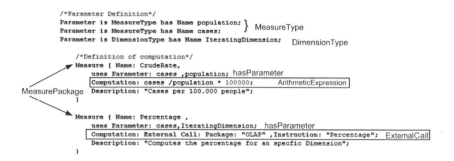

Figure 4.6: Measure Definition for crude rate

In the project measure definition, a distinction between measures and base measures is necessary, not only to fulfill requirement M1, but also to distinguish whether a measure has to be computed or gathered from the data sources. Base measures are based on data sources and, for those, analyses, as they will be introduced in section 4.4.2, must be defined. All these elements have to exist in the resulting project. Here, a distinction between measures and base measures is needed because they are treated differently in the resulting AIS. A *ProjectMeasure* has a *ParameterType*, that defines which elements play what role in a measure definition. For example, in a crude rate definition, this mapping would include which base measure plays the role of population in this particular project. In this way, it can be assured that all needed parameters are included and the type mapping is correct. With this separation, it is possible to reuse domain knowledge and, therefore, M4 is fulfilled.

4.4.1.4   Concrete Syntax

After the abstract syntax has been defined in the previous section, now the concrete syntax is defined. First, it has to be decided if the resulting language is a textual or a graphical language. To decide this, the goal of the measure language is recalled. It is to describe computations and their dependencies, and their relation to a concrete project. A good way of showing dependencies could be the use of a dependency graph. In this graph, the computations could be visualized as trees. This kind of notation has to be learned by the users of the measure language, because they are not used to such a notation. If a graphical notation is chosen, it has to be considered that a large number of elements has to be visualized and, therefore, a graphical notation might be a little bit confusing.

To provide a better understanding of the concrete syntax, first an example is given, and then the corresponding EBNF is presented. In figure 4.6, a small example of a

MeasureDefinitionPackage is given. In the first block, the *Parametertypes* are defined. Here, *Measurestypes* for population and cases are described. Then the measure definition itself is done with the *MeasurePackage* in the next block. Here, the general computations are defined. In the first measure, a crude rate computation is shown. In the second measure, an external call is shown.

In listing 4.4, the Xtext-based grammar, as introduced in section 2.2.5, is given to describe *MeasureDefinitionPackage*. It shows how the concrete syntax is built up. The grammar is based on the abstract syntax from the previous section. It is based on a programming language syntax style that includes brackets and colons to organize elements.

```
 1  (p+=Parameter)+ (m+=MeasureDefinition)+ ;
 2
 3  MeasureDefinition:
 4      'Measure { Name:' name=ID ','
 5      'uses Parameter:' params+=ParameterDefinition (',' params+=
            ParameterDefinition)* ';'
 6      'Computation: ' comp=Computation';'
 7      'Description: ' description=STRING';'
 8      '}';
 9
10  ParameterDefinition:
11      p=[Parameter]|m=[MeasureDefinition];
12
13  Computation:
14      term=Term | ex=ExternalCall ;
15
16  ExternalCall:
17      'External Call: ' 'Package: ' (package=STRING)? ',' 'Instruction:'
            externalCall=STRING;
18
19  Term:
20      m=MultExpr (('+'|'-') term=Term)?;
21
22  MultExpr:
23      Unary (('*'|'/') multi=MultExpr)?;
24
25  Unary:
26      '(' unary=Term ')' | BaseExpression | -UNARY;
27
28  BaseExpression:
29      op=[Parameter] | faktor=INT;
30
31
32  Parameter:
33      'Parameter is' type=ParameterType 'has Name' name=ID ';' ;
34
35  enum ParameterType :
36      DimensionType | MeasureType;
```

Listing 4.4: Grammar for the measure definition

For the definition of measures for a concrete project, the other package, the *Project-MeasurePackage*, is used. In figure 4.7, an example is provided. It shows the project definition for the Gesundheit NRW project. Here, the *MeasurePackage* from the example above is used. In a concrete project, *BaseMeasures* and *Dimension* are defined.

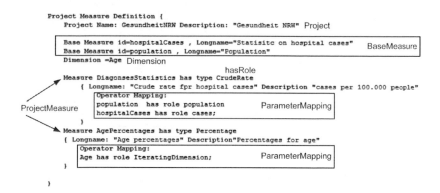

Figure 4.7: Concrete instance of an project measure

Then the concrete *ProjectMeasures* are defined. Within these, next to the naming, the definitions for the *Parametertype* and *MeasurePackage* are mapped.

In listing 4.5, the EBNF for this concrete syntax is provided.

```
 1 ProjectMeasure:
 2     'Project Measure Definition {'
 3     'Project Name: ' name=ID 'Description: 'description=STRING
 4     (baseMeasures+=BaseMeasure)+
 5     (measure += Measure)+
 6     '}';
 7
 8 Measure:
 9     'Measure ' name=ID  'has type 'mea=[MeasureDefinition]
10     '{ Longname: 'longname=STRING
11     'Description' description=STRING
12     'Operator Mapping: '
13     (parameter+=ProjectParameter)+ ';'
14
15     '}';
16
17 ProjectParameter:
18   (m=[ProjectMeasureparamater] 'has role' p=[Parameter]);
19
20 ProjectMeasureparamater:
21     BaseMeasure | Measure | Dimension;
22
23 BaseMeasure:
24     'Base Measure id='name=ID ', Longname='LongName=STRING;
```

Listing 4.5: Grammar for project measures

4.4.1.5   Conclusion

In this section, a measure language was introduced. Based on the requirements, base artitmethic expressions have been chosen as the base for a concrete syntax. This enables a clear definition of mathematical expressions. During the language development, it has been shown that mathematical description is not the most important. The focus of the measure language is more about configuration and connecting of analysis. This impression was strengthened by the fact that the description of mathematical procedures is limited because all operations have to be mapped to multidimensional structures. The general possibility of this has been shown in this section, but it has also been clarified that this is not always useful. Therefore, a call to an external function has been realized.

The measure language enables distinction of domain knowledge and a concrete project within the target domain, as there is one block for the definition and one for the project. With these distinctions, domain knowledge can be reused. The provided concrete syntax fulfills the requirements.

The developed language enables description of facts for the resulting AIS. This language can be used to communicate with target domain experts and can therefore be well integrated in the process.

4.4.2 Analysis

In this section, the analysis language is introduced. This language describes possible analysis in the resulting AIS. The measure language, which was introduced in section 4.4.1, is also used to describe analyses in the resulting AIS. The measure language, however, only describes the general kind of analysis that should be performed with the resulting AIS. With the analysis languages introduced here, analyses are made more concrete. Concrete AIS analyses are based on a multidimensional model, as introduced in section 4.2. This multidimensional analysis structure is described with the analysis language. The provided language describes analysis so concrete that, based on these language instances, data transformations, as will be introduced in section 4.4.5, can be defined and executed.

This section is structured as follow: First, the general requirements for an analysis language are introduced. After this, existing languages are introduced in section 4.4.2.2. Then the abstract syntax is introduced in section 4.4.2.3. In section 4.4.2.4, the concrete syntax is introduced. This section ends with a conclusion.

4.4.2.1 General Requirements for an Analysis Language

The goal of the analysis language is to describe analysis in the resulting AIS. As defined in section 4.2, the resulting AIS should able to support OLAP. The concrete requirements are:

- **A1. Assignment of base measures** In the measure language in section 4.4.1, base measures were introduced as facts in the target domain. These facts can be observed in data sources and have different attributes and forms. The properties of facts are described with the help of the multidimensional model. Therefore, it must be possible to assign an analysis to one base measure from the measure language. It must also be possible to describe the properties of the base measure. This includes an aggregation function .

- **A2. Support of multidimensionality** In the resulting AIS, the use of the OLAP paradigm is required. Further, as OLAP requires a multidimensional data structure, the analysis schema must support these structures.

- **A3. Appropriate definition of hierarchies:** As described in section 3.1, hierarchies in the multidimensional model can have complex structures with many different categories. The analysis language must be able to describe these structures appropriately and be easy to handle; otherwise, modeling would be impossible.

- **A4. Reference of hierarchies** As described in section 2.1.4.1, in an AIS, a global dimension model exists. In an analysis definition, these global dimensions are only referred to. The resulting language should be able to deal with this aspect. This includes the definition of data levels. By reference, it is meant that only a subset of a global dimension can be referred, and a single dimension can be referred more than once in a single analysis.

4.4.2.2 Existing Languages

Existing languages for describing have been introduced in section 2.1.4.3. There, graphical languages were introduced that describe analysis in an AIS with the use of the multidimensional model. For the analysis language that should be realized in this thesis, one requirement (A2) is to support the multidimensional model. Therefore, it might be useful to use one of the languages from section 2.1.4.3. Only one languages can be used, so, it has to be decided which language is chosen as the foundation. It is possible to define a more detailed catalog of criteria. This detailed catalog is also needed because the analysis language is a central part of the autoMAIS approach. The introduced languages only provide a concrete syntax and no abstract syntax. For the semantics of the language explanations are given.

To choose the right languages foundation, the following aspects should be considered.

- **Adequateness :** Can all aspects of the multidimensional model be described adequately. This means, in detail:

  - Difference between measures and dimensions.
  - Clear appearance of complex hierarchies.
  - Difference between levels and categories.

- **Maturity:** Is the language sufficiently researched scientifically and / or proven in practice?

- **Usability:** In this field, the following aspects are relevant:

  - Are notation elements intuitive or is a long introduction needed?
  - Clarity of the overall presentation.
  - Level of learning curve.

Based on this criteria, the following estimation can be made:

- **Adequateness:** All three languages are able to model multidimensional structures, that contains dimensions and cubes. In all three languages, the cube is the central data structure. In all languages, levels can be modeled. ADAPT, as introduced in section 2.1.4.3, provides more flexibility when modeling subsets of dimensions. MERM and DFM provide a strict distinction between quantitative and qualitative attributes. ADAPT is not able to model different facts into one cube. It is possible only in DFM to model an aggregation function.

- **Maturity:** No case studies on these languages exist. Therefore, it is difficult to say which language is more popular. [HPN03] says that ADAPT and DFM are more popular. ADAPT is often used in the US and has more response after publication. [TJ98] claims that ADAPT is most proven in practice.

- **Usability:** The understandability of the ADAPT notation is very high. Based on the clear elements, it is easy to learn. For a user who already familiar with ER-notation, MERM will also be easy to learn. In DFM, relations between levels in a single dimension are not clear, nor is it clear where the aggregation takes place. ADAPT has an element that identifies a dimension. In the other languages, the definition of a dimension is implicit.

A big disadvantage of ADAPT is that it does not differentiate between quantitative and qualitative attributes, but it allows the modeling of complex structures and has a high usability factor. For the concrete syntax of the analysis schema, ADAPT has been chosen. However, it has to be extended to be able to differ between attributes.

4.4.2.3   Abstract Syntax

ADAPT has been chosen as the foundation for the analysis language. Now, in this section, the abstract syntax of the analysis language is introduced. The abstract syntax describes the internal structure of the analysis language.

The abstract syntax of the analysis schema is given in figure 4.8. It represents the multidimensional model, because the goal of this language is to support these structures, as defined in requirement A2. A *Cube* is the central part of the abstract syntax. It contains *CubeMeasures*. The *CubeMeasure* is mapped to a *BaseMeasure*. And so, requirement A1 is fulfilled. Each *CubeMeasure* has an *AggregationFunction*. These functions are limited to ones that are typically used in such systems, including sum, count, average, minimum, and maximum. They can also be extended, if needed. For a measure, a minimum or maximum value can also be defined. This helps to ensure data quality. If, during modeling, it is known that a cube will not contain negative values, for instance, this can be specified here. A cube contains *CubeCells*, and these values are described through a set of *Categories*. A cube also has *CubeDimensions*. This is a link to the referred *Dimension*. The reason for this reference is the concept of the global dimensions and therefore, to fulfill requirement A4. Global dimensions are not defined in this language, because requirement A3 demands an appropriate way of modeling these global dimensions. This requirement cannot be fulfilled completely within the analysis language, therefore the dimension modeling aspects has been transferred to a different language. This hierarchy language will be introduced in depth in section 4.4.3, but some of the elements of this languages are displayed here to show that the complete multidimensional model is covered with this abstract syntax. There is no need to define dimensions here, as they are only referred. The abstract syntax also contains data layers. These describe at what level

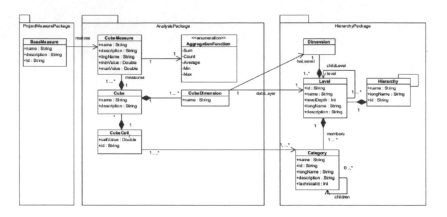

Figure 4.8: Abstract syntax of the analysis schema

of granularity data is available. This is also only a reference, because levels are defined within the hierarchy language.

With the abstract syntax introduced here, it is possible to cover the required elements for an analysis, and that plays a central part in the resulting AIS. It describes major parts of the multidimensional model and integrates parts of the hierarchy language from section 4.4.3 as well as the measure language from section 4.4.1.

4.4.2.4   Concrete Syntax

The concrete syntax of the analysis schema languages is based on ADAPT because it fits best to the requirements, based on the estimations. ADAPT has a large number of notation elements, and that sometimes makes it difficult to learn. For this reason, the number of notation elements has been reduced. Another reason for the reduction is that not all elements provided by ADAPT are needed. To fulfill requirement A3, the definition of hierarchies has been transferred into a separate language, the hierarchy language. The ADAPT languages also includes elements for the logical modeling of dimensions, but due to requirement A3, these are not needed here. The elements from the ADAPT language that are used are: (Hyper-) cube, dimension, dimension hierarchy, hierarchy level, category, connection between notations elements, and loose and strict connections between levels. These elements have been mapped to the same named elements in the abstract syntax.

In figure 4.9, an instance of an analysis schema language is shown which displays the multidimensional structure for the hospital cases from section 3.1.1.1. The prototype development of this language has been done in [Bur08], which was formed during this thesis. The languages can also be used for ad hoc data integration, as presented in [TRA10]. With the chosen concrete syntax, a well-established language has been used. This language has been reduced to fulfill the requirements of the analysis language. In figure 4.9, the corresponding elements of the abstract syntax are shown in gray boxes. The boxes display that all elements within the box correspond to this element of the abstract syntax. The element that is not shown is the *AggreationFunction* because it is defined in a menu in the language editor. In addition, the *CubeCells* are not displayed because they are not part of the domain knowledge which has to be modeled. They are implicitly based on the chosen hierarchy instances. The *categories* are also not displayed because the concrete categories are not important for an analysis. The categories and their definition are discussed in section 4.4.3.

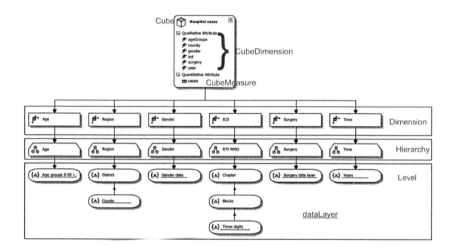

Figure 4.9: Concrete instance of the Analysis language

4.4.2.5 Conclusion

In this section, a language for analysis has been defined. To do so, first, requirements for the analysis language were set. Based on these requirements, an abstract syntax was presented. This abstract syntax is more or less congruent with the multidimensional model, as introduced in section 2.1.4.1. The concrete syntax of the analysis languages is based on ADAPT. An abstract syntax of ADAPT is not included in its original definition. The provided language can be used to model analyses in an appropriate way and, with the meta model, it can be ensured that instances can be processed by tools. The modeling of hierarchies is not part of this language. It will be introduced in section 4.4.3.

4.4.3   Hierarchies

In this section, the hierarchy language is introduced. This language describes the subset of dimensions from the multidimensional model, as introduced in section 2.1.4.1. This section is structured as follows: First, it explains why a separate language for describing dimension is necessary, and why the analysis language from section 4.4.2 is not enough. Then, the requirements of a hierarchy language are introduced in section 4.4.3.2. Based on the requirements, the abstract syntax is presented in section 4.4.3.4. Based on this abstract syntax, the concrete syntax is introduced in section 4.4.3.5. This section ends with a conclusion.

4.4.3.1   Characteristics and Need of a Hierarchy Language

The analysis language from section 4.4.2 is used to describe the central element of the multidimensional model, cubes, and dimensions. The hierarchy language in this section is used for describing dimensions. The description of definition is separate from the definition of the multidimensional model though, as described in section 4.4.2.1, as well as in requirement A3 and A4. The definition of dimension is a central aspect, therefore some more attention has to be paid to this aspect. This is done in this section.

ADAPT and the other describing languages as noted on page 22 are able to model dimensions, but there are different reasons why it is necessary to develop a new language or to extend an existing one. As described in section 2.1.4.1, dimensions and their elements are the central integration point for AIS. The integration is done by the common elements of the dimensions. Dimensions are global for a AIS. If, within an AIS, different cubes with the same dimension names exist, these dimensions are the same. The cubes do not have to contain the whole dimension. In most cases, a cube only contains a subset of a dimension. In different cubes, this can be a different subset but they still refer to the same dimension, and they may share some dimension elements. In this thesis, the difference is called global and local dimensions, as introduced in section 2.1.4.1. A global dimension is valid for the whole resulting AIS. Here, all hierarchies, levels and categories used are defined. A local dimension is used in an analysis. If hierarchies would only be modeled in the analysis language, it would be difficult to create a clear image of the global dimensions. Of course, it would be possible to model global dimensions based on the local ones in the analysis schemas, but dimensions are the integration point for the whole system and so a clear structure is necessary. When generating the global dimension, a lot of semi-automatic work by a domain expert has to be performed. The domain expert has to check to see whether the generation is correct or not. It is therefore better to define the global dimension and then refer subsets of this global dimension in a concrete analysis, as introduced in section 4.4.2.

4.4.3.2 General Requirements for a Hierarchy Language

All together, the following requirements for the modeling of global dimension exist:

- **H1. Support of different hierarchy types** Ability to model different types of hierarchies. These were introduced in section 2.1.4.1 and displayed in figure 2.6.

- **H2. Appropriate conceptual modeling of dimensions** As introduced in section 2.1.4.1, the modeling of dimensions consists of two parts, conceptual modeling and logical modeling. Conceptual modeling describes the hierarchy types and the relationships of levels. The resulting language should be able to describe these relationships in a clear and appropriate way.

- **H3. Appropriate logical modeling of hierarchies** The conceptual modeling of dimensions describes the categories and their relations within the different levels. With appropriate logical modeling of dimensions, it is meant that the resulting languages provides possibilities to associate categories to levels. Furthermore, the language should provide mechanisms to connect a large number of categories in a relationship. It also means that a large number of categories can be modeled easily with additional describing attributes.

4.4.3.3 Existing Languages

In general, it could be said that the existing languages for describing hierarchies are the same as the existing languages introduced in section 4.4.2.2. This is not uncommon because the hierarchy language describes a real subset of the analysis language, which describes the multidimensional model. But, as said in section 4.4.3.1, there is a need to describe the hierarchies in a different language. The introduced languages for multidimensional modeling all enable conceptual modeling of hierarchies, but only ADAPT provides elements for logical modeling.

4.4.3.4 Abstract Syntax

To show how the provided languages meet the requirements, the abstract syntax is introduced first, before introducing the concrete syntax.

In figure 4.10, the abstract syntax of the hierarchy language is shown. To satisfy requirement H1 (the different types of hierarchies) no strict cardinalities between *Levels* exist. The meta model itself checks whether the model connections are valid hierarchies. A *Level* contains categories. These categories are connected to other categories. These relations can be parent- or child-relationships. Categories have an identifier and a *technical ID*. The identifier helps to identify the category during the modeling, and the *technicalId* is used in the resulting system. Categories can have a *ConcreteAttribute*. Attributes assign additional values to a single category. These attributes have a name and a value. Attributes are defined for each *Level*, thereby, it can be assured that the same

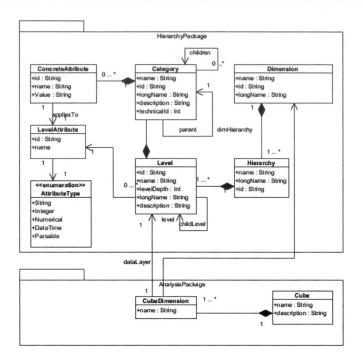

Figure 4.10: Abstract syntax for hierarchies

attributes exists within a level for each category. A more detailed distinction is not necessary because of the technical limitations of AIS systems. For this, the *LevelAttribute* is used. The *LevelAttribute* also specifies the data type for a particular attribute, called *AttributeType*. Levels are connected with other levels via a parent- or a child- relationship. Levels are grouped together in *Hierarchies* and hierarchies are grouped together in a *Dimension*.

Also displayed in figure 4.10 is the connection to the *AnalysisPackage*, which was introduced in section 4.4.2. Here, the reference is made to *Cubes* via the *CubeDimension* that stores the data level and the referred global *Dimension*. This again shows the fulfillment of A3.

4.4.3.5   Concrete Syntax

Based on the requirements, the concrete syntax is chosen. The concrete syntax for hierarchy language is based on the Analysis language, that is based on ADAPT because, in section 2.1.4.3, it was said that ADAPT provides an adequate representation of com-

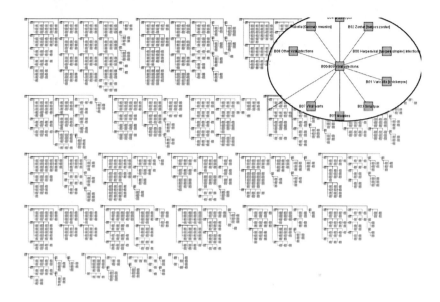

Figure 4.11: Concrete instances of categories for the ICD dimension

plex dimension hierarchies. So it is reasonable to use ADAPT as the foundation for the hierarchies languages. ADAPT provides a good way to conceptualize modeling for hierarchies. The notation elements are reduced to the the following ADAPT notation elements: dimension, dimension hierarchy, and hierarchy level. So, the use of ADAPT fulfills requirement H2. In general, ADAPT also provides the possibility for logical modeling of dimension, but in practice this is not appropriate, because in ADAPT, a concrete category within a level is one graphical element with a connection to the parent level. For a concrete time dimension as introduced in section 2.1.4.1, in figure 2.5, 120 of such graphical elements have to exist next to the conceptual model, when only modeling two years. This is not appropriate, because all these categories have to be defined by the user of the hierarchy language since the definition of categories is domain knowledge and, therefore, it can not be generated. As a result, defining categories in the same way as levels is elaborate. This way of modeling would also not be clear because, in general, a dimension consists of thousands of categories and each single category has, in general, a few attributes. Therefore, the overall view on the dimension cannot be clear because so many graphical elements exist. How this would look is displayed in figure 4.11. Here, the concrete categories of an ICD dimension are displayed, but only for chapter, blocks, and three digit codes. This figure shows that a clear overview of the dimension is not possible with such a representation. To show the instances, a magnifier view is displayed in the upper right corner.

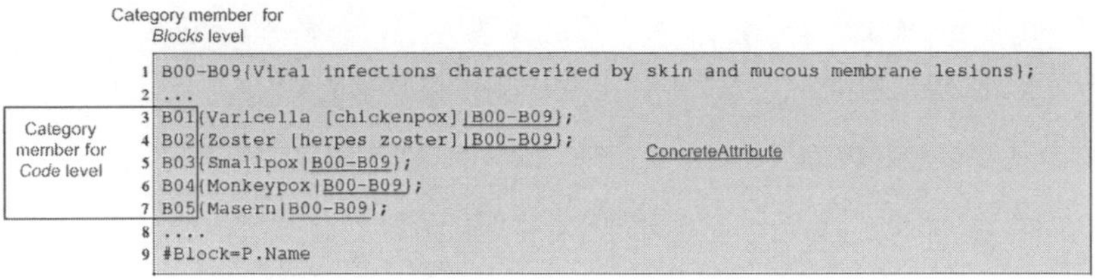

Category member for
Blocks level

```
 1 │ B00-B09{Viral infections characterized by skin and mucous membrane lesions};
 2 │ ...
 3 │ B01{Varicella [chickenpox] |B00-B09};
 4 │ B02{Zoster [herpes zoster] |B00-B09};
 5 │ B03{Smallpox|B00-B09};
 6 │ B04{Monkeypox|B00-B09};
 7 │ B05{Masern|B00-B09};
 8 │ ....
 9 │ #Block=P.Name
```

Category
member for
Code level

ConcreteAttribute

Figure 4.12: Example of defining and linking categories

To be able to fulfill requirements H2 and H3, the hierarchy language is split into two language parts, one for the conceptual modeling and one for the logical modeling. The conceptual part is a graphical language based on ADAPT, and includes the elements *Dimension*, *Hierarchy*, and *Level* from the abstract syntax of the hierarchy language. An instance of this language part is given in figure 4.13. The modeling of categories and their attributes is done with the other part of the language. This is a textual language. An instance of the textual language part is given in listing 4.12. Both languages instances show the definition of the ICD dimension. The language parts are connected via levels and their attributes. For each level, categories and their connections can be defined with the textual language. In listing 4.12, in line 1 the category definition for an ICD group is given. This definition has the concrete ICD code as a name and the long name as an attribute. In lines 3 to 7, concrete instances for the blocks are given. Next to its three digit code and long name, a concrete code has an attribute that defines the block in which the code is in. In line 9, the rule for the definition of parent-child relationships is given. These connections are specified for a concrete level, in this case, the group level. It says that if the block of an instance is identical to the name of an instance in the parent level, then there exists a parent-child relationship. The corresponding elements of the abstract syntax are displayed in gray boxes.

Now the grammar of the textual language is introduced. To be able to model a large number of categories within a level, the category definition is given in listing 4.6 as EBNF. This helps to model a large number of categories. This query defines categories within a level. Categories have a name and are identified by them. Within a level, the name must be unique. The values for the attributes (*AttributeList*) are defined in curly braces. With this category definition, it is possible to model a large number of categories in an expedient way. It is faster to drag and drop and connect drawing elements.

```
1 │    <CategoryName>';'
2 │    <CategoryName>'{'<AttributeList>'}';'
3 │    <AttributeList> ::= <ConcreteAttribute> { '|' <ConcreteAttribute> } ';'
```

Listing 4.6: Query extension for defining categories

With ADAPT, levels are conceptually connected to each other to build up hierarchies. For logical model hierarchies, categories between levels have to be connected. Because of large numbers of categories within a hierarchy, two kinds of operations for this task are introduced. The operations are executed on the child layer to connect parent categories. The first extension can be seen in listing 4.7. This is also called simple connection. In this operation categories are connected through aspects of their names, as equal or non-equal substrings of a particular length. This can be used to structure postal or ICD codes. In Germany, postal codes have 5 digits. For geographical analysis, regions are combined over digits (two-digit postcode areas, for example). Categories can be connected to their first or last digits.

```
1 SimpleCategoryConnection ::= <Position> <Operation> <Number>
2 <Position> ::= 'Last' | 'First'
3 <Operation> ::= '=' | '!='
```

Listing 4.7: Simple category connection extension

The first query extension is good when category names contain hierarchical elements. When category names do not have this structure, attributes can help to build up hierarchies. For example, take a geographical hierarchy which contains region name, as categories and postal codes as attributes. A concrete attribute could be a category named 'Oldenburg-Bürgerfelde' and has the attribute postal code with the value '26121'. The hierarchy in this case can be built up on the attribute postal code. Another example of attribute connection is age groups. In the field of public health, single ages are, in most cases, grouped in 3 or 5 year age groups. To build up a hierarchy, a single age group can have a minimum and a maximum age value, and based on this, attribute connections are made. In listing 4.8, the operations to fulfill these tasks are shown. Connections can be made by comparison of name or attribute values (lines 2 to 5). The comparison can be made on the child or parent category with string values, and the names or attribute values themselves can be connected. Another possible way of connecting categories is the between operations (line 6). Here, connection can be made by defining a range of possible categories. In listing 4.9, the remaining statements to complete the textual language are displayed. These are statements to map non-terminal symbols to terminal symbols.

```
1 <ComplexConnection> ::= <HierarchyQuery> | <BetweenQuery> ;
2 <HierarchyQuery> ::= <Identifier> <Operator> <Value>;
3 <Identifier> ::= <CategoryIdentifier> | <ParentIdentifier>;
4 <CategoryIdentifier> ::= '#'<AttributeName> | <Name>;
5 <ParentIdentifier> ::= 'P#'<AttributeName> | 'P.'<Name>;
6 <BetweenQuery> ::= 'Between('<Identifier>';'<Identifier>')='<Value>;
7 <Value> ::= <Identifier> | <String>;
8 <Name> ::= <String>;
```

Listing 4.8: More complex category connection

With the introduced operations, many cases of parent-child relationships can be defined. If there are no rules on category names or category attributes, the connection between parents and children must be modeled by hand, as it would be done without the

```
1 <ConcreteAttribute>   ::= <String>;
2 <AttributeName> ::= <String>;
3 <String> ::= <AlphabeticCharacter> | <Digit> { <AlphabeticCharacter> | <Digit>
    };
4 <Operation> ::= '=' | '!=';
5 <Alphabetic character> = 'A' | 'B' | ... | 'Z' | '(' | ')' | '[' | ']' ;
6 <Number> ::= <Digit>, {<Digit>}
7 <Digit> ::= '0' | '1' | '2' | '3' | '4' | '5' | '6' | '7' | '8' | '9' ;
```

Listing 4.9: Remaining statements for the definition of the textual hierarchy language

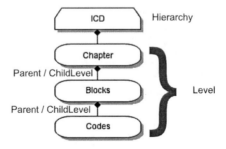

Figure 4.13: Concrete instance of the hierarchy DSL in conceptual modeling

introduced operations. For this kind of connection, a search could be introduced. This search would find categories by name and/or by attributes in different levels and connect them afterward.

In figure 4.13, an instance of the graphical hierarchy language is displayed. It shows the conceptual modeling of an ICD dimension from the hospital cases from section 3.1.1.1.

4.4.3.6 Conclusion

In this section, a hierarchy language has been introduced. It describes the special part of dimensions from the multidimensional model. To fulfill the language requirements, the language has been split into two language parts, graphical and textual. With this distinction, an appropriate and complete modeling of hierarchies is possible. The complete modeling is important because, otherwise, the overall requirement O5 from section 4.1 cannot be fulfilled. Generation is only achievable if all possible knowledge is stored within the language instances. Without the complete hierarchy instances, the generation of a ROLAP AIS, as introduced in section 2.1.4.2, with, for instance, a star schema, would not be possible. However, complete hierarchies are also important for data integration and, therefore, for the data transformation language in section 4.4.5. This is because transformations can be made more specific, and it can be assured that no invalid data are integrated into the AIS, with complete hierarchies.

4.4.4   Data Sources

Data sources are the sources for the resulting AIS. Data from the sources are copied to the AIS as facts. In this section, a language for describing data sources is introduced. For this, first, the requirements for a data source language are introduced. Then, in section 4.4.4.2, existing languages for describing data sources are introduced. The abstract syntax for this language is introduced in section 4.4.4.3. Here, the three different aspects, data connection, data structure, and information, are covered. In section 4.4.4.4 the concrete syntax for the data source language is introduced. This section ends with a conclusion in section 4.4.4.5.

4.4.4.1   General Requirements for a Data Source Language

Data sources exist within an organization that issues an AIS. Data sources can be operational systems like Customer Relationship Managements systems or Enterprise Resource Planning systems. In this thesis, only structured data is considered. These kinds of systems are used for operational business, and each of these systems may contain valuable information. In most organizations, data is distributed in different departments with different systems. Alternatively to operational systems, data can be provided by a service provider. An example of this in the Gesundheit NRW project is population data, which was provided by a statistical office.

To integrate data from different sources, they have to be described. This language must fulfill the following requirements:

- **D1. Support of different source systems:** In an organization, a variety of hardware and software systems exist. Because of this diversity, it is impossible to model all these systems in advance. A language must therefore offer the ability to deal with all possible systems. It must also deliver some kind of abstraction.

- **D2. Data structure description:** With the language itself, it must be possible to describe the structure of data. The goal of this language then, is to describe the data sources in enough detail to enable data transformation to the integrated schema. Therefore, the structure of the data is important.

- **D3. Describing connections:** The resulting language must be able to deal with different types of connections to different systems, including database systems and different kind of files, such as flat- or XML-files.

- **D4. Describing content:** The kind of information stored in a data source is important for the resulting AIS. This kind of information is important for a domain expert. Therefore, the resulting language must contain structures that help to describe the stored data.

- **D5. Automation:** Most of the introduced requirements for the resulting language deals with technical information and accessibility. This kind of information is structural, and the sourcing of it does not need much domain knowledge. Also, the definition of each attribute and its type is schematic work. One goal of autoMAIS is to reduce schematic work in AIS creation automation. For this, the language must be useful. Structures and types can be gathered automatically and it is faster than doing it by hand. Therefore, there is no benefit for the domain expert to do it manually.

4.4.4.2 Existing Languages

For describing data sources, different languages and formats exist. Most of these existing formats are very specific for their use cases. One example of this kind of languages is Universal Business Language (UBL) [OAS10]. UBL is based on XML. It is a widely-used standard for electronic message interchange between business partners. UBL provides techniques to extend the standard to custom needs. With this extension, it would be possible to describe data sources and their distribution. However, UBL is specialized in electronic processing and perhaps would be too costly to adapt, as only a simple language is needed.

Another, less complex approach of describing data sources is the Tuple Attribute language by [IIol02]. This textual language was developed to describe graphs with attributes in a relational way. It would be possible to use this language to describe the content of a data source, but to describe connections, it has to be extended.

Another way to describe relational data sources are ER diagrams by [Che76]. These types of diagrams describe the structure of data sources, as well as relations and their attributes. If using this language, requirement D2 would be fulfilled, but not the others.

Another language in this field is Data Documentation Initiative (DDI). It is a "standard for describing data from the social, behavioral, and economic sciences." [Dat11] The concrete syntax, as UBL, is based on XML. The goal of DDI is to describe the complete data life cycle for data in social studies [Dat09]. The requirement for such a language differs from the requirements in the data source language. In this language, the structure and connection of data is more on focus. Therefore, DDI would be a little bit over-sized.

All the introduced languages are not really suitable. They have different scopes and, in most cases, they provide much more functionality than is needed in this language. Therefore, relevant concepts of the language should be adopted and be integrated into a new customized language.

4.4.4.3 Abstract Syntax

As described in section 4.4.4.2, it is necessary to develop a customized, simple language for data sources. In this section, the abstract syntax of it is introduced.

The description of data sources can be divided into the following three aspects: connections, data structures, and information. These three aspects are independent from each other.

Connections are used for describing the technical accessibility of data sources. They describe how data can be queried. The access is independent of the content of the data source. If it is clear, how data can be accessed, the other aspects can be specified. A change in the connection does not interfere with the other aspects because it is still the same data source.

The data structures describe the format of the data that is stored in data sources. The data structure is independent from the other aspects because it must be clear how the data is built up, but this does not describe the content or stored information.

The third aspect of data sources is the information stored. This aspect is neither technical nor structural, but is for the domain expert. The domain expert knows what kind of information is stored in the data sources. He also knows the value of the data and what this data is used for. This information has to be described, but it is independent from any technical or structural aspect.

Data Connections

Connections describe the technical access to a data source and fulfill requirement D3, as this thesis deals only with structured data, and this structured data can always be transformed into a relational structures. Therefore, it can be assumed that relational databases that are used for OLTP Systems support ODBC. ODBC is an open standard database interface used for accessing databases with SQL. ODBC is implemented in ODBC drivers, which enable connectivity to the databases. Therefore, a connection string is needed for dynamic data sources. A single relational database is managed in a RDBMS. In most cases, a RDBMS contains more than one database, therefore the database itself is needed for connections. A relational database contains many relations. In most cases, one OLTP systems has one database. This database stores all relevant information for the corresponding application. For the resulting AIS, not all relations are relevant, so connections must be able to include or exclude relations. Another important aspect for dynamic data sources is authentication. Connections must therefore be able to provide credentials.

For connecting to files, a path is necessary. This method of connection is considered in this language, but other ways of connecting data sources like URI or WebDAV [Whi10] are also possible. They are not considered here, because access would be technically different, but the sources themselves can be treated the same way. So, including this is only a technical aspect. Also, the type of the static data source is needed. Common types are CSV, XML, or Excel. The type is not needed to establish connections, but it helps to automate the structure access because the structure is independent from the connection. This provides a higher level of abstraction for the automation because the structure is not dependent on the connection. This fulfills D1.

In figure 4.14 the abstract syntax for data connection is shown. This meta model enables connections to both kinds of data sources. A *Connection* contains a URL. The

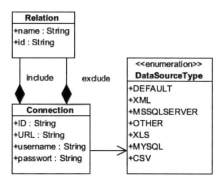

Figure 4.14: Abstract syntax for data connections

URL includes, in the case of a static data source, the file path. In the case of a dynamic data source, the *connection* contains the connection string to the RDBMS, including the database name. For authentication, two fields, *username* and *password*, are used. It would also be possible to use other means of providing credentials, for example, key-based access, but this would only be a technical aspect that would not change the general concept. To identify the data source type, the enumeration *DataSourceType* exists. Based on the *DataSourceType*s it can be determined what kind of data source is present. This enumeration does not do a simple distinction between the two types, but specifies the concrete technology within which data is stored. In the case of dynamic data sources, these are XML, CSV, and XLS(X), the common data exchange formats for organizations. In the case of static data sources, the enumeration specifies the RDBMS type. The reason for this is that this distinction is better for automation.

Data Structure

Next to the connection, the data structure of a data source is needed. To fulfill require-ment D2, data structures describe how data is stored and formatted. A common model for structuring data is the relational model. The relation model is a simple model for rep-resenting data and is the foundation for RDBMS. It has a simple structure and is based on mathematical relations [EN10]. It consists of the elements: relations, attributes, enti-ties, and tuples. The relevant OLTP systems and data sources that are used in this thesis are based on this model. For this reason, the relational model is used for defining data structures.

In section 4.4.4.3, it was said that there are data formats other than relational. These formats can all be converted into the relational model, but it is necessary to show how the elements of the relational model can be mapped. A single CSV file can be seen as one single relation, or entity. The file headers are the attributes. The single lines are the tuples. An Excel file can be threaded similarly to a CSV file. A spreadsheet can be mapped to a relation and the row header can be seen as attributes. Taking into account that Excel provides the use of multiple spreadsheets, each spreadsheet can be seen as a relation. Some may compare this fact to the relational database concept. A spreadsheet can contain relations to other spreadsheets. These can be mapped to a foreign key constraint. In this concept, limitations exist. The formation of a single spreadsheet may sometimes not be as strict as in a CSV file, so attributes could also be found horizontally. Also, it is possible that cells could contain values that cannot be converted to relational concepts. In these cases, a domain expert must allot these structures by hand.

Another format for a static data source is XML. It has two characteristics that makes it difficult to map XML to the relational model. XML data has an order, and this order is based on the tag position in the containing file. The relational model does not contain an order. The missing order is no problem, because the resulting AIS does not need an order because the data is ordered by the analysis.

The hierarchical structure is a more complex problem. In [LN05], it is shown that in general, all kind of XML formats can be converted in the relational model. For automation, some algorithms exist. In [ML03], an algorithm for conversion with regular tree grammars was introduced. When using an automatic approach, the quality of the resulting relational models may not be as high as if it was done by hand. Sometimes a semi-automatic conversion may be necessary. In this thesis, instances of the structured data will be processed automatically. For this reason, the created relational model may reduce performance during querying.

Information

Connections and structures of data sources are technical aspects. The third aspect to consider is information. Information describes the content of a data source and therefore fulfills D4. It describes what kind of valuable information is stored and the usage of it within the organization. This aspect is used by a domain expert to map data sources to analyses.

In figure 4.15, the abstract syntax for describing data sources is shown. Together with figure 4.14, this describes the complete aspect. This abstract syntax is based on the relational model. Every *DataSource* has describing attributes like Name and ID and it has a relation to a *Connection*. The *DataSource* contains relations. These relations have at least one *Attribute*. These attributes represent the concrete values and descriptions of a data source. An *Attribute* can contain information about itself for the domain expert. It also contains some elements for data description. The enumeration *DataType* describes the type of data. This enumeration contains only abstract data types because then it can be used for all kinds of data sources. The attributes *scale* and *precision* describe arity and decimal places for a single attribute.

In the introduced abstract syntax, the aspect of information is covered only briefly. This can be done with the *DataDescription* class. It contains the department in which

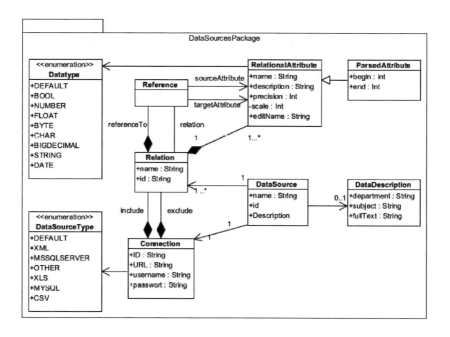

Figure 4.15: Abstract syntax for describing data sources

the data is produced or used. It also describes the *subject* and users of the data source. In *fullText*, some text can be stored to provide additional information to the data source. The reason why all the attributes of the *DataDescription* are modeled as strings is simple. It is because this description is not planned to be automatically-processed. It is used by the domain expert, who needs some structured information to decide the usage of a data source and, for this, strings are enough because the domain expert will be able to deal with this. For further development for the aspect of information it can be wise to use ontologies or linked open data [Lin11].

4.4.4.4   Concrete Syntax

The aspect of data sources does not need as much domain knowledge as the other aspects. Therefore, it has a big technical part. For the technical part, an automation is possible. Because of the automation, this aspect has been divided into three parts. For identifying the structure of data, automation tools can be written. For each kind of data source, as seen in figure 4.15, a kind of program can be written that builds up the structure. An excerpt of such a tool is shown in listing 4.10, as introduced in [Mas11]. This listing shows how relations can be detected by using foreign key constraints. The query shown is specific for MS SQL Server; for other SQL dialects, this query has to be adjusted. With this kind of program, the bigger part of the data source instances can be generated. The connection must be known, then these programs can build up the structure. The developed tool for this is called **DQ2MM** and fulfills requirement D5.

```
1  SELECT
2      K_Table = FK.TABLE_NAME,
3      FK_Column = CU.COLUMN_NAME,
4      PK_Table = PK.TABLE_NAME,
5      PK_Column = PT.COLUMN_NAME,
6      Constraint_Name = C.CONSTRAINT_NAME
7  FROM INFORMATION_SCHEMA.REFERENTIAL_CONSTRAINTS C
8  INNER JOIN INFORMATION_SCHEMA.TABLE_CONSTRAINTS FK ON C.CONSTRAINT_NAME = FK.
9  CONSTRAINT_NAME
10 INNER JOIN INFORMATION_SCHEMA.TABLE_CONSTRAINTS PK ON C.UNIQUE_CONSTRAINT_NAME =
       PK.
11 CONSTRAINT_NAME
12  INNER JOIN INFORMATION_SCHEMA.KEY_COLUMN_USAGE CU ON C.CONSTRAINT_NAME = CU.
       CONSTRAINT_NAME
13  INNER JOIN (
14     SELECT i1.TABLE_NAME, i2.COLUMN_NAME
15     FROM INFORMATION_SCHEMA.TABLE_CONSTRAINTS i1
16     INNER JOIN INFORMATION_SCHEMA.KEY_COLUMN_USAGE i2 ON i1.CONSTRAINT_NAME = i2
           .
17     CONSTRAINT_NAME
18     WHERE i1.CONSTRAINT_TYPE = 'PRIMARY KEY'
19 )PT ON PT.TABLE_NAME = PK.TABLE_NAME
```

Listing 4.10: Identifying relations by using foreign key constraints [Mas11]

Therefore, for a concrete syntax of data sources, only the aspects of data connections and information have to be considered in depth. The target domain expert should be able to see the automatic structure to be sure that it was correctly identified. He also must be able to include or exclude relations, because it can be possible that not all extracted relations will be used.

The representation of data connections can be made simple because a single data connection will be specified by database experts, so no qualified language will be necessary. For that reason, the generated syntax of the EMF Framework will be used. The concrete syntax is based on the abstract syntax in figure 4.14. An instance of the concrete syntax is shown in figure 4.16. It shows the connection to a data source that is an Excel file which is stored on the hard disk. This connection has to be defined by hand. Based on this definition, the data structure can be extracted automatically. The result is shown in figure 4.17. For this, it would also be possible to use another concrete syntax like the already-mentioned ER diagrams. It would be possible to generate an ER-diagram based on the information provided by the DQ2MM tool.

Figure 4.16: Instance of the concrete syntax for the aspect of data connection

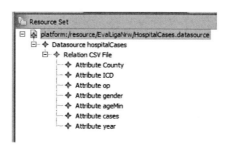

Figure 4.17: Instance of the concrete syntax for the aspect of data structure

4.4.4.5   Conclusion

In this section, a language for describing data sources has been introduced. This languages fulfills the requirements set out. The developed concrete syntax is made simple, but it can be extended to certain needs. With this language, all needed data sources in the resulting AIS can be cataloged. The automatic generated structures can be used to describe transformations, as they will be introduced in section 4.4.5 into the integrated dataset. This language is used as a foundation in the data transformation language in section 4.4.5.

4.4.5   Data Transformations

When data from different sources are integrated into an AIS, the source has to be transformed so that they fit the needs of the integrated schema. In section 2.1.6, this was introduced as ETL. If ETL is not done during an AIS creation project, combined analyses on different sources within the resulting AIS, are impossible. In section 4.4.4, a language for describing data sources was introduced. There, it was described how different types of data sources and their structure can be cataloged. In section 4.4.2, a language for describing analysis in the resulting AIS was introduced. With instances of this language, the integrated schema is defined implicit; One the one hand, as said in section 4.4.4, data sources can have different formats and schemas; but on the other hand, the analysis language defines one integrated schema for all kinds of analysis, with integration on common hierarchy language instances, as noted in section 4.4.3. So, there is a need for describing transformation from the data sources to the integrated analysis schema. A language for describing these transformations is introduced in this section.

This section is structured as follows: First, the requirements of a language for data transformation are introduced in section 4.4.5.1. After this, existing languages are described briefly, then the abstract syntax of the data transformation language is given in section 4.4.5.3. This is followed by the concrete syntax in section 4.4.5.4. This sections ends with a conclusion.

4.4.5.1   General Requirements for a Data Transformation Language

In this section, the general tasks for data transformations are described. Based on these demands, general language requirements can be derived. The resulting language should be able to cover the complete ETL process as described in section 2.1.6. The concrete requirements are:

- **T1. Define mappings on schema and attribute level:** Mapping in an ETL process can be defined on different levels. The resulting language should be able to describe schema as well as attribute mapping. This can lead to at least a two-step process because a mapping on attribute level can only be defined when the schema mapping has been completed.

  As an example, take the infections and population data sources from section 3.1.1.1. If applying a simple name matcher on these two sources and targets, this would lead to the result that all gender, age, and region attributes from the sources would match both targets. This is not textually correct because population source has to be mapped to population analysis, and the infection count source has to be mapped to the infection count analysis. If a mapping exists between these schemas, the name matching on the attributes would be correct. Taking the properties of an AIS into account, this double-matching is not surprising. The attributes, in most cases, are dimensional attributes, so every source and target must include dimensional information. And, because there is this dimensional information, these double-matching results are normal. It would be more useful first to map the source and targets in general.

- **T2. Multiple sources for one target:** In some cases, one integrated schema has more than one source schema. This factor can have different reasons: First, different tables have to be combined to get the needed information. This can be foreign-key constraints, for instance. Second, the data for one target originates from different data sources. An example of this is given in section 3.1.1, where data for the infections rate come from different sources.

- **T3. Import of data sources and analysis:** To be able to model transformation, the sources and targets must be part of the data transformation language, otherwise, the mapping cannot be defined, because there is nothing to define. To enable a better, or, better said, conformable usage, these elements should not be modeled by hand because this is rather time-consuming. An ideal way to handle this could be to enable instance imports from data source instances as described in section 4.4.4, and analysis schema instances as described in section 4.4.2.

- **T4. Automatic generation of mappings (schema matching):** To fulfill the automation requirement from section 4.1, the transformation language should provide some automatism. A useful automation is to provide an automatic mapping between schemas and attributes. This is also called schema matching, as introduced in section 2.1.6.2, matching.

- **T5. User defined mappings:** The users of the language should be able to define mapping between attributes and schemas by themselves. This is important because only the user can decide which matchings are correct. As described in [RB01], a good matching algorithm exists, but a full automation is impossible, so the final decision must be made by the users. A language for data transformation should consider this.

- **T6. Definition of transformations:** As described in section 2.1.6, in most cases, data has to be transformed to conform to the integrated schema. The resulting languages should provide a mechanism to describe transformations.

- **T7. Clearly-arranged hierarchically structures:** Data sources, as well as analysis, are hierarchically-structured. In the resulting language, these structures should be easy to identify. This supports a clear assignment for the mappings.

4.4.5.2 Existing Languages

In section 2.1.6.1, existing languages for describing the ETL process have been introduced. In this section, mainly languages in commercial tools have been introduced because many research works are based on these tools' concepts. Also, in the foundation section, more formal languages have been introduced, but these languages are not suitable here because they have been designed for a more specific target domain. So in this

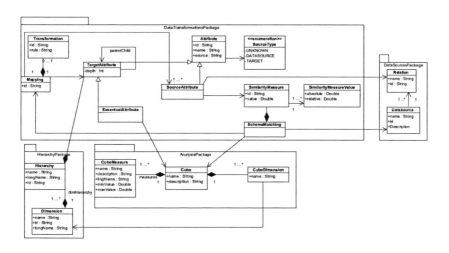

Figure 4.18: Abstract syntax for the data transformation language

thesis, a similar approach, as in the introduced related work, will be used: a graphical language for describing mapping and enabling matching. For transformation, a textual language will be used.

In the field of transformation languages, existing languages have been introduced not only in section 2.1.6.1, but also in section 2.2.4. These languages differ in their target domain. The software engineering field provided languages for model transformations. In section 2.2.4, ATL and QVT were introduced. The domain of these languages are model transformations in the sense of MDSD. The domain of the data transformation language is data integration, therefore it is useful to search in this domain for an appropriate language. Such a language has been introduced on page 28. The general concept of R_2O and the autoMAIS data transformation are quite similar. R_2O maps from relational sources to ontologies, and autoMAIS maps from relational sources to meta model instances. The mapping targets are conceptually quite similar, because they are both based on object-oriented concepts. Therefore the approach fits well. R_2O provides the ability to describe complex transformations. Because autoMAIS uses a general approach, it cannot be determined what transformation will be needed, therefore the ability to write complex queries, as is possible in R_2O, is needed. Another positive quality of R_2O is that it is fully declarative and can therefore be used for self-verification. In this way, inconsistencies and ambiguity can be detected.

4.4.5.3   Abstract Syntax

In figure 4.18, the abstract syntax for the data transformation language is given, but this only describes the mapping, and not the transformation itself. This is done to fulfill T1 and T6. The definition of the transformation is independent from the mapping.

This abstract syntax also contains elements for the matching to fulfill T4. There are two kinds of matching: one for schema and one for attributes. Both kinds use *Schema-Matching*. Based on the *SchemaMatching*, *Mappings* are defined. These are defined on *Cubes* from the Analysis schema and *DataSources*. These are imported from the particular languages as introduced in sections 4.4.2, 4.4.3, and 4.4.4. So, this fulfills T3.

For T4, to support the introduced concepts from section 2.1.6.2, more is needed. Matchings and mappings are defined on *Attributes*. These *Attributes* can be a *SourceAttribute* or a *TargetAttribute*. The difference is realized by inheritance. To find mappings, matchers are executed for each source-target-attribute combination on schema and on attribute level. Each source target attribute combination has different matching results. These results are described with *SimilarityMeasure*. Each matcher has a *SimilarityMeasureValue* that contains the absolute and relative matching results. The absolute value describe the concrete matching result of a concrete matcher, and the relative value considers the match threshold value. These matching results are not an explicit part of the concrete syntax, but the automated mapping is part of the language and is performed in the background, so these elements are needed for the language.

The concrete mapping is modeled with *Mapping*. These are suggested based on the matching result that is stored within the *SimilarityMeasures* mappings. However, these mappings can also be defined by the language user, so T5 is fulfilled. The cardinality from mapping to the source attributes ensures T2.

With the introduced abstract syntax, it is possible to describe mappings on attribute and schema levels. For the population data from the Gesundheit NRW project as described in section 3.1.1.1, this means that the population data source can be mapped to the defined population cube. Also, each attribute within the population data source can be mapped to an attribute within the population cube, which contains elements from the *HierarchyPackage*. Depending on the attributes, these mappings can be user-defined or based one matching results.

The introduced abstract syntax describes the *Transformation* within a mapping as a string, so next to the mapping, a transformation language has to defined. Because of its properties, as introduced in section 4.4.5.2, R_2O has been chosen as a transformation language. The abstract syntax is not introduced here because it is a pre-existing language and its abstract syntax is defined implicitly through it's concrete syntax. The link between these two languages is the *Transformation*.

4.4.5.4 Concrete Syntax

To describe the data transformation language, first the mapping language is described. This is a useful separation because first it has to be clear what should be transformed, and how. Then the logical modeling can be performed.

In figure 4.19, the concrete syntax of the data mapping language is given. In this figure, the corresponding elements of the abstract syntax are displayed in gray boxes. Data sources as well as analysis schema are display as rectangles. The data sources are displayed on the right side of the figure. They can be identified as they contain the Relation which are shown by a rectangle within a data source. A concrete relation contains attributes, in this case *SourceAttributes*. Each attribute is displayed as a box. The analysis is displayed on the left side of the figure. The rectangle consists of one rectangle for each of the different data levels and one measure. These are all used as *TargetAttributes* because, in this language, these are handled equally, and therefore, are converted to attributes. The reason why only the data levels are displayed, and not more elements of the multidimensional model, is that mappings can only be defined on the data levels. In most cases, the data layer should be enough to derive the necessary informations, but if information about the whole dimension is needed, then the hierarchy language from section 4.4.3 can be used. In that case, this information is stored in the abstract syntax. With this containment rectangle style, the hierarchical structure of the relational model can be expressed. The analysis is also handled equally because then the user does not have to learn a new notation for nearly the same concepts. The mappings are defined with the help of lines between attributes and data levels, or attributes and measures. To decide if a transformation has been defined or not, a circle is displayed on this line. If a circle contains a bold dot, this indicates that a transformation between these elements has been defined. This is also where the relation between the graphical mapping language and the textual transformation language occurs. All elements that deal with matching, such as *SimilarityMeasure* or *SchemaMatching*, are not part of the concrete syntax because they are not defined by the languages, but are user-generated. For further realization details, refer to [Mas11].

The concrete syntax of data transformation is R_2O. As the syntax has already been introduced in section 2.1.6.1, it is not introduced here. However, the concrete syntax that is defined with the help of an EBNF can be found in the appendix on page 207, from listing A.3 to listing A.6. The only aspect of interest might be which parts of R_2O have been used in this thesis, as R_2O consists of six main parts. The first two parts are not used int this thesis, because this functionality has been covered with the mapping language from section 2.1.6.2. These two parts describe import of sources and targets. The other four introduced parts are used. With R_2O, an appropriate language is provided that can execute transformation. More examples of the transformations can be found in chapter 5.

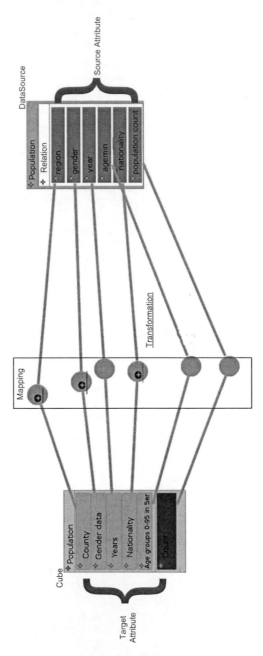

Figure 4.19: Concrete instance of the mapping language

4.4.5.5   Conclusion

In this section, a language for data transformation to describe the ETL process was introduced. To reduce schematic work, matching is part of this language. This helps to define mappings automatically. The data transformation language is split into two parts, graphical and textual, as was also done in the hierarchy language in section 4.4.3. This division was made because the mapping language provides a good overview on the defined mappings since, with the provided concrete syntax, it is clear which schema and attributes belong together. On the contrary, describing transformations with the help of a graphical language would be not clear, therefore an existing textual language was used.

With the introduction of this language, the complete AIS architecture as introduced in section 2.1.2 is covered. So, it is possible to describe a complete AIS with the introduced languages. With the language introduced here, it is possible to describe a transformation from the data sources noted in section 4.4.4 to the implicitly-defined integrated analysis schema from section 4.4.2.

4.4.6   Data Quality

Data quality is an important factor for AIS. If it is not possible to achieve defined quality criteria, the project will fail [BG09]. Therefore, in this section, a language that deals with this aspect is introduced. Data quality is a huge aspect that covers many different fields. A taxonomy of data quality that was defined in [Hin02] identifies 16 regions of data quality. For each AIS, different quality criteria exists. These criteria were defined individually. Depending on the sources and the quality criteria, effort has to be made to achieve quality goals, and this has to be done individually. Therefore, the treatment of data quality as a whole is a very complex and costly problem. To address this aspect in its entirety is beyond the scope of this thesis. However, it is an important aspect of AIS that should not be neglected. An aspect of data quality is integrated in this work. The reason for this integration is to show the ability to treat this important aspect with the developed methods. The aspect shown is consistency.

Before introducing languages for consistency, it must be clear where to deal with data quality issues. Three possible areas can be found: in the data sources, data transformation, or after data integration. An advantage to dealing with data quality at the data sources is that all contextual information and the knowledge of the domain expert who maintains the data, is still present. So, only some extension to the data source languages from section 4.4.4 would be needed. A disadvantage is that every data source must be treated individually. No unified format for data exists, so this would be costly. During data integration, in the staging area, the data from different data sources have a unified format, but in most cases, the contextual knowledge is lost. It would be possible though, to extend the data transformation language from section 4.4.5. Dealing with data quality after data integration is not in the original definition of an AIS and is only rarely done. In some cases, it may be useful to consider quality issues after integration. The usefulness is shown in [SA10], but can be only applied in a few cases. The disadvantage of this approach is that data does not stay the same. In the resulting AIS, the same analysis can have different results. For economic reasons, it is best to deal with data quality issues during data integration because all data has the same format, so in the case of autoMAIS, this would mean to use the analysis schema from section 4.4.2. The lack of context information can be partly adjusted through the information aspect of the data source in section 4.4.4.3. It can also be insured then that the data stays the same after integration.

In this section, now a selected data quality issue is introduced. This aspect deals with inconsistent data and is applied after data transformation, when all instances have a common format, so that rules can be easily applied on the AIS. This approach has been published in [TBA10] as well as in [BTA10]. This approach defines a language for defining consistency constraints for target domain experts.

This section is structured as followed: first, requirements for the data quality language are introduced in section 4.4.6.1. Then existing languages are discussed briefly in section 4.4.6.2. In section 4.4.6.3, the abstract syntax for the data quality language is introduced.

This is followed in section 4.4.6.4 by the concrete syntax of this language. This section ends with a conclusion.

4.4.6.1   General Requirements for a Data Quality Language

The introduced data quality language aims to describe the special issue on consistency constraints. Consistency constraints, in this particular case, means dependencies of categories on different hierarchies. As introduced in the analysis languages from section 4.4.2, a concrete analysis always refers to a set of hierarchies with categories. These categories from the different dimensions could depend on each other. For instance, an analysis that describes cancer cases refers to the hierarchy ICD to define the concrete diagnosis and a gender dimension. For ICD C53 (Malignant neoplasm of cervix uteri), only female cases are valid. This means that it is not possible to have male cases with this diagnosis. Each category, C53 and male, are valid categories that refers the right dimension and level, but for this particular analysis, this combination is invalid because they are not consistent. The InDaQu language deals with this kind of consistencies. It is the definition of valid category combinations from different hierarchies.

The scope of the data quality language is very limited, therefore, only the few following requirements have to be met:

- **Q1. Definition of consistency constraints for categories:** This means that the resulting languages should be able to model the introduced consistency constraints from the example.

- **Q2. Appropriate language for target domain experts** The defined consistency constraints are specific to a particular target domain so, in most cases, only the target domain expert is able to define such specific rules. Therefore, the resulting language should be appropriate for the target domain expert.

- **Q3. Finding inconsistencies:** With instances of this language, it should be possible to find inconsistencies and not to repair them. As will be shown in section 4.4.6.2, there are approaches that do so. This should not be done by the InDaQu language because in AIS, depending on the target domain, these uncommon cases might be important for analysis results, and an automated correction would lead to invalid analysis results. Therefore, here an automation of schematic work, as it was done in other languages, is not possible here.

- **Q4. Usage of the multidimensional model:** The central aspect of an AIS is the analysis and integrated schema, which, in the case of autoMAIS, is the multidimensional model, as noted in section 4.2 and section 4.4.2. This schema has the advantages that clear navigational structures exist. The properties of the multidimensional model should be used to improve definition of constraints for the target domain expert.

4.4.6.2   Existing Languages

In the field of InDaQu, some languages exist and these are briefly introduced here.

In the target domain of health care edit and imputation systems are spread to solve the addressed problem of inconsistency. The general idea of these systems are described in [FH76]. The goal of these systems is to find inconsistent data and replace it with consistent data. This replacement is based on statistical functions. Inconsistencies are defined as edits. These kind of rules are, in [FH76], specified as textual language that defines valid or invalid combinations of attributes based on a set notation. These languages do not make use of the multidimensional model. The use of such a language might be a little bit difficult because it is not intended to import existing instances.

It can be said that, more or less, any languages that provide the ability to define constraints are suitable candidates for InDaQu. This includes programming languages and/or languages that are based on predicate logic. An example of a language that is based on predicate logic, and is of common use in the database domain, is datalog [EN10]. It is a programming language that is based on Prolog. In the field of software engineering, OCL [Obj11b] is a language candidate. It is a textual language defined by the OMG and helps to define constraints and queries on MOF objects.

Datalog and OCL are both languages that fit in their target domain. But neither are suitable here, because they are both specialized for their domain. This might make it difficult for a target domain user to learn such a language. Therefore, a more general approach has to be applied here.

4.4.6.3   Abstract Syntax

The language **InDaQu** was originally developed for the domain of public health care systems [TBA10]. Inconsistent data can be found in hospitals, cancer registries, and other data producers. These data quality problems often result in high costs and low medical quality [Bai03].

One example of such a problem is that, in 2010, 43 % of the checked insurance bills had coding errors [Ste10]. Inconsistent data does not only exist in the health domain. It also occurs in other domains, including criminal proceedings [ES05], legal systems, and federal statistics.

To deal with these kinds of inconsistencies, InDaQu defines rules on hierarchy elements. In figure 4.20, the abstract syntax is displayed. A *Rule* has a left side and a right side. In general, a rule defines a mapping between dimensions. This is called *left-* and *rightDimension*. This defines that consistency dependencies exist between a set of dimensions. The concrete rules are defined on *categories* from the hierarchy language from section 4.4.3. With the use of the hierarchies, Q4 is fulfilled. To ensure that *Categories* fit to their *Dimension*, the OCL constraints in listing 4.11 are used. A *Rule* can be used for different analysis; therefore, the *AnalysisPackage* is used.

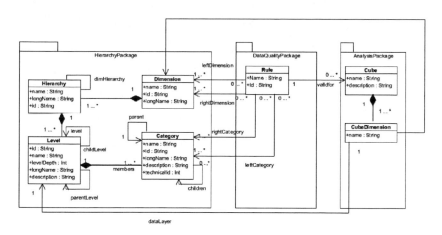

Figure 4.20: Abstract syntax for data quality

With the introduced abstract syntax, the definition of constraints is possible because category instances can be combined to valid tuples, so Q1 is fulfilled. The abstract syntax does not have any other elements than the one shown. Therefore Q3 is met.

For a better understanding of the abstract syntax, the following example is provided. ICD and T, N, and M [Int01] are hierarchies that are used within a cancer cases analysis for an AIS in the target domain of a population-based cancer registry. ICD defines categories for diseases (in this specific case, malignant neoplasms) and T, N, and M define a coding set of tumor-describing attributes. ICD was already introduced before, and T, N, and M are new hierarchies. The coding standard provides many different values for T, N, and M. Not all combinations are valid, and the valid combinations depend on the diagnosis. Which combinations are valid can only be defined by a domain expert, because much knowledge about the coding standards and the cancer domain is needed.

For each specific neoplasm, only some T, N, and M values are valid. Therefore, the following rule can be specified: $ICD \rightarrow \{T, N, M\}$. This is the described dimension mapping. As the concrete rules are applied on categories, an example is: $C11.0 \rightarrow \{T = 0, N = 1, M = 1\}$ This rules expresses that in an analysis that uses all four dimensions, a new value is integrated and the ICD code is C11.0. Then, the values for the tumor classification must be T=0, N=1, M=1, otherwise this is an invalid tuple. Medical experts agree that such rules exist for the description of tumors. These rules are defined by the previously-described IARC, UICC, or another institution.

```
1 Context Rule inv: rightCategory.Level.Hierarchy.Dimension = rightDimension;
2 Context Rule inv: leftCategory.Level.Hierarchy.Dimension = leftDimension;
```

Listing 4.11: OCL constraints for rules

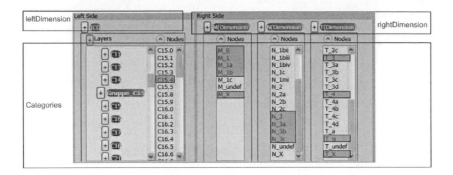

Figure 4.21: Language editor for the InDaQu language

With the introduced meta model, consistency constraints can be defined. These can be applied during the data integration process. A bigger challenge is how to provide a concrete syntax for the provided abstract syntax.

4.4.6.4   Concrete Syntax

In this section, the concrete syntax of the data quality language is introduced.

As shown in the example rule $ICD \rightarrow \{T, N, M\}$, the definition of the introduced consistency constraints requires a lot of domain knowledge. Therefore, it is difficult for an AIS design expert or a system administrator to have the ability to model such detailed domain knowledge. The only role that could perform this task is the target domain expert. The target domain expert, as introduced in section 4.3.1.1, is not familiar with languages or software development. So the languages OCL and datalog introduced in section 4.4.6.2 do not fit here. It is also not possible to develop languages that are realized with model-driven tools like EMF, GMF, Xtext or DSL tools as these languages are hosted in an integrated development environment (IDE). The realized languages and their editor tools will be introduced in section 5.1. As these languages are hosted within IDE, it is not easy for target domain experts to use these languages. It would be possible that the target domain expert defines the concrete instances, but as seen in section 4.4.3, a hierarchy has many instances, so this would be a lasting process. For these reasons, another way of realizing the data quality language was used.

A screen shot of the developed editor is displayed in figure 4.21. This prototype implementation has been devolved in [Pio09], which has been formed in this thesis. It shows the modeling of a concrete rule for $ICD \rightarrow \{T, N, M\}$. It can be seen that the developed language is a tabular-based layout, with each of the table rows representing one hierarchy. The concrete rules are defined by selecting the categories. On the left side the ICD-code 'C15.4' is selected (highlighted). Then, on the right side the T-,N-, and M-values are shown that are valid for this ICD category. The highlighted T-,N-, and M-values are currently valid for the given ICD-code, but the user can simply select other values and modify the selection. These defined rules are stored and can then be executed after data integration. It would also be possible to apply these rules on an existing AIS. This can be useful if new rules have been defined, and it has to be ensured that the data within the AIS follows these rules. If data violates these rules, it can be changed. This is against the AIS paradigm, as introduced in section 2.1, but in some cases, this is needed. As the language instances are defined by target domain experts, this might occur more often because they are working with the resulting AIS and, during this work, rules are more likely to come out. So it can be said that Q2 is fulfilled. The concrete syntax has been developed together with target domain experts.

As described in [TBA10], the InDaQu approach has been applied in the cancer register of Lower Saxony. There, different consistency rules have been realized. The users of the language were able to define the rules by themselves with the help of the InDaQu language. These rules are then transformed so that they can be used during the data integration process. These rules were able to find consistency errors.

4.4.6.5 Conclusion

With the introduction of the InDaQu language, it has been shown that special instances of data quality issues can be integrated as language into the autoMAIS approach. As said before, this is a specialized approach for modeling consistency constraints only. A specialty of this language is that the concrete syntax has been designed for target domain experts, so that they can define and execute the domain models. It has been shown that such an approach is applicable by introducing this language in the cancer register of Lower Saxony. However, the development costs for such an editor are much higher than for IDE-based languages . Because the editor has been developed from scratch, no code generation was possible.

The language introduced here is specific for a particular data quality issue. This issue of consistency does not always occur in AIS creation projects. For instance, in the evaluation in chapter 5, InDaQu has no application. But this section should act as a general example of data quality issues in the context of the autoMAIS approach.

There are more aspects of data quality to consider during an AIS creation project, but these aspects cannot all be addressed with the autoMAIS approach as they are specific to the target domain and the data sources.

4.5   Meta Models and Their Integration

In the previous sections, 4.4.1 to 4.4.6, all relevant aspects and their languages for AIS creation have been introduced. In this section now, it will be shown how these aspects are integrated with each other and the advantages of such an integration is provided. The integration is part of the autoMAIS requirements from section 4.1. There, it was said that integration can reduce schematic work and improve verification.

First, the advantages of an integrated meta model are presented in section 4.5.1. Then, in section 4.5.2, the integration itself is described. Then the modeling architecture of the autoMAIS approach is presented in section 4.5.3. After this, the section ends with a conclusion in section 4.5.4.

4.5.1   Advantages of Integrated Languages

Each concrete syntax of the languages in section 4.4.1 to section 4.4.6 have been developed independently. The reason for this is that the different aspects have to be adjusted to their problem domain, so it is a separation of concerns. It has to be ensured that the aspect can be modeled satisfactorily for the users of this aspect. So, when designing the languages for the different aspects, the aspect itself was part of the consideration; not the integration. This is because the needed concepts are the same and, therefore, the abstract syntax of the languages are integrated with each other.

For each aspect, some kind of software can be generated for the resulting AIS, independent from the other aspects. Next to the reuse of already existing elements, the integration has more benefits, as also introduced in [TF08]. There exist two kinds of advantages which are introduced now. The first kind describes how a single aspect, or a few aspects, benefits from the integration or import of the integrated element instances from other aspects. The second kind are those that concern all introduced aspects and therefore benefit the whole AIS creation process.

- **Analysis schema and hierarchies** The analysis schema from section 4.4.2 and the hierarchy language from section 4.4.3 together can be combined as a multidimensional aspect. Based on instances of this aspect, software for creation of the integrated schema can be generated. Examples of the integrated schemas have been introduced in section 2.1.4.2.

  If the multidimensional aspect is integrated with the data sources aspect from section 4.4.4, then both general and specific interfaces for data integration and transformations can be generated.

  With an integration of the multidimensional schema with the measure aspect from section 4.4.1, it can be said in what analysis a measure is used and vice versa. Another advantage of this integration is that it can be determined what categories are useful for an analysis.

- **Data quality:** Using the InDaQu language from section 4.4.6, integrated with the hierarchy language, the hierarchies with all their defined categories can be used in the data quality language, and do not have to be defined within the language. During data integration, the incoming tuples are checked for consistency. In these tuples, it can be assured that the categories within the tuples corresponds to a category within the resulting AIS.

- **Data source transformations:** In the case of an integrated data source transformation from section 4.4.5, these transformations are not specific for the target schema (e.g., a specific to a concrete instance of a snowflake schema). So the target schema can be changed, for example, to a star schema without changing the data source transformation.

All the points discussed before affects only certain aspects. The following points refer to the complete AIS creation process. If the different aspects are integrated, the following can be done with less effort, but with great benefit for the resulting AIS.

- **Source usage analysis:** With the help of an integrated meta model, it can be said which sources are used for which measure computation. This can done because data sources are integrated via the data transformation aspect to the analysis, and analyses are connected to measures. If this was done by hand, the different technical systems involved would have to be checked manually.

- **Measure dimension mapping:** When the measures and analysis are not integrated with each other, this can lead to problems during runtime. An example of this was given in section 3.1.2. There, the measures and analysis were not integrated. This means that hierarchies were used in the measure definition and not in the corresponding analysis. This leads to errors at runtime because only then the computation was executed, and if this mapping was incorrectly defined, this leads to errors.

- **Useful categories for an analysis:** When defining measures , cubes are combined at runtime. These combined cubes can have different dimension sets. The resulting cube has the union of dimension set as dimensions. So it is possible to perform analysis for all these categories, but one useful result is the intersection of the dimension set, because valid data exists only at the intersection. This can also be applied at the categories and levels as well. When combining cubes with a age dimension, but different data levels, only the intersection will provide valid results.

- **Handle technical limitations:** The resulting AIS will be deployed in a technical infrastructure. Based on the type of infrastructure, some limitations exist for particular problems. Some of these problems can be handled by integration. Examples of these limitations are: assurances of unique names and support for parallel hierarchies. Some OLAP servers, like Mondrian [Pen11], need unique identifiers for their level definitions. For only one hierarchy instance, this can be done by the model itself, but to ensure that all instances for the resulting AIS do not have double level names, all the levels and all hierarchy instances have to be checked within the integrated meta model. Such a check can be easily applied on the integrated meta model; without this, the issue is difficult to find. Another technical problem is that Microsoft Analysis Service [Mic12b] does not support parallel hierarchies. In the case that the resulting AIS should be based on this system, all hierarchies must be checked for this issue. This also can be done easily within the integrated meta model.

- **Integrated documentation:** The different languages and their instances are good for the documentation of the specific aspect, but more documentation can be generated based on the integrated meta model. An example of this kind of documentation is DWH Schema creation as described in [GR09a]. Such types of documentation can be generated from the integrated meta model.

- **Single point of truth for design decisions**: The integrated languages and their defined instances provide a single point of truth for design decisions. It can therefore be said what measures, analysis schemas, and transformations are defined in a particular AIS instance. It can also be determined which instances are related to each other. If something is not stored within the integrated model, it does not exist in the resulting AIS. So, all design decisions can be reproduced here.

All these points show that an integration of the different models is useful and the integration provides great advantages for the AIS creation process.

4.5.2   Technical Language Integration

In this section, it is introduced how the different languages are integrated technically with each other, with more detail than in the previous sections. A good example of an integrated meta model is the CWM, which was introduced in section 3.2.1.

In [KT08a], two ways of model integration are suggested: via common elements, and via transformations. These two approaches are shown schematically in figure 4.22. When doing integration via transformation, the different languages are kept separate, as shown in figure 4.22 (a). When one wants to integrate a language into another, this is done by transformation to the model of the target language. These kinds of transformation are possible over a large number of languages, as is displayed in figure 4.22 (a). When using this approach, the order of languages is fixed. It is not possible to create an instance of language 2 and then go back to language 1 without defining an additional transformation. Also, with this integration approach, the overall requirement O4 from section 4.1 cannot be fulfilled. Another way of integrating languages is via common elements. This approach is shown in figure 4.22 (b). In this approach, the integration aspect is present during language design time, so there is also a search for common elements.

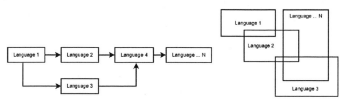

(a) Integration via transformation taken from [KT08a] (b) Integration via common elements taken from [KT08a]

Figure 4.22: Integration of meta models

[KT08a] suggests using integration via common elements, if possible, because when using the other alternative, the same concepts are modeled separately in every language. This makes them more difficult to maintain and does not support reuse.

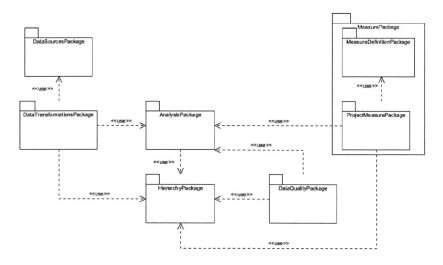

Figure 4.23: Integration of languages

In this thesis, the integration approach by common elements is used because, in the different languages, elements exist that can be used as common elements. These common elements have also been shown in the definition of the abstract syntax of the particular aspects in section 4.4.1 to section 4.4.6. For instance, in the data quality language from section 4.4.6, the abstract syntax of this language consists of only one element. All other needed concepts were used from other packages (hierarchy and analysis).

used package \ using package	Measure Definition	ProjectMeasure	Analysis	Hierarchy	DataSource	DataTransformation	Dataquality
Measure Definition		•					
ProjectMeasure							
Analysis		•			•	•	
Hierarchy		•	•		•	•	
DataSources						•	
DataTransfomration							
Dataquality							

Figure 4.24: DSM for packages

In the particular language, elements from other languages have been used, as they describe the same concepts. Another advantage of this approach is that integration via common elements is done here, so no other work has to be done. Now, the overall integration is presented. It describes how the different packages and classes are integrated with each other.

First of all, a general overview on the integration is provided. To do so, the package integration is shown. In figure 4.23, the packages from the different aspects are given. They show which package uses elements from the other. For a better overview, a **Dependency Structure Matrix** (DSM), as it was introduced by [CBB⁺10], is shown in figure 4.24. A DSM is a square matrix that lists the packages as columns and rows. A 1 in i^{th} column and j^{th} row indicates that i uses j. In [CBB⁺10], it is said that this is a form of the uses style. It can be used for debugging, testing, and gauging the effect of changes. In addition, the uses style is good for showing integration.

In both representations of the package integration, it can be seen that the *Analysis* and *HierarchyPackage* are used by most packages. This is not surprising because both of these packages represent the the data warehouse in the resulting AIS. Since the data warehouse is the central part of an AIS, the analysis and hierarchy packages are the central part of the autoMAIS meta model.

A more detailed integration can be seen in figure 4.25. Here, a UML diagram of the complete autoMAIS meta model is presented. It shows which classes in which packages depend on each other. For a better overview on the integration, only those elements that have a connection to an element in another package are displayed. Also, for the detailed integration, a DSM is shown in figure 4.26.

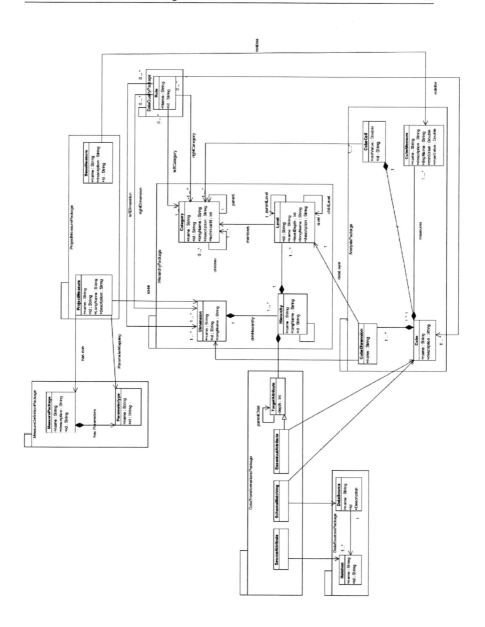

Figure 4.25: Integrated meta model

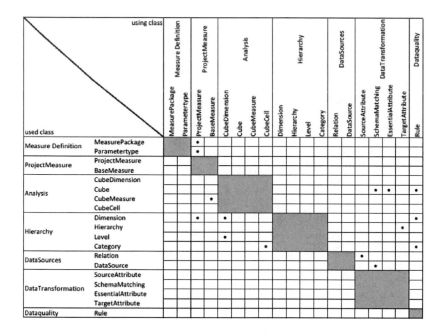

Figure 4.26: DSM for classes

4.5.3 Modelling View

In the previous section, it was shown how the meta model elements are integrated with each other. Now, in this section it describes what the integration for the autoMAIS user looks like. Therefore, the modeling architecture is described here. It shows how the integration from section 4.5 is realized in a software architecture. This architecture describes the modeling environment for creating all introduced language instances for an particular AIS creation project. This modeling architecture supports the engineering part of AIS creation.

The modeling architecture is displayed in figure 4.27. This figure represents a component-and-connector style as introduced by [CBB$^+$10]. To be precise, a repository styled as a UML component diagram is shown. The goal of this figure is to visualize the integration of the languages and their meta models to enable integration and a repository functionality. The architecture consists of the following elements.

- **Data accessor components:** Each of the languages and their meta models act as data accessor components for the modeling repository. In the figure, each language is described with two components. One represents the meta model, and the component above represents the concrete syntax and the editor. They are connected via an interface. This separation has been done to support changeability. The developed meta model for each language should be able to describe the aspect completely to enable integration and generation. The concrete syntax can be exchanged, if needed. For example, a concrete syntax for the analysis language ADAPT was chosen, but the meta model is not specific to ADAPT, but, rather, to the general multidimensional model. If needed, the concrete syntax can be changed to DFM, for example, as introduced in section 2.1.4.3. It must be ensured that the new concrete syntax supports the meta model. Then, nothing has to be changed in the other components' integration, and generation will be possible in the same way as before. So, there is a loose coupling between the languages and their meta model.

  Each meta model accesses the repository component to store a concrete instance to the repository. Each component can store a complete instance or a segment. These writing connectors are displayed with the *Store* interface. For some languages, as for the analysis or the data transformation language, a reading connector is also needed, because they refer to other modeling languages. Therefore, they need these instances to enable the generation.

  The generation of the AIS project is done by the *AIS Generation* component. To do so, this component also has a reading connector to the repository. To ensure that a valid configuration will be generated, the global AIS checks are performed by a *global AIS* component. This component realizes the *Check plausibility* activity from the autoMAIS process model from section 4.3.

- **Repository components:** The *Integrated meta model repository* is the repository component. It stores and loads all languages instances. But it does more than that.

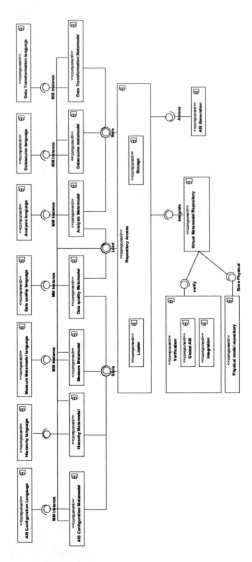

Figure 4.27: Automais Component and connector Style

To enable the integration as introduced in section 4.5, each new model is reviewed in the *Verification* component. So, for every new or modified instance, it is checked to determine whether it fits into the integrated meta model or not. This is done by the *Integration* component. All model instances are physical stored, using the *Physical model repository* component. To access the repository, the *Repository Access* component has been introduced. It acts as a facade [GHJV94].

4.5.4   Conclusion

In this section, the integration of the different aspects was introduced. The different aspects are integrated via common concepts. So, requirement O3 from section 4.1 is fulfilled. It has been shown that integration provides many advantages. One great advantage is the single point of truth for design decisions for AIS creation. Everything that will be used in the resulting AIS is described within the integrated meta model instance; otherwise, it does not exist. In this section, the modeling architecture was also presented, which shows how integration is presented to the autoMAIS user. This shows how the integrated meta model can be used in practice.

4.6   Transformations

In this section, the transformations for generating an AIS based on the autoMAIS models
are described schematically. In section 4.5, the integration of the different meta models
has been introduced. These models are now used to describe the transformations for
the resulting AIS and, therefore, fulfill the overall requirement O5 from section 4.1.
The integrated meta model has the advantage for the transformation that, not only the
different meta models have to be considered, but the definition can be based on the
integrated meta model directly. With the description of the transformation, here the
requirement O5 from section 4.1 is fulfilled.

This section is structured as following. First, the general overview on the transformations is provided in section 4.6.1. After this, in section 4.6.2, the autoMAIS transformations are related to the terms of MDSD. In particular, the platform for the autoMAIS
approach is introduced. Then, transformations within the autoMAIS approach are introduced in section 4.6.3. This sections ends with a conclusion in section 4.6.5.

4.6.1   Transformations Overview

Before the transformations are introduced in depth, an overview of the different transformations is provided. The goal of an AIS creation project is to build up an architecture
of different systems and components that, all together, build up the AIS. The required
components and their roles in the resulting AIS were introduced in section 2.1.2.1. In
that section, a reference architecture for AIS was introduced and it was said that the
components of the reference architecture must exist in every AIS. To describe the transformations, this reference architecture is used.

In figure 4.28, the AIS reference architecture is shown with the autoMAIS meta models and their transformations. The gray components are covered within the autoMAIS
approach, and transformations for these components exist. The analysis is not shown because it is not part of the AIS creation process. When an AIS is built up properly, which
is one of the autoMAIS goals, all kinds of analysis software can be used to access the
AIS easily. Data sources are not shown in gray because they are not part of the AIS creation process. On the left side, the autoMAIS packages are displayed. The arrows show
which autoMAIS package is used to build up a particular component of the reference
architecture. The arrows forming the original reference architecture are now displayed
with dashes. The integrated meta model, as introduced in section 4.5, is displayed as a
UML component because it is the result of the integration process. Therefore, it can be
seen as a component rather than a package.

The following packages build up the AIS within the transformation. To make the
transformations easier to understand, it can be said that one element of the reference
architecture is defined by one transformation. These transformations use one or more
packages from the autoMAIS models.

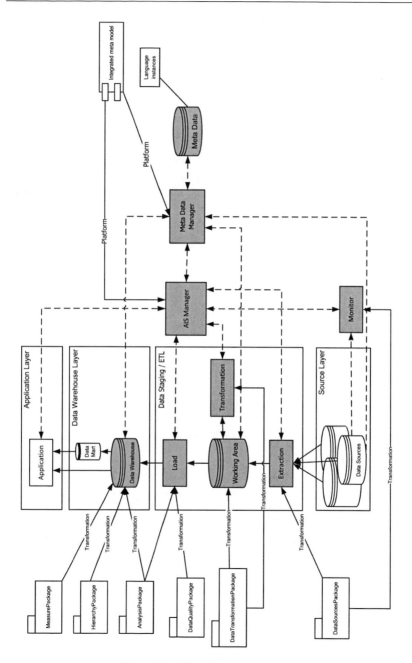

Figure 4.28: Transformation overview

- **DataSourcesPackage** → **Monitor:** The DataSourcesPackage contains information about how to access the structure of the data source. A monitor needs access to the sources to identify changes. The transformation could generate a program for this task or, in the case of a SQL-based data sources, triggers could be generated.

- **DataSourcesPackage** → **Extraction:** As information about accessing relevant attributes is stored within the DataSourcesPackage, a transformation could generate a program that extracts relevant data from the sources. Alternatively, a configuration file for an existing ETL tool could be generated to fulfill this task.

- **DataTransformationPackage** → **Transformation:** The DataTransformationPackage contains information on how to transform source attributes to attributes in the integrated analysis schema. For the transformation itself, the transformation rules are needed. As this information is stored in the package, SQL scripts or a configuration file for an ETL tool can be generated based on this information.

- **DataTransformationPackage** → **Working area:** The working area is the place where extracted data from the sources is temporarily stored for transformation and loading. As the DataTransformationPackage contains information about which sources exist and how these are structured, this can be used to generate temporary tables.

- **(DataQualityPackage, AnalysisPackage)** → **Load:** The AnalysisPackage contains information about what kind of data is required as fact data for a particular analysis. In the DataQualityPackage, the combination of fact data that is invalid for a particular analysis is defined. This information can be used to generate a Load component that only allows the integration of valid fact data. For this, a SQL script or program can be generated.

- **(MeasurePackage, HierachyPackage, AnalysisPackage)** → **Data warehouse:** The AnalysisPackage, together with the HierarchyPackage, contains information about the multidimensional model within the data warehouse. This information can be used to generate, for example, a snowflake schema which contains all facts and dimensional data in an OLAP server configuration. Alternatively, a program could be generated that stores the multidimensional model. The MeasurePackage contains information about how to combine analysis in computation. This can be used to generate calculation rules within the OLAP server configuration, or a configuration for an external computation engine like R.

- **Integrated meta model** → **AIS manager:** The integrated meta model fulfills, as was introduced in section 4.5, tasks of the AIS manager, because the integration and checks that are performed are identical to the monitoring and control of the AIS manager. This functionality is not the result of a transformation, but of integration.

- **Integrated meta model** → **Meta data manager:** The tasks of the meta data manager are also done by the integrated meta model because the autoMAIS process enables collection of meta data and their relations.

- **Meta Data:** The meta data of an autoMAIS-enabled AIS are the different integrated language instances.

This section only provided an overview on the required transformations. Some of these transformations will be introduced more deeply in section 4.6.3.

4.6.2   AutoMAIS in the Terms of MDSD

In section 2.2.1, the general terms of MDSD have been introduced. Now these terms are applied to the autoMAIS approach. In figure 4.29, the general MDSD terms, as shown in section 2.15, have been applied to AIS creation with autoMAIS.

The languages that describe the domain concepts are now made concrete. In autoMAIS, six different languages for these tasks have been developed, as seen in section 4.4.1 to section 4.4.6. These languages describe the AIS configuration model. Based on these language instances which are combined to an integrated meta model, transformations are defined. These transformations are shown in more detail in this section. There are several transformations that are based on one or more language instances. The result of the transformation is the configuration code for the platform. The platform has been split up into three parts because an AIS consists of different software components and tools, as said before. So, an AIS configuration is not based on one single platform, but on several platform parts. These parts are:

- **Computation engine**: This stores and executes the computation rules within the data warehouse. This can be, for instance, a computation engine within an OLAP server.

- **Data staging**: This component performs all tasks related to the ETL process. For this, commercial tools like Kettle, as well as self-defined components, exist.

- **Data warehouse**: The scenario addressed in this thesis is ROLAP. Therefore, for the data warehouse, a relational database like PostgreSQL and an OLAP server like SSAS, is required.

- **Management components**: These component control and monitor the AIS process. Parts of these components can be ETL tools or self-defined components.

For each part of the platform software, concrete tools exist. A transformation has to be defined for a concrete software tool. For instance, in the evaluation in chapter 5, several transformation have been developed. For the computation engine, the MUSTANG platform which is based on R project [RPr11] has been used. The corresponding transformation generates SQL statements to describe the parameter within the data warehouse and R functions to describe the computations. For the data staging, a self-defined component has been used, so the corresponding transformation generates a configuration file for these components. The data warehouse in the evaluation was built on Microsoft SQL

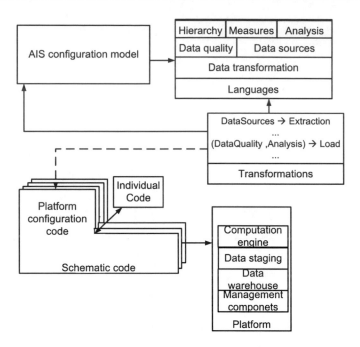

Figure 4.29: MDSD terms in the autoMAIS approach

Server and SSAS. Thus, the transformation generates a snowflake schema in T-SQL and a configuration file for the SSAS.

If one of these components is exchanged with another software, a new transformation for this platform part and this particular software has to be defined. The other transformations can be left untouched. If, in the evaluation scenario, the data staging component is exchanged, a new transformation for this new component has to be defined.

So, with autoMAIS it is possible to generate AIS that are based on different platform components, which can be chosen individually for each AIS creation process.

4.6.2.1   A MUSTANG Configuration

As said in the previous section, to be able to develop a transformation, concrete instances of the component from the references architecture must be chosen for the resulting AIS. An example configuration of the reference architecture for an AIS, that is based on MUS-TANG, has been introduced in section 2.1.2.2. Here now, the components that will be used in the evaluation of the autoMAIS approach in chapter 5 are described. Now, not only the components, but also the configuration of them, are described. For a configuration of an AIS, only the data warehouse and the data staging layer must be considered, because the data sources are outside the resulting AIS as they cannot be configured, but just used. Also, the application layer is fixed to the CARESS application.

- **Data Staging:** The MUSTANG platform does not provide any mechanisms to integrate data. Therefore, some software has to be realized that reads the data sources, executes the R_2O scripts, and generates insert scripts for the fact-tables of the specified SQL script. For this, a simple data staging component has been developed. This component uses autoMAIS model instances to integrate data. In this component, all transformations from section 4.6.3.1 are included.

- **Data warehouse:** The data warehouse consists of two elements: the configuration of measures, and an OLAP server. For the description of measures, C# code is used. This code describes the definition of measures and their computations, as well as the calls of R functions. Executed, this code stores the definition within the Microsoft SQL Server. As shown in section 4.6.1, for a ROLAP data warehouse, relational tables and OLAP server configurations are required. Within the MUSTANG platform, there is functionality that generates the relational tables and the OLAP configuration from a multidimensional object structure and therefore provides functions for storing dimensions and cubes. This structure can be built up by using .NET. For the transformation, C# code generates the multidimensional structure. This multidimensional structure can be executed and generates a snowflake schema for Microsoft SQL Server or PostgreSQL.

4.6.3 Transformation Within autoMAIS

In this section, now the autoMAIS transformations are described more deeply. However, they are not described with complete technical realization, as this would be inappropriate. Therefore, the transformations are described by the target component of the reference architecture from section 2.1.2.1, and the concrete components from section 4.6.2.1. The transformations are ordered by layers of the AIS reference architecture.

4.6.3.1 Data Staging Transformations

Extraction

For extracting the data from the data sources, instances from the *DataSourcePackage* are used. For each instance, the *Connection* is used to provide data access. Based on the *DataSourceType*, different connections are possible. For each connection type, the access was implemented. For instance, the *CSV* type is connected by *FileInputStream*. For the database connection types, a JDBC connection is used. So, for each data source, one of these implementations is configured with the language instance that describes the concrete access to the data sources.

Next to the connection, the data from the sources has to be extracted. To extract the data, the *Relation* and the containing *RelationalAttribute* are used. For each *RelationalAttribute* and the corresponding *DataType*, a Java object is created. Together with the connection to the data source and the transformed type information, the data from the source can be extracted line by line. The extracted data is then stored in memory for further processing.

Working Area

The working area was realized in memory, as described in the previous paragraph. Here, the data is extracted based on the *Relation* and its attributes. This way of realization is adequate for the scenarios described in this thesis, because the amount of data is not so huge. It is more likely MBs than GBs. It would also be possible to generate a working area within a relational database. To do so, for each data source a temporary database table would be created. The attributes and their types are derived from *RelationalType*, but in this case, the types do not have to be mapped to Java, but rather, to SQL types. If the table has been created, Insert-statements can be generated to fill the temporary tables.

Transformation

The data transformations are performed in two steps. First, the source data is transformed into plain text for the corresponding analysis instance and, after this, transformed into the technical representation of the relational data warehouse. For the data transformation, instances from the data transformation language are used. In these instances, the *SchemaMatching* defines which *AnalysisPackage* and *DataSourcePackage* instances belong together.

For the transformation, the R_2O defined functions and conditions have been implemented in Java, so that it can be configured with a concrete R_2O Xtext instance. A transformation is executed if a *rule* is defined within the *Transformation*; otherwise, the source attribute can stay the same. This is the case for each *Mapping* and *TargetAttribute*. At the end of this transformation, the attributes are transformed into the representation of the analysis schema. This means that a tuple consists of the *category names* and, if the *AggregationFunction* within the analysis instance is not *count*, a number is added. This plain text representation is then transformed into the technical representation of the snowflake schema within the Microsoft SQL Server. This means that the instances are transformed into SQL Insert-statements. The generated Insert-statements are executed immediately with a JDBC connection. This is the most simple form of a load component.

4.6.3.2 Data Warehouse Transformations

Computation

Within the MUSTANG platform, the computation on cubes are stored within the data warehouse in relational tables. To create and fill these tables, the MUSTANG platform provides an API. So, for a transformation to generate computations, C# code must be generated. The central object of the measures API is the *SummaryVO*, which describes a cube. A *BaseSummaryVO* describes one cube that is stored in the data warehouse. For each measure language instance, the following is generated. For each *MeasurePackage* instance, a method is created. This method has a number of parameters. These parameters can be a Dimension or another *SummaryVO*, which can also be a *BaseSummary*. These two types depend on the *ParameterType*. Within the method, the computation is based on the given parameters. If the computation is within the *MeasurePackage* instance, an external call is defined, and then the R function with the given parameters is called. Otherwise, the given computation is transformed into an R statement which can be directly executed by the MUSTANG platform at runtime. This is possible because all computations within MUSTANG are executed by using R. Next to the call, a function to store the resulting summary is also generated.

The generated methods are called by the code that is generated based on the *ProjectMeasureInstance*. The code uses this method to define computations for a concrete project. For each *BaseMeasure*, code is generated that stores this as *BaseSummaryVO*. For each *ProjectMeasure*, one of the previously-defined methods is called. The needed parameters are defined by the *ParameterMapping*. Based on the integration from section 4.5, the referred dimension can be loaded from the data warehouse, so there is no integration gap.

ROLAP Schema and OLAP Server Generation

To generate a data warehouse that enables OLAP analysis, as introduced in section 2.1.5, and based on a RDMS, two elements are needed: first, the relational representation of the multidimensional structure, and second, an OLAP server configuration that maps the relational structures back to multidimensional structures of the OLAP server. As described in section 2.1.4.2, one way to describe a multidimensional structure in the relational method is the snowflake schema. The described transformations create such a schema.

Within the MUSTANG platform, there are components that generate a snowflake schema and the OLAP Server configuration based on C# code. Therefore, the described transformations do not generate SQL and XML files, but this code. The central object that the MUSTANG platform provides is the *OlapMetaVO* object. Within this object, the multidimensional structure of all cubes and dimension for the resulting data warehouse are stored. So, the transformations generates C# code that describes these objects. For each hierarchy instance from the integrated meta model, a dimension object is created.

In this dimension object, the *Hierarchy* and *Levels*, and their *LevelAttributes*, are stored. Also, objects for the *Categories* and their *concreteAttributes* are generated and put in relation with levels and each other. Each category object requires an ID that is unique for the resulting data warehouse. This can be assured by the transformations because an ID generator is also generated. The general structure of the object is provided by the platform, and a concrete hierarchy instance is used to fill this.

To generate the cube for the *OlapMetaVO*, the analysis instances of the integrated meta model are used. For a cube instance, the previously-defined dimension objects are referred. For this reference, the *CubeDimension* is used. The framework also provides elements to store *CubeMeasures* and their aggregation function. It can be said that the provided framework describes the complete multidimensional structure. An advantage for the transformation is that the different language instances are integrated with each other, and that the transformation generates valid C# code. This means that is can be assured that a referred dimension and level exists.

The generated C# code can be executed to generated the ROLAP schema and the OLAP server configuration. What is done during the execution of this code is the same as if the transformation directly generates a snowflake; therefore, it is described here.

For each level, a relational table is created. This table has as attributes, next to names and descriptions, one attribute for each *LevelAttribute* and one foreign key constraint of the parent. Each tuple of this table is one *Category* that has been modeled as a *member* for this *level*. For each cube, a fact table is generated. The fact table contains a foreign key constraint for each *dataLayer* table. The information about the dimension and hierarchy is not stored within the ROLAP schema, but within the OLAP server configuration. The generated OLAP configuration stores the names of the dimensions and hierarchies. In this configuration, the mapping of the concrete tables is defined, too.

4.6.4   Execution of the Transformations and Generation of the AIS

To understand the transformations including the dependencies, a UML activity diagram is given in figure 4.30. First, the autoMAIS modeling and integration is done as introduced in the autoMAIS process model from section 4.3. If the modeling is completed and the checks are successful, the instances are transformed as described in this section. First, the code to generate the data warehouse, and then the measures, are generated. After the generation, the C# code is executed. During this, the snowflake tables and the measure configuration are stored in the database. After this, the data transformation can be executed to fill the snowflake tables with fact data.

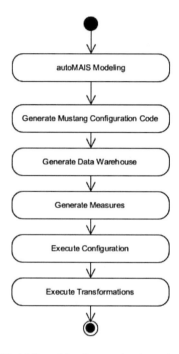

Figure 4.30: UML activity diagram for the code generation

4.6.5   Conclusion

With the description of the transformation, it has been shown that the generation of an
AIS configuration is possible, and requirement O5 from section 4.1 is fulfilled. In this
section, only the general concepts of transformations, and an example of the MUSTANG
platform, have been provided. The autoMAIS approach in general is more flexible than
this. To support different technical components of the reference architecture, new transformations have to be developed. For instance, if the measure computation should not be
executed within R, but within the OLAP server, a new transformation for MeasurePackage $\rightarrow$ data warehouse has to be written by the transformation developer. The development of a new transformation is only needed if, during an AIS creation project, a new
component is used. Existing transformations can be reused in every project. Therefore,
the autoMAIS is flexible enough to support different target architectures and platforms.

4.7 Conclusion

In this section, the autoMAIS approach was introduced. In this conclusion, first, issues of verification and correctness are introduced, and then the concept is summarized.

4.7.1 Verification and Correctness

In the language sections, nothing has been said about verification and correctness of the different languages. The general concepts are identical for each language, therefore they are introduced here.

Verification is one of the challenges of AIS creation, as introduced in section 3.1.3.2. Verification is a process to ensure that an AIS meets its specifications. To do so, the different aspects and their integration must be correct. There are two kinds of correctness, syntactical and semantical.

Syntactical correctness for a concrete aspect means that defined instances correspond to their abstract syntax. Each language in the autoMAIS approach provides mechanisms to provide syntactical correctness. For instance, it is not possible to define measures with the use of an undefined base measure within the measure language. In the hierarchy language, it is not possible to define categories without a parent category. Or, within the data transformation, it is not possible to define a mapping without a target. So, it can be assured that only syntactically-correct languages can be defined within the autoMAIS languages. This means that the result of a transformation, as will be introduced in section 4.6, generates valid artifacts, on the condition that the transformations are correct. So, syntactical correctness can be provided for each aspect.

Semantical correctness is a little bit different. It means that there are no logical errors within the different model instances. This is part of the validation process. Validation ensures that an AIS corresponds to its requirements. In general, this means that, within an AIS, the right data for analysis exists. In the case of the Gesundheit NRW project, this would means that the resulting AIS fulfills the task of health reporting and that all measures are correctly defined, as well as the data transformations and analyses. This must be done not only for the complete AIS, but also to ensure that the different language issues of semantic correctness exist. In the measure language instance, for example, that means that a crude rate definition must be based on a measure that describe populations, and not some other cases. In the hierarchy language, the parent-child relationships are set, but they are not semantically-correct for a particular instance. An example of data transformation is that the transformation from an age year to age groups is not correct. Each of the examples can be modeled syntactically-correct. These semantical error cannot be automatically detected, because domain knowledge is needed. This domain knowledge is provided, as introduced in the autoMAIS process model in section 4.3, by the target domain expert. Therefore, semantical errors must be detected by him. All the autoMAIS languages have been designed in a way that the target domain expert is able to understand the model instances with the help of the AIS design expert, although he is not able to define them. Therefore, the model instances defined by the AIS design expert can be reviewed by the target domain expert to identify semantical errors. As a result, the introduced semantical errors might be found within the design process. Another issue here is that the autoMAIS approach raises the level of abstraction so that semantical errors are reduced, because the instances are defined within the target domain, so it is possible to identify semantical errors with the help of the autoMAIS models.

In section 3.1.3, it was also shown that a big challenge in AIS creation is verification among the different aspects of an AIS, because in traditional approaches, it cannot be assured that the different aspects fit together. This is different within autoMAIS as introduced now. For the integration among different aspects, two integration points within the autoMAIS process, from section 4.3, exist. In the process model, there exists one activity, called *check plausibility*, where one part of the integration is done. Here, it is checked if all model instances fit together. This plays more or less the role of syntactical correctness of integration, which will be introduced later. The bigger part of the syntactical correctness is done within, or better stated, between the different design activities from the process model. Some design activities like *define hierarchies* and *define analysis*, depend on each other. This can be seen in the hierarchy and analysis languages. This means that hierarchies are imported into the analysis languages to define syntactical correct analysis instances. So there is syntactical integration for these two languages. This is not only true for the analysis or hierarchy definition, but for all other languages that depend on other languages, as shown in the process model. These dependencies were modeled because there are elements needed from another languages's abstract syntax. So, the language are integrated by design. However, not all parts of syntactical integration can be done in this way. The definition of measures can be done without the existence of analysis, although a *BaseMeasure* depends on the *CubeMeasure* from the analysis languages. This integration must be checked within the *check plausibility* activity of the autoMAIS process. Otherwise, it is not possible to support a top-down AIS design (see section 2.1.3).

Next to syntactical correctness issues, the *check plausibility* activity can also be used for semantical correctness of integration, because there are some integration issues that can be solved with the implicit integration based on the language's abstract syntax. These issues deal with different languages instances. These issues are data sources, data quality, or analysis without a data transformation defined, or hierarchies that are not used within one of the analyses, or the deepest layers within a hierarchy which have not been used as data level within any analysis. These missing references indicate semantical error. These instances cannot be used in the resulting AIS because they are not completely integrated. For instance, an analysis without a data transformation would lead to an analysis without any data in it. In some cases, like in an agile approach, they might be intended because in the next iteration, the data transformation for the analysis might be defined. The reason why an empty analysis was defined was to discuss the analysis model with the target domain expert so it can be determined whether these issues are errors which would prevent an AIS generation, or just warnings, and the AIS will be generated with the non-integrated instances. However, these integration issues can be only be checked when all design activities are completed and the integrated AIS meta model exists.

4.7.1.1 Conclusion on the autoMAIS Approach

In this section, the autoMAIS approach was introduced. The five requirements for the autoMAIS were defined in section 4.1. O1 consists of a set of languages which describe the whole AIS creation process. The languages are integrated with each other, and how the languages can be combined is described within the process model. The described elements fulfill the requirements from section 4.1. In O1, it was said that the complete AIS creation process should be covered with autoMAIS. That the whole AIS creation process is covered can be seen in the transformation discussed in section 4.6. There, in figure 4.28, it was shown which meta model instances are used to generate particular components of the reference architecture. Here, all components were covered. Therefore, O1 is fulfilled.

The requirement O2 requested appropriate languages for each of the identified aspects. The autoMAIS languages are introduced in section 4.4.1 to section 4.4.6. For each of the languages, existing languages have been evaluated and, if appropriate, the existing languages have been used. So it can be said that O2 is also fulfilled.

The integration of the languages, and also the advantages of the integration, were shown in section 4.5, so requirement O3 is also met. The autoMAIS process model was discussed in section 4.3. Here it has been shown that autoMAIS is able to work with different AIS creation methodologies as well as different software engineering processes. Therefore O4 is also met.

The last requirement, O5, is the generation of an AIS. In section 4.6, this generation has been introduced. In this section, it has been shown which meta model instances are needed to generate particular components. Also in this section, concrete transformations for the MUSTANG platform were described in more detail. That the generation of an AIS is possible will be shown in chapter 5 and, therefore, O5 is also fulfilled.

Now, as the autoMAIS approach is completely introduced, this approach can be evaluated to determine if it helps to improve the AIS creation process in the fields of schematic work, verification, and documentation. This will be done in the next chapter.

5   Evaluation

In this section, the autoMAIS approach is evaluated. First, the prototype implementation is introduced in section 5.1. The languages from section 4.4.1 to section 4.4.6 and the transformation for the MUSTANG platform, as introduced in section 4.6, have been implemented. Two AIS creation projects, that have been implemented with the autoMAIS prototype, are introduced in section 5.2 to show the applicability of the approach. This section shows that it is possible to generate an AIS using autoMAIS. In the AIS, described first, the complete autoMAIS process, as introduced in section 4.3 has been covered. A part of Gesundheit NRW project from section 3.1.1 is redeveloped with autoMAIS. In the AIS, only a part of the complete project had been redeveloped. In the second AIS, a real project with customers has been developed with the autoMAIS. This AIS and the application of autoMAIS are shown in section 5.2.3.

After the applicability of autoMAIS has been shown, the goals of autoMAIS, improvement of the AIS creation process, are estimated with the help oft the GQM approach in section 5.3. This sections end with a conclusion in section 5.4.

5.1   Prototype Implementation

In this section, the prototype implementation of autoMAIS is introduced. First, the realization of the languages and, afterward, the developed transformations, are shown.

5.1.1   Prototype Implementation of the autoMAIS Languages

For the implementation of the developed languages and their integration, the introduced technologies as introduced in section 2.2.5 were chosen. The Analysis and Hierarchy language from section 4.4.2 and section 4.4.3 were realized using Microsoft DSL Tools [CJK07]. These have been chosen to show the interoperability of the approach with other technologies. During this time, the used .NET technology was an advantage because the MUSTANG platform is also .NET-based. An advantage of the Microsoft DSL Tools is that they are easy to learn and performant at execution time. It also enables code generation, but does not support M2M-transformation and a real modeling API. This makes integration of the different languages difficult because models cannot be edited outside the generated editor in a reasonable way.

Therefore, for all meta models, EMF was used. There are multiple reasons for this decision. First, the EMF platform is a well-established platform that has existed for several years. In addition to the definition of each meta model, an API for manipulation, persistence, and creation of model instances and graphical editors can be generated with no effort. Furthermore, EMF is constructed to integrate models with each other. The biggest advantage of using EMF and Ecore is that other technologies are based on (or

Aspect or Language	Technology
Meta model	Ecore
Measures	Xtext
Data source language	Ecore
Analysis	Microsoft DSL Tools
Hierarchies	Microsoft DSL Tools
Data transformation language	GMF
Data mapping language	Xtext
Code transformations	Xpand

Table 5.1: Used technologie for the protype implementation of autoMAIS

use Ecore models and provide implementations based on) Ecore. Examples of this are ATL and QVT as model-to-model transformation languages, as well as Xtext and GMF as language creation tools. There are also many different tools like query languages or visualizations. Using Ecore, it can be assured that there is tool support which will likely continue over the coming years. In table 5.1, all realized tools and other aspects with their technology are displayed.

The analysis and hierarchy languages stay in their original .NET-based implementation. The reason is that the autoMAIS architecture supports the separation of the concrete and abstract syntax. Therefore, the concrete syntax of the Analysis and Hierarchy language can stay in .NET, but for the abstract syntax Ecore and Java is used. Technically, this can be achieved by using IKVM [Fri11] as a connection between .NET and Java. IKVM is a Java Virtual Machine for the .NET platform. In this, Java byte code is translated on the fly into CIL code and can be executed just as .NET code. Another advantage of this separation is that the language editor can be exchanged without changing anything else.

5.1.2   Prototype Implementation of the Transformations

To be able to generate an AIS that is based on the MUSTANG platform, the transformations, as introduced in section 4.6.3, have been realized. The transformations have been realized with Xpand, as introduced in section 2.2.5. These transformations generate C# projects that generate the data warehouse. The data integration has been realized as components that are configured by instances of the data transformation languages. For the data integration, a Java-based tool has been developed that is configured with instances of the data transformation language. This Java tool executes the R_2O transformations and realizes the extract and load component.

5.2   Applicability of the Approach

This section shows that the generation of an AIS is possible using autoMAIS. This can be viewed as a feasibility study.

The first scenario is the Gesundheit NRW project that was introduced in section 3.1.1. Parts of this project have been used to describe some language examples. For this project, a complete AIS has been generated and all activities of the autoMAIS process model have been performed. This shows how the different languages are integrated with each other and that the overall autoMAIS approach works. In the resulting AIS, it is possible to analyses the hospital statistics as in the original project.

The other scenario is a description of a project that has been issued by the RKI, under the project name CARESS@RKI. The AIS architecture of this project has already been introduced in section 2.1.2.2. The project started in October 2011 and was still ongoing when finalizing this thesis. In this project, an AIS was built up and autoMAIS was used to generate the data warehouse component of this AIS. As this is a real project, which has not been reduced in scope for the evaluation, the described models are more complex than in the first scenario. This means that the prototype implementation could be used for a real project.

5.2.1   AutoMAIS in Gesundheit NRW

In this section, the whole autoMAIS process is completed with the Gesundheit NRW project, which was a real project done by OFFIS. As the project was huge, the whole project has not been redone, but just the part required to show the proof of feasibility. It has to be shown that the AIS generation with autoMAIS is possible in general. To do so, all layers of the reference architecture have to be covered. In the autoMAIS process model in section 4.3, it is said that the definition of one base measure would be enough to generate an AIS. However, this will not show that it is possible to describe computations with measures. So, at least one non-base measure has to be defined.

Using the resulting AIS of the evaluation, an analysis of hospital statistics, with the help of the MUSTANG frontend, CARESS, should be possible. The provided measures should be crude rate and age-specific rates. For a crude rate, population data is required, so two analyses and two data transformations have to be defined, one for the hospital cases and one for population. If this can be described with the autoMAIS languages and generated with the transformations, the applicability is proven.

A proof that this approach is scalable can be shown by providing arguments. A real project, as the Gesundheit NRW project, consists of more data source than the two described. In the real project, 38 data sources were provided by LIGA. This would mean that within the autoMAIS, 38 analysis and data transformation instances have to be defined, as well as more hierarchies. These hierarchies would be more complex than the one that will be provided in this section, but in the end, they also consist of levels and hierarchies. As shown in section 4.4.3.4, all kinds of hierarchies can be modeled with the hierarchy language, so this would be no problem. The same is true for measures because nesting (requirement M3) is supported, so there is no difference between a base measure and a measure. Another issue with scalability is performance. During the modeling of the language instances, performance is not an issue because the user is the bottleneck. During integration and transformation, performance might be an issue because more complex models need more time to be processed. This can be a problem when dealing with really huge models that contain more than 100,000 instances. However, as the transformations are a sequential process, the overall integration and transformation process will take longer. If the time is too long, one option is to improve the transformations. The results of the transformations are configurations of existing components. In most cases, the issues that these components have with performance are independent of their configuration.

In the following, first the use of the autoMAIS process model is introduced. Then the different developed language instances are presented. These include all languages introduced in chapter 4. After this, the integration and the generation of the resulting AIS is introduced.

5.2.2   Use of the autoMAIS Process Model

The autoMAIS process model, as it was introduced in section 4.3, was used to build up the resulting AIS. It was completed many times. First, only the hospital cases as single base measures and the corresponding analysis instances, were modeled. Not all hierarchies were modeled at once, but only in some iterations. This was also true for data integration. After finishing the hospital cases, population data was designed and integrated. After the complete integration, the measure instances were defined. This shows that the process model is flexible enough.

5.2.2.1   Measures

An instance of the measure language is given in figure 5.1[1]. The instance consists of two parts: the definition of a few measures for health reporting, and the project measure. The definition part starts with the parameters used by the measures. These parameters include numerous parameter types. The first measure describes the crude rate definition per 100,000 people, which is a simple calculation. The measure *Percentages* shows how percentages can be expressed as an external call of an external package. The last definition shows the age-specific rate. The concrete computation was introduced in listing 4.3 in the measure section 4.4.1.

---

[1] All provided model instances are in their original form in German language because the target domain language for the different real world projects is German. For readability, these instances have been translated into English. For traceability, the original instances without the translations are provided in Appendix A.3

```
Parameter is MeasureType has Name population;
Parameter is MeasureType has Name cases;
Parameter is DimensionType has Name IteratingDimension;
Parameter is DimensionType has Name ageDimension;
Parameter is MeasureType has Name StudyPopulation;


    Measure ( Name: CrudeRate,
        uses Parameter: cases ,population;
        Computation: cases /population * 100000;
        Description: "Describes crude rate";
    )
    Measure ( Name: Percentage ,
        uses Parameter: cases,IteratingDimension;
        Computation: External Call: Package: "OLAP" ,Instruction: "Percentage";
        Description: "Computes the percentage for an specfic Dimension";


    )


    Measure ( Name: AgeSandardizedRate ,
        uses Parameter: Rate,population,ageDimension ;
        Computation: External Call: Package: "ekn" ,Instruction:"FunctionDmdr";
        Description: "Computation of DMDR";


    )


Project Measure Definition (
    Project Name: GesundheitNRW Description: "Gesundheit NRW Liga"

    Base Measure id=hospitalCases , Longname="statistics on hospital cases"
    Base Measure id=population , Longname="Population"
    Dimension =Age
    Dimension =Gender
    Dimension =Region

    Measure CasesCrudeRate has type Rate
        { Longname: "Crude rate hospital cases" Description "cases per 100.000 people"
            Operator Mapping:
            population  has role population
            hospitalCases has role cases;
        )

    Measure PercentageAge has type Percentage
        { Longname: "Age percentages" Description "percentages for Ages"
            Operator Mapping:
            CasesCrudeRate has role cases
            Age has role IteratingDimension;
        )

    Measure PercentageGender has type Percentage
        { Longname: "Gender percentages" Description "percentages for Gender"
            Operator Mapping:
            CasesCrudeRate has role cases
            Gender has role IteratingDimension;
        )

    Measure AgeStanHospital has type AgeSandardizedRate
        { Longname: "Standardized Rate" Description"Age Standardized Rate "
            Operator Mapping:
            CasesCrudeRate has role cases
            Age has role ageDimension;
        )
)
```

Figure 5.1: Instance of Measure Language

The project measure part uses some of these definitions. Here, the two base measures *Hospital statistics* and *population* are defined. After this, the crude rate definition for hospital cases is done.

To conclude, from this section on measures, this language makes it possible to differ between procedures and project definitions. The syntax does not provide the clear mathematical form as expected. As seen in section 4.4.1, the mathematical representation has an important role in this language, but complex mathematical procedures are not defined within this language except via external calls. More important is the configuration of existing procedures and mapping them to projects. Based on the measure language meta model, it is possible to transform the concrete syntax to a more mathematical expression. For instance, OpenMath content dictionaries [Dav09] could be used to represent the measure definition. OpenMath also provides other representations for mathematical structures. This works the other way, too. Also, other transformations are conceivable to provide a more mathematical view on the measure definitions. The provided measure language makes it possible to reuse previously-defined procedures, so the measure definitions can act as a repository. As the bigger part of the language is a new language, the usage has to be learned. However, due to the structure and the built-in validation the effort required to learn it will be low.

5.2.2.2 Analysis

Two analyses have been modeled during this evaluation, one for hospital cases and one for the population. These two analyses have been modeled with the analysis language from section 4.4.2. In figure 5.2 the multidimensional schema for the hospital statistics is shown. In the hospital analysis, six global dimensions are referred (*Age*, *Region*, *Gender*, *ICD*, *Surgery*, and *Time*). All dimensions, except for the dimension *Age*, refer to the data layer of the global dimension as their data layer.

The analysis schema for the population data is displayed in figure 5.3. This analysis refers to five global dimensions (*Age*, *Region*, *Gender*, *Nationality*, and *Time*). For all dimensions, the data layer of the hierarchy has been chosen as the data layer for the analysis.

The analysis language supports differentiating between global and local dimensions. Each analysis requires a single model instance, which could lead to confusion in managing all the different instances. To give a better overview on the different analysis language instances, it would be possible to provide transformations that deliver a more compact view on analysis. Nevertheless, the analysis language makes it possible to model analysis in proper and common notation in little time. Using a common notation results in a possible documentation for the project. The language-integrated validation also ensures some quality.

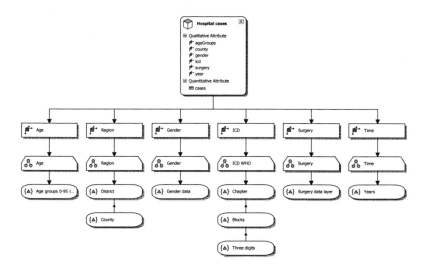

Figure 5.2: Analysis schema instance for hospital cases

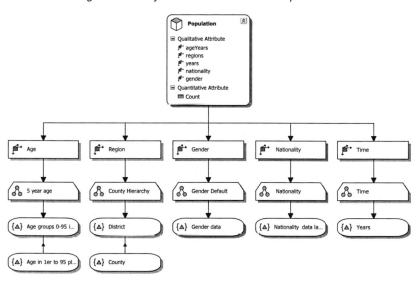

Figure 5.3: Analysis schema instance for population

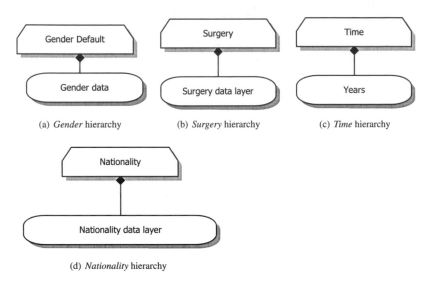

(a) *Gender* hierarchy   (b) *Surgery* hierarchy   (c) *Time* hierarchy

(d) *Nationality* hierarchy

Figure 5.4: Simple hierarchies in the evaluation

5.2.2.3   Hierarchies

For the definition of hospital cases, six hierarchies are required. These hierarchies have
been modeled with the hierarchy language from section 4.4.3. The modeled hierarchies
are *Gender*, *Nationality*, *Time*, *Surgery*, *Region*, *Age*, and *ICD*. The hierarchies can be
divided into two types: simple and complex ones. The simple hierarchies are *Gender*,
Surgery, *Nationality*, and *Time*. These hierarchies only have one level, called a data
level, and this level contains only a few categories. In all cases, there are three or less
categories. The conceptual modeling of these hierarchies is shown as a language screen
shot in figure 5.4. The more complex hierarchies are *Region*, *Age*, and *ICD*. These
hierarchies have more than one level, and more than three categories within these levels.
The *Age* hierarchy is shown in figure 5.6. For instance, the *Three digit layer* of the *ICD*
hierarchy contains 1687 categories. For these levels, parent-child relationships have to
be defined. A language screen shot for these hierarchies is displayed in figures 5.6 to 5.8.
These modeled hierarchies act as global dimensions for the evaluation. In the original
Gesundheit NRW project, some of the modeled dimensions consisted of more levels
than those modeled here, which are not needed to fulfill the scenario. In figure 5.5, a
screen shot of the hierarchy language editor is shown. It shows the modeling of the *ICD*
dimension, which is shown in figure 5.7, in its original German language representation.
Next to the conceptual modeling, the logical modeling is shown. Here, the children are
of the *Category A50-A54*.

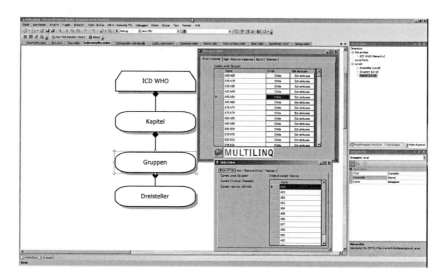

Figure 5.5: Hierarchy language editor displaying ICD hierarchy

The *Region* dimension, shown in figure 5.8, describes the regional structure of North Rhine-Westphalia. The required categories were provided by LIGA and transfigured to the structure by macros. Community Identification Numbers are used to describe the categories within the levels. In listing 5.1, an excerpt from the category definition, as introduced in section 4.4.3.5, is shown. Overall, the 65 categories within this hierarchy have been modeled. In this definition, the name attribute and one or two other attributes have been defined. In line 1, an administrative region is shown and, in line 2, a county which is part of the administrative region is shown. Line 3 shows the statement that connects the categories within the two levels to each other, introduced as conceptual modeling of hierarchies. It uses the properties of a Community Identification Number which has a hierarchic structure included.

The modeling of the *Age* dimension is a little different because no data has been provided by LIGA. *Age* is a numeric dimension, so the categories can be realized by little algorithms using *for* statements. The age group layer (Age 0 - 95+ in 5 year groups) contains two attributes, the minimal and the maximum age value of this group. These attributes are used to link the categories between the different levels. The linking statement is displayed in listing 5.2. The general concept for this was introduced in listing 4.8. It can be seen that the between statement is used based on the attribute definition.

```
1  Between(#minimalAge,#maximumAge)=Name
```

Listing 5.2: Category linking for dimension *Age*

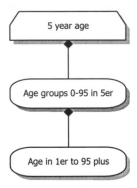

Figure 5.6: Age hierarchy in the Gesundheit NRW project

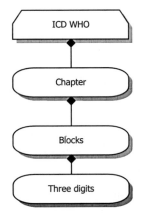

Figure 5.7: ICD hierarchy in the Gesundheit NRW project

```
1 -- Region with attribute Community Identification Number
2 Cologne {53};
3 Euskirchen{5366|eu};
4 First(2,#gkz)=#gkz
```

Listing 5.1: Category definition for dimension *Region*

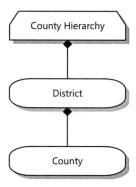

Figure 5.8: Region hierarchy in the Gesundheit NRW project

The last model dimension is ICD. The category definition is provided by DIMDI [DIM11] in a CSV file. This file was integrated into a database using simple SQL queries, and the categories for a particular level were extracted. After this, macros were used to transfer these categories to the autoMAIS category definition.

This kind of preparation is always needed when more complex hierarchies have to be defined, and is not particular to autoMAIS. This also has to be done during AIS creation using a traditional approach. An advantage of autoMAIS is that this format is near natural language because there are no SQL and descriptors needed.

5.2.2.4   Data Sources

For the evaluation, two data sources are required, one for the population and one for the hospital cases. Both have been provided by LIGA. In the case of the population data, the original data source was an Excel [Mic11b] spreadsheet. This spreadsheet contains information in a human-readable form in three dimensions. The rows contain the region and the number of people for a specific age group. The columns have data for gender, nationality, and sums of this information. For example, one column contains population data for female, and another column contains the population for male non-German. Identifying this information is not possible with the autoMAIS approach because it is limited to two dimensions. Therefore, the population has been transformed into a two-dimensional format. The same has been done with the original data during the data integration process. More details on the hospital cases have been provided in section 3.3.

Based on the transformed data and the original hospital data, the two data source descriptions have been generated based on connections, as introduced in section 4.4.4.

These descriptions are shown in figure 5.9. Each of the attributes of the data sources has been identified, as well as the data types.

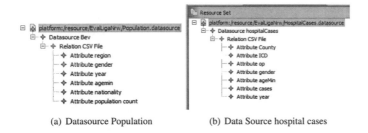

<table>
<tr><td>(a) Datasource Population</td><td>(b) Data Source hospital cases</td></tr>
</table>

Figure 5.9: Data source languages instances in the evaluation

5.2.2.5   Data Transformation

To perform the data transformation from the sources to the analysis, two steps are required, as introduced in section 2.1.6. First, the schemas are matched. For the hospital cases, a correspondence has been found, so a mapping is suggested. For the population, this is more difficult because the naming of the data source does not match. However, for humans, this correspondence is easy to find and, therefore, the mapping has to be defined by the language user.

Based on this, schema matching for the attribute matchings can be performed. This attribute mapping makes suggestions based on the provided schema mapping. For this suggestion, the same matchers are used as for the schema matching. In figure 5.10, the matching results for the population attributes are displayed. As this is a screen shot and the computation results are based on German language, this has not been translated. This figure also shows the editor for this language and the values for the attribute matchers. The values are not very high but, at least based on the configuration, three correct correspondences have been found. This correspondence is always found when words within the attribute description are equal. To find other correspondences like *Region* and *County*, some more detailed domain knowledge has to be integrated into this approach. For example, the synonym matcher does not work properly for some of the attributes, as for example *ageMin*, does not exist in natural language. When using a synonym matcher that is based on domain knowledge, correspondences would be easier to find. The complete defined mapping for the hospital cases can be found in figure 5.12 and, for population, in figure 5.11.

Next to the mapping, transformations for the attributes have to be defined. In figure 5.12, a screen shot of the complete mapped hospital cases including the transformations is given. The definition of transformation is indicated by the black dot within the map-

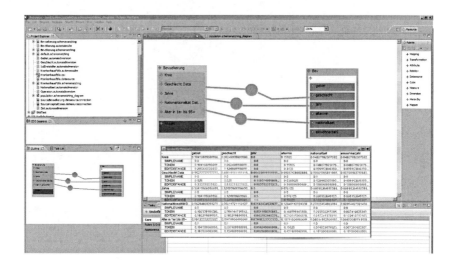

Figure 5.10: Result for schema matching for population

```
1  ...
2  conceptmap-def name "Hamm" identified-by "Hamm"
3      uri-as constant arg-restriction on-param 'const' has-value string 'Hamm'
4      applies-if
5          equals_str
6              arg-restriction on-param 'value1' has-column 'hospitalCases.county_0
                   '
7              arg-restriction on-param 'value2' has-value string '5915'
8  conceptmap-def name "Kleve" identified-by "Kleve"
9      uri-as constant arg-restriction on-param 'const' has-value string 'Kleve'
10     applies-if
11         equals_str
12             arg-restriction on-param 'value1' has-column 'hospitalCases.county_0
                   '
13             arg-restriction on-param 'value2' has-value string '5154'
14 ...
```

Listing 5.3: R2O excerpt from *county to county* transformation

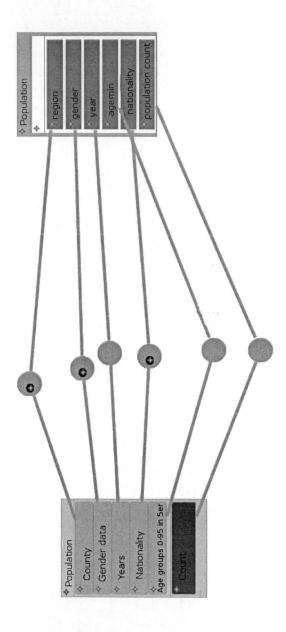

Figure 5.11: Complete schema mapping for population

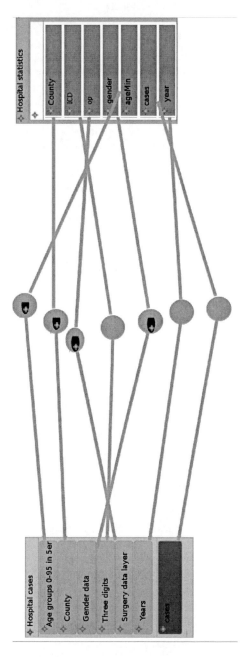

Figure 5.12: Complete defined schema mapping for the hospital cases

ping. It can be seen that all target attributes have been mapped. For the definition of transformation, R_2O is used, as introduced in section 2.1.6.

For some transformations, like gender, the transformation is quite short. It is displayed in figure 2.1. The meaning of defined transformation is quite simple but a few lines are needed for this statement. The R_2O statements are getting longer, but not more complex, when defining transformations on hierarchies that contains more categories. An example of such a hierarchy is *Region*. An excerpt of the *County to County*-transformation is given in listing 5.3. In this listing, each category in the level *Region* has a transformation defined. The problem is that the names of the categories are real natural language names, and the source contains the community identification number (CIN). So this mapping is defined here. This mapping has already been modeled in the hierarchies within the attribute definition. Consequently, the analysis model has this information and the transformation definition is redundant. However, R_2O does not have a mechanism to support these kinds of attributes. To circumvent this, the language should be extended on category attributes, and something as presented in listing 5.4 would be possible. Here, the power of R_2O functions can be used to specify the transformation. The changes in the language are displayed within <>. The category used contains information about the CIN in the attributes, as shown in listing 5.1. This extension would be useful, but during the evaluation, another approach has been used and the required transformation has been generated with Java code.

```
1  conceptmap-def name "Region" identified-by "Region"
2    uri-as constant arg-restriction <on-attribute> 'const' <has-attribute 'CIN'>
3      get_substring
4        arg-restriction on-param "str" has-column "population.county_0"
5        arg-restriction on-param "lo_limit" has-value integer 0
6        arg-restriction on-param "hi_limit" has-value integer 3
```

Listing 5.4: R2O transformation with language extension

In the integrated meta model, all instances, and hence all categories, exist. Therefore, the R_2O statements for longer transformations are generated. Although the generated transformation is quite long, the required Java code to build the transformation is short.

Regarding the data transformation and data sources, it can be said that the matcher does not provide satisfying results. Better results could be achieved by integration of abbreviations or the complete hierarchy into the matching. In this case, mappings for *Region* and *Population* could be found. Another way to achieve better matching results could be to create project-specific matchers. Such a matcher could contain information that indicates that *ageMin* describe ages. The question, however, is what effort reduction of these newly-introduced matchers would provide. Compared to the data transformation effort, the mapping will probably not be huge.

For the definition of the R_2O statements, more effort is needed. The language provides all functions to transform data. As the definition of the statements is a little costly, it could be useful to generate these statements automatically. In this case, the matcher improvements described above should be realized because then they are executed on the attribute values. To do so, some verification has to be made by the user to ensure that the described transformations are correct.

The execution of the transformation has been done and the data provided by LIGA has been integrated. For the hospital cases in the year 2008, 831,801 tuples have been integrated, and, for population, 19,657 tuples have been integrated. The execution has some performance issues. For a prototype implementation this is fine, but outside the prototype, the execution of the language with their complete trees could lead to problems. Therefore, an array-based transformation could be useful to improve performance. The described data transformations do not cover the complete ETL process. Based on the work of [TLM03], aspects of logging, correction, and aggregation are missing in the autoMAIS approach. Maybe a workflow-based approach as suggested by [VSS02] would be useful. In this case, a transformation to a configuration of an established ETL tool, such as Microsoft Integration Services [Mic11e], could be used. To maintain the integration, the data sources and the transformation to the data warehouse should be read-only because these are the first and final steps of the ETL process. Between these steps, every data flow could be possible, but it is assured that the R_2O transformation can be executed and the data sources are known. However, such an approach would reduce the traceability.

Another advantage of the introduced data transformation process is that matching and mappings are identified with text descriptions and not their identifiers. This makes them more easy to learn and maintain because it is clear what is done.

5.2.2.6 Data Quality

According to the process model, the first step would be to define consistency constraints. In this evaluation, no consistency constraints can be found. Therefore, this step is left out.

For general quality assurance, autoMAIS provides some mechanisms to ensure quality. Within the autoMAIS approach, no invalid tuples can be integrated into the data warehouse. The transformation definition is tied to categories within the data warehouse. If a single category does not exist, the whole tuple is not integrated. Technically, this tuple is kept and reported to the user. In the example project, a problem with an unmatched ICD code was introduced. In autoMAIS, this tuple was not integrated and the user was notified. To integrate the tuple, an additional transformation rule had to be defined.

One big advantage of this approach is that it uses more or less natural language to describe the domain elements, and not meaningless identifiers. All the language instances introduced deal with natural identifiers, not synthetic ones. As shown in the case of the *County* transformation from page 171, this can lead to more effort, but with this approach, the single steps are more traceable than in a traditional approach. In the case of the transformation, it can be clearly seen that *County* is mapped to *County*, rather than identifier x is mapped to identifier y. In that case, an additional SQL query would be necessary to identify x and y correctly. This is also true for the transformation. A single tuple is transformed into the natural language representation. For instance, the source tuple (5120;C66;1;1;80;1;2008) for the hospital cases is mapped to tuple (Olpe;C66;OP;M;1;2008), and then it is transformed to the technical representation of the data warehouse. This might be redundant for the execution of the transformation, but helpful for the user to do verification.

5.2.2.7   Integration and Transformation

As introduced in section 4.5.2, some of the integration is done during the autoMAIS process, as the different languages depend on each other. In addition, the following checks have been applied to the complete integrated model:

- **Base measures to analysis mapping:** This check ensures that, for each defined base measure, an analysis has been defined for mapping. This assures that all defined measures can be computed. It also checks the opposite to ensure that all defined analyses have been used. The check to determine whether all measure definitions are coherent is done by the measure language itself. This check connects the two different layers, analysis and data warehouse, with each other.

- **Unambiguity:** Checks if all model elements have different names. As already mentioned, unambiguity can lead to technical problems during transformation or at runtime of the resulting AIS. Therefore, it is prevented at modeling time. The unambiguity check can be restricted on certain modeling instances or models.

Artifact	Language	LOC
Liga evaluation	C#	6,979
Snowflake script	SQL	2,156
ASSL Script	XML/A	1,174

Table 5.2: LOC of the generated artifacts

The realized transformations, as introduced in section 5.1.2, have been applied to the modeled instances. The generated C# code, based on the language instances introduced in this section, has 6979 LOC. This number has been computed by the code metrics measurement component inside Visual Studio 2010 [Mic11a]. With this code, 2156 lines of SQL for the generation of the snowflake schemas and 1174 lines of XML/A code, is generated. These values are displayed in table 5.2.

In figure 5.13, an Analysis Services Scripting Language (ASSL) screen shot of Business Intelligence Development Studio [Mic11c] shows the generated and executed OLAP configuration. It shows the generated snowflake tables and their relation to each other. It also shows the modeled cubes and dimensions.

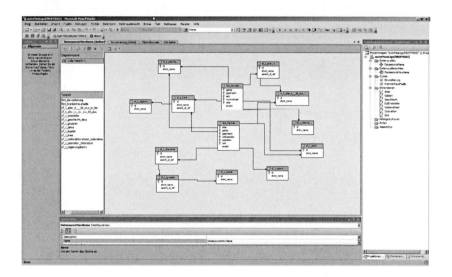

Figure 5.13: ASSL screenshot of generated snowflake schema

After the data warehouse has been generated, it can be filled with fact data. This fact data is stored within the data sources, as introduced in section 5.2.2.4. For the data integration, no transformation was needed because a prototype implementation of the ETL layer has been done. This ETL layer accepts as configuration, instances of the *DataTransformationPackage*. The developed components of the ETL layer can be executed and then the data is integrated. The result of the integration is that OLAP analysis, as introduced in section 2.1.5, is possible. In figure 5.14, a result of a simple OLAP analysis is shown. Here, the hospital cases are given for age and ICD groups, but it has been filtered to only those cases where a surgery has been done.

5.2.3   AutoMAIS in CARESS@RKI

The CARESS@RKI is an AIS creation project which is done within OFFIS and was still ongoing when finalizing this thesis. The customer for this project is the German Center for Cancer Registry Data at the Robert Koch Institute (RKI). The goal of this project was to provide an analysis software for their data. The RKI gets data from all the population-based cancer registries in Germany with diagnoses, except for Baden-Wuerttemberg. One task of this center is to analyze the data and publish the findings on cancer incidence [HKK+10]. The goal of the project was to provide an analysis software that helped to improve their analysis workflow. As analysis software, CARESS was chosen, which is part of the MUSTANG platform [FHTA09]. The goal of the project was not only to

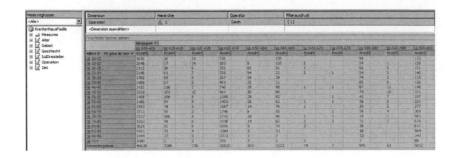

Figure 5.14: Example of a simple OLAP analysis with autoMAIS-enabled AIS

provide an analysis software, but also an integration of their relevant data. So, the project called CARESS@RKI was an AIS creation project.

The project consists of several milestones. The first milestone, which is described here, was completed on time. The goal of the first milestone was to integrate all of their data about cancer cases in Germany, and to enable first analysis within CARESS. To achieve this, next to cancer data, population and standard population were included in the resulting AIS.

As the fact data was provided by the RKI, the AIS bottom-up methodology was used. The description of the cases is complex and is based on the Federal Cancer Registry Data Act (Bundeskrebsregisterdatengesetz, BKRG). This Act also describes the data format, which consists of three parts:

- Personal details

  - Gender
  - Month and year of birth
  - First five digits of the Community Identification Number residence

- Information of tumor diagnosis

  - Tumor diagnosis based on the current ICD classification
  - Histology code
  - Localization of the tumor
  - Month and year of the first diagnoses
  - Earlier tumors
  - Diagnostic confirmation
  - Stage of disease based on the TNM classification

- Primal therapy

- In case of death

  - Month and year of death

  - Cause of death

  - Autopsy determination

The case data was provided within a Microsoft SQL Server database. The RKI had already unified the data that came from the different registries, so only one data source had to be integrated, instead of 15 different ones. For population and mortality data, RKI provided CSV files as data source.

For building the data warehouse component with the Microsoft SQL Server and Analysis Services as technical components, autoMAIS was used. So again, C# code is generated to build up this component. In a traditional approach, as is often done in OFFIS, the C# code that is generated by the autoMAIS transformation is written manually. Due to the dense timetable there was the expectation that autoMAIS would help to master the tight schedule.

The ETL layer was not done with autoMAIS because it was a requirement that the whole ETL process is done only with SQL scripts. This is a very uncommon requirement because, in general, for this task commercial data integration tools would have been used as they are more convenient to use and maintain. The prototype implementation, as introduced in section 5.1.2, is Java-based and configured with autoMAIS model instances. Due to the script restriction of the RKI's infrastructure, the deployment of these components would be impossible with the existing transformations. A redevelopment of the transformations was not possible because of the tight schedule, and it would have been to risky to try this based on a prototype implementation.

In the next section, the implementation of the data warehouse is introduced to show that it is possible to use autoMAIS within a real project.

5.2.3.1 Measures

The measure definition was not a complex tasks within the CARESS@RKI project because the computation definition could be taken over from the CARLOS project. Within the CARLOS project, the Mustang platform and the analysis frontend CARESS is used to build up an AIS for a population-based cancer registry. The CARLOS project was issued by the Cancer Registry of Lower Saxony (EKN). The EKN fulfills similar tasks to the German Center for Cancer Registry Data at the Robert Koch Institute, but the EKN is limited to cases that occur within Lower Saxony and the analyzed data has a greater level of detail. Still, the computations in general are the same, although the data warehouse is built up differently.

```
Parameter is MeasureType has Name population;
Parameter is MeasureType has Name cases;
Parameter is MeasureType has Name standardPop;
Parameter is DimensionType has Name Age;

Measure { Name:Personyears,
    uses Parameter: population;
    Computation: External Call: Package: "ekn",Instruction:"Pop";
    Description: "Definition of person years";
    }

    Measure { Name: CrudeRate,
        uses Parameter: cases ,population;
        Computation: cases /population * 100000;
        Description: "Cases per 100.000 people";
    }

    Measure { Name:CumulativeRate,
        uses Parameter: cases,Age;
        Computation: External Call: Package: "ekn",Instruction:"CUMULATIVERATE";
        Description: "Describes the comulative rate";
    }

    Measure { Name:ConfidenceIntervall,
        uses Parameter: cases,population;
        Computation: External Call: Package: "ekn",Instruction:"ci_crude_rate";
        Description: "confidence interval";
    }

    Measure { Name:DMDR,
        uses Parameter: population,cases,Age;
        Computation: External Call: Package: "ekn",Instruction:"direct_std";
        Description: "direct standarized rate based on standard population";
    }
```

Figure 5.15: Measure definition for the CARESS@RKI project

Within the CARLOS project, R packages have been defined that cover the most important computations for the domain of cancer registration. These R packages are reused in the CARESS@RKI project. An excerpt from the *MeasureDefinition* instance is given in figure 5.15. As seen here, five different measure definitions are provided. All definitions, except for *CrudeRate*, have external calls to R packages. The defined computations and their usage are explained in [OFF11]. Based on these definitions, the concrete project measures can be defined. In the first milestone, 39 *ProjectMeasures* have been defined in total. An excerpt of this definition can be found in figure 5.16, where eight project measures are shown.

Measure definitions are used in different project measures. In most cases, all project measures are defined on a population as well as a standardized population. Also, nesting is enabled. For instance, the *CrudeRateIncidenceCI* is based on the *CrudeRateIncidence*. All measures could be defined for the first milestone.

```
Project Measure Definition {
        Project Name: CaressRKI Description: "Definition of measures for the first milestonre"

        Base Measure id=population , Longname="Population"
        Base Measure id=incidence   , Longname="Tumor inforamtion from 15 different cancer registires"
        Base Measure id=standPopulation , Longname="Standard population"
        Dimension =Age

        Measure PersonYears has type Personyears
        { Longname: "person  years" Description"Person years"
                Operator Mapping: population has role population;
        }

        Measure CrudeRateIncidence has type CrudeRate
        { Longname: "Crude rate for incidence" Description"Description"
                Operator Mapping:  population has role population
                        incidence has role cases;
        }

        Measure CrudeRateIncidenceStandardPop has type CrudeRate
        { Longname: "Crude rate for incidence standard population" Description"Description"
                Operator Mapping: incidence has role cases
                        standPopulation has role population;
        }

        Measure CumluativeRateIncidence has type CumulativeRate
        { Longname: "Cumulative rate for incidence" Description""
                Operator Mapping: CrudeRateIncidence has role cases
                Age has role Age;
        }

        Measure CrudeRateIncidenceCI has type ConfidenceIntervall
        { Longname: "Crude rate (CI) Incidence" Description""
                Operator Mapping: CrudeRateIncidence has role cases
                population has role population;
        }

        Measure CI has type ConfidenceIntervall
        { Longname: "Crude rate (CI) Incidence" Description""
                Operator Mapping: incidence has role cases
                population has role population;
        }

        Measure DmdrIncidence has type DMDR
        { Longname: "DMDR Incidence study population" Description""
                Operator Mapping: population has role population
                 CrudeRateIncidence has role cases;
        }

        Measure DmdrStudyIncidence has type DMDR
        { Longname: "DMDR Incidence study population" Description""
                Operator Mapping: standPopulation has role population
                 CrudeRateIncidence has role cases;
        }
```

Figure 5.16: Project measure definition

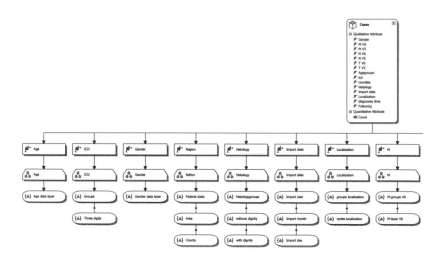

Figure 5.17: Cases Analysis, left side

5.2.3.2   Analysis

In the first milestone, four analyses have been defined, one for the case data which is based on the law definition as introduced before. The defined analysis is displayed in figure 5.17 and figure 5.18. (For readability the figure has been cut into two pieces.) In this figure, it is shown that many of the introduced hierarchies are used, but not all properties of provided data are integrated in the analysis model. For instance, earlier tumors and therapy is not include. The reason for this was simply the customer did not want to analyze these attributes.

To enable computations, other analyses have to be defined which are introduced now. To enable crude rate definitions, population data is needed. The population analysis is displayed in figure 5.19. One issue with population was that this data could not be provided on county level, but only on the level of federal states. So, the analysis has this level defined as a data layer. The population analysis does not refer to many hierarchies because it is just population data.

Another analysis that was modeled to enable computation is standard population. It is displayed in figure 5.20. The standard population is used to make computations results comparable because it provides a fixed age distribution. So, this is a very simple analysis but important for computation results.

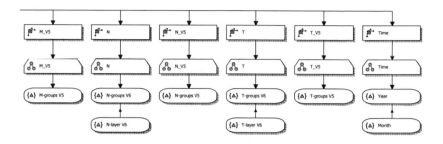

Figure 5.18: Cases Analysis, right side

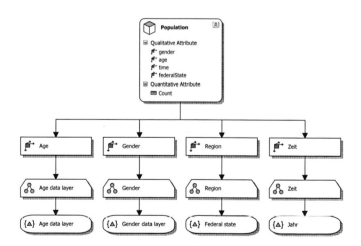

Figure 5.19: Population

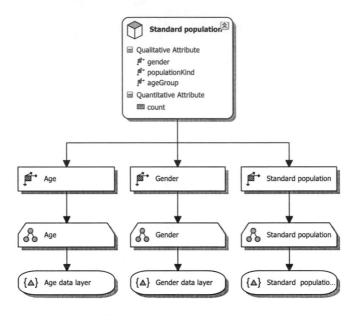

Figure 5.20: Standard Population

5.2.3.3   Hierarchies

Within the CARESS@RKI project, 17 different hierarchy instances have been modeled. Due to the high number, not all instances will be introduced here. An overview of these hierarchies is given in figure 5.3. In this table, dimension names, the number of levels, and the overall number of categories within this hierarchy are displayed. Additionally, the conceptual model of the hierarchies can also be seen in the analysis instances in section 5.17.

Most of these hierarchies are straight forward and based on classifications like *ICD*, *TNM*, *Histology*, and *Localization*. TNM has been split up into 6 hierarchies because T, N, and M provide information about different tumor properties as introduced in section 4.4.6. As a result, a hierarchy was modeled for each property. As there are different versions of the TNM classification within the data source, three dimensions for every version (5 and 6) have been defined. For the *Region* dimension, all counties within Germany have been modeled.

Dimension name	Level count	Category count
Age	2	22
DCO	1	3
ICD	3	1013
Gender	1	3
Region	4	497
Histology	3	1855
Import date	3	446
Localization	2	402
M	2	12
M_V5	1	5
N	2	23
N_V5	1	7
Standard population	1	4
T	2	40
Death	1	3
T_V5	1	9
Time	3	2314

Table 5.3: Overview on hierarchy instances at CARESS@RKI

5.2.3.4   Integration and Transformation

The different model instances have been integrated with each other. The hierarchies and analyses are integrated based on their dependency, as introduced in section 4.4.2. The measures and analyses have been integrated by the the the introduced check.

Artifact	Language	LOC
RKI modelling	C#	51,173
Snowflake script	SQL	6,770
ASSL Script	XML/A	3,750

Table 5.4: LOC of the generated artifacts in the CARESS@RKI

Based on the integrated meta model, the transformations introduced in section 5.1.2 and used in the Gesundheit NRW evaluation example, have been used to generate 51,173 lines of C# code. This code generates SQL scripts and the configuration file for the OLAP server. The generated SQL script consists of 6,770 LOC and the OLAP server configuration file as XML/A consists of 3,750 lines. The amount of C# code compared to the resulting SQL code is much higher than in the Gesundheit NRW project. The reason for this is that more attributes for the hierarchy instances have been defined. To assign one *ConcreteAttribute* to a category, three LOC are generated. In the generated SQL script, one category with all attributes is one line. Attributes have been modeled

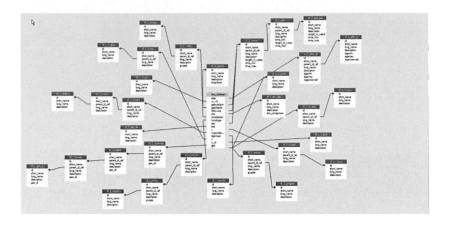

Figure 5.21: Generated snowflake schema based on the introduced models

for the *Time*, *Age*, and *Region* hierarchies. For instance, for the *Age* hierarchy, there are the attributes *ageMin*, *ageMax*, and *LengthInYears*.

These two generated artifacts, next to the manually-written SQL insert scripts, were provided to the customer. In figure 5.21, the generated snowflake schema with relations are displayed. Based on this data warehouse, the manually-created integration scripts were executed and CARESS was used as analysis software. In figure 5.22, a screenshot of CARESS is given which is based on the data warehouse described here. It shows a map of Germany on the county level and, with colors, the number of cases within the county are visualized.

5.2.3.5   Estimation of autoMAIS Within the CARESS@RKI Project

The data warehouse with CARESS as the analysis frontend was successfully put into operation at the RKI. In this section, the role of autoMAIS within this project is rated. The advantages and disadvantages of using the prototype implementation in this project are discussed.

One disadvantage of the project setting is that an autoMAIS-enabled ETL layer could not be used in this project. The data integration in this project was done manually in plain SQL and was, therefore, a little error-prone. Some data integration problems that occurred during this project might have been prevented. Additionally, the development of the data integration layer would have been faster. It would have been interesting to see the limits and capabilities of the autoMAIS approach in a real data integration project.

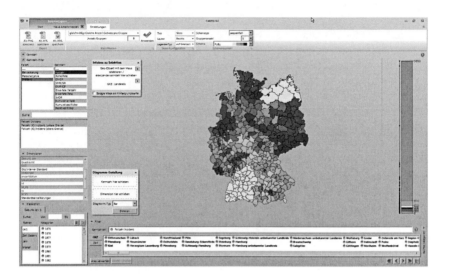

Figure 5.22: CARESS screenshot showing a map with case data

In the used autoMAIS elements, issues exist as well. Within the hierarchy instances in nearly every level, an unknown category had to be included. This is used if an attribute is not given in the data source, not detailed enough, or not valid in the analysis model. In this case, the attribute in the hierarchy instance is mapped to the unknown category to enable an analysis to be as detailed as possible. For instance, it can be unknown in which county a case occurs, but the federal state is known. In this case, the case is mapped to the specific federal state's unknown category. Hence, this case is not lost in data integration and can be used in every analysis.

In some cases, it is imprecise when using the region hierarchy. The unknown category does not exist in specifications like ICD, so this instance had to be added manually. This is also true for the autoMAIS hierarchies. This task must also be done in a traditional AIS creation process. This is a little wasteful, because the other instances could be modeled easily and the unknown categories require extra work. Perhaps this modeling strikes out a little bit because the other categories where modeled more easily. In a traditional approach, this effort has to be more or less made for every category. So, the autoMAIS approach provides advantages when modeling categories. It would be better to have the possibility to model these kinds of categories within the approach. This is an issue in the language realization or within the transformations, but not in the concept generally. In principle, the implementation is possible as there are unknown categories within the models.

Another issue is that measures could not be modeled in blocks. The excerpt from the measure definition in section 5.2.3.1 shows that the same measure definitions are used for each base measure. For the cases (incidence), there is a definition for crude rate DMDR and confidence intervals. This definition exists for population and the standard population. This is schematic work. The same effort will have to be made when integrating mortality cases. If it would be possible to apply blocks on the definitions, this schematic work would be reduced.

The graphical notation of the analysis is, when using real world scenarios, not very clear, as can be seen in figure 5.17. A consideration is to use a different concrete syntax for the analysis language, for example, a textual one which is more compact. This textual syntax could be changed without changing the meta model, as introduced in section 4.5.3.

Within the project, some iterations have been made to complete the first milestone. The hierarchies were modeled one after another, as well as the analysis and measures. Some of the hierarchies were not correct at the first attempt. For instance, the *Region* dimension has been changed. The county definition was provided by the RKI and used to build up the hierarchy instance. However, during data integration some missing counties were found, so a new definition was provided. In the corresponding hierarchy instance, the county level was deleted and the new definition was used to define the categories. The other levels and categories were not touched. As the general structure of hierarchies did not change, the analyses, which used these hierarchies, had not to be touched again because they were automatically updated. AutoMAIS enables changing of instances.

The automatic detection of syntactical correctness was a big help when defining the *Histology* dimension. The customer wanted, for this hierarchy, a combination of histology and dignity. There is a definition for this combination within our working group, so this was used. This definition was syntactically-incorrect because some categories were missing. This could be easily determined, because it was an invalid model. The missing categories were added.

Another advantage was the traceability of measures. The customer found that the computation of crude rate was not done in the way he had expected it. So, the measure language instance was used to explain how the measure was computed. This showed that another kind of population computation was expected. Person years were expected as the measure, instead of population as defined in the measures in section 5.2.3.1. Person years defines an average population instead of the population data. This was easily found out and could be changed.

Reuse is another advantage. The *ICD* hierarchy which was modeled during the Gesundheit NRW example from section 5.2.1 was used in this project as well. This could be done because each hierarchy instances can be used individually. In the *ICD* hierarchy in the Gesundheit NRW project, the complete ICD scope was included; in this project, only those codes which deal with cancer are needed. The categories not needed were deleted from the hierarchy instance. This shows the possibilities of the autoMAIS approach.

The AIS creation projects realized at OFFIS often have the same target domains, and many hierarchies like *ICD* or *Region*, or analyses like *Population*, are realized in many AIS creation projects. With autoMAIS, parts of an AIS creation project could also be reused. This is independent from the concrete architecture and the concrete technical representation, because this is done by the transformations and these transformations are independent from the domain. Even if the target domains are independent from each other, like in PEIS and the Gesundheit NRW project, reuse can be done. The program that was used to generate the autoMAIS instances for time could be used in the PEIS project to generate a time hierarchy. Therefore, reuse is a promising attempt within autoMAIS.

One overall advantages of the usage of autoMAIS within the CARESS@RKI project was that the focus was laid on modeling within the target domain, and not the technical representation of the domain. The overall process might have been completed a little faster because some issues were found more easily than in previous projects, because it can be checked if the language instances are syntactically correct. If the instances are correct, the generated solutions can always be executed and generate a data warehouse. Finding and fixing errors within the technical representation was reduced, and more focus could be laid on the domain issues.

The first milestone of the project had a tight schedule. A big advantages of the autoMAIS usage was that it could always be assured that a valid data warehouse, that works properly together with the CARESS application and the MUSTANG platform, will be generated. There was no need to care about a valid OLAP server configuration or wrong foreign key constraints that lead to wrong aggregation within an analysis. After a few days, it was always possible to provide a data warehouse for internal testing. In this first attempt, only the case data was integrated but not all hierarchies that were there. Hierarchies were added step by step, as well as the integration. As soon as possible, a new AIS instance was generated. This approach helped to develop a good sense for the resulting project and the tight schedule as there was something that could be delivered. This deliverable was not complete, but was technically without error, so that an analysis with this AIS would be possible. It has not been measured, but the development with autoMAIS seemed to be faster than in the traditional approach, and the level of abstraction was raised.

This shows impressive application of the autoMAIS approach and its benefits for real AIS creation projects.

5.3   Estimation of the autoMAIS Approach

In the previous section, it has been shown that autoMAIS is able to generate an AIS, but this was not the main goal of the autoMAIS approach as defined in the motivation in chapter 1. There, different issues of AIS creation were introduced. These issues were made concrete in chapter 3. The main goal of the autoMAIS approach is to improve the

AIS creation process. To estimate this improvement, the Goal Question Metric (GQM) approach [BCR94] is used.

The GQM approach is a hierarchical approach in software metrics. It consists of three levels: conceptual, operational, and quantitative. On the conceptual level, the goal is defined for an object, and this is the target. On the operational level, questions are formulated. These questions describe how the goal is reached. On the quantitative level, metrics are defined. For each question, a set of metrics exists. These metrics provide quantitative answers to achieve the goal.

The goal of the thesis can be defined as:

Goal: AutoMAIS improves the AIS creation process

compared to traditional approaches.

This section shows if autoMAIS improves the AIS creation process compared to traditional approaches. These traditional approaches have been introduced in chapter 3. There, experience from real world projects as well as literature work was introduced to describe traditional AIS creation processes. In chapter 4, the autoMAIS approach was introduced and now, in this section, it has been shown that the developed approach can be applied. Now both approaches will be compared.

For this comparison, one particular real world project is chosen. This project is the Gesundheit NRW project, introduced in section 3.1.1. This project was an AIS creation project for a real customer and was developed with the traditional AIS creation approach. In the evaluation, parts of this project have been redeveloped with the autoMAIS approach as introduced in section 5.2.1. The approaches in this project can be compared with each other to show the improvement.

In the next sections, the comparison based on the GQM approach will be performed. The question deals with the three subjects: schematic work, verification, and documentation of AIS creation projects. These questions describe the challenges in AIS creation, as derived in section 3.1.3. These challenges are schematic work, verification, and documentation. The question now is if autoMAIS improves these challenges.

5.3.1 Q1. Does autoMAIS reduce schematic work within the AIS creation process?

5.3.1.1 Q1.M1: Amount of generated code

One goal of the autoMAIS approach is to enable the generation of large parts of an AIS (see O4 from the autoMAIS requirements in section 4.1).

With the autoMAIS approach, nearly the complete AIS can be generated based on the defined models. The transformations as introduced in section 4.6 generate all needed artifacts. As introduced in the application section, some model instances have been defined using Java code. This individual code was used in the definition of hierarchies and data transformation. All together, there have been 183 LOC written within the Gesundheit NRW application part. This value is compared to the 6,973 LOC of generated C# code. This makes 3% of individual code.

In contrast, in the traditional approach there is no generation done at all. All artifacts have been written by hand. Hence, the bigger parts of an AIS creation project can be generated, as it has also been shown within this evaluation. So the results for this metrics is that 97% could be generated in the autoMAIS approach, and 0% in the traditional approach.

5.3.1.2   Q1.M2: Development time

One of the promises of MDSD and DSM is reduced development time. The question is, if the autoMAIS approach is faster then the traditional approach. To show this, the effort of each project is compared to get an impression on the different development speeds.

The development speed of the original Gesundheit NRW project for the chosen particular subset is not available. Therefore, the effort has been estimated by experts. The estimation was only done for development time, but not for documentation or requirement analysis.

For estimating the development time, the three-point estimation, as introduced in [OW07], has been used. Four persons were involved in the estimation, two AIS design experts that have more than 10 years experience in AIS creation, one AIS designer with three years of AIS creation experience, and one AIS inexperienced developer. The task and the corresponding data was presented to the attendees. They were asked to estimate the definition of the computation, which in this thesis is done with the measure language, the creation of the integrated schema, for which the analysis language and the hierarchy language from section 4.4.3 are used, and the data integration. For each task they provided the best, worst, and average case. The overall results can be seen in table 5.5 and in table 5.6. The estimations are displayed by persons. The estimation result is 9.57 days and the standard deviation is 1.93. One interesting point is the difference between the two AIS design experts with over 10 years of experience. Their estimates differed by more than 14 days, as seen in table 5.6. In this table, the different estimations are displayed. The reason why these persons differed so much was that, among other things, Expert A indicates that he would reuse artifacts from existing projects. He said that SQL scripts for the definition of *ICD*, *Age*, and others already exist, so he will use them. The other expert assumed that the project was completely developed from scratch.

The autoMAIS effort was measured during evaluation. Here, only one person who is an autoMAIS expert, was recorded. The measures are displayed in table 5.7. The realization time with the autoMAIS approach was a little longer then the estimation of

Task	Best	Average	Worst
Measure	0.83	1.63	4.00
Integrated schema	2.63	5.13	8.13
Data integration	1.19	2.38	4.13
Overall	4.64	9.13	16.25

Table 5.5: Estimation result in days of the Gesundheit NRW project with the traditional approach

	Expert A			Expert B			AIS Designer			AIS Developer		
Task	B	A	W	B	A	W	B	A	W	B	A	W
Measures	0.2	0.5	1	2	3.5	10	1	2	3	0.13	0.5	2
Integrates schema	0.5	1	2	5.75	10.5	16	2	3	4.5	2.25	6	10
Data integration	0.5	1	2	1.25	2.5	4.5	2	5	8	1	1	2
Sum	1.2	2.5	5	9	16.5	30.5	5	10	15.5	3.38	7.5	14
Estimation	2.7			17.6			10.08			7.90		

Table 5.6: Estimations by persons (B=Best, A=Average, W=Worst)

Expert A, but with the autoMAIS approach, nothing was reused. It was completely developed from scratch. It would be interesting to see how much time the realization by Expert A would actually take.

The result is that the autoMAIS approach is faster, or required the same time. For a more competitive result, an experimental evaluation should be considered. As seen in the estimation results, this would take much time when being performed with different people. Before they can do the realization of the AIS creation projects, they have to be trained on the concepts of AIS creation, which includes all of the elements that were introduced in section 2.1. Then they have to learn the tools of the particular approach. This kind of evaluation would be required if reduction of development time is the only aspect for the estimation of the autoMAIS approach. This is not the case, because only one measure deals with development speed, and other aspects are important as well.

Task	Effort
Measure	0.5
Integrated schema	1.5
Data integration	1
Overall	3

Table 5.7: Measured autoMAIS effort

5.3.2 Q2. Does autoMAIS improve verification of AIS creation?

Verification is an issue during an AIS creation project, as introduced in section 3.1.3.2. This section determines whether autoMAIS improves the verification. For this, metrics about code quality, correctness, and testing are used.

5.3.2.1 Q2.M1: Can coding conventions be kept?

In a traditional approach, this was difficult to assure because different developers with different skill levels were part of the team. The team included one skillful developer who was involved in AIS creation projects over ten years, and developers who had just recently graduated. The code produced from the experienced developer had a better code quality and better-kept conventions than from the other developers. In this case, it is also difficult to assure coding convention like in [Mic12a].

Within the autoMAIS approach, this is different. The code within a particular project is generated, which means that code conventions are maintained if they are kept within the transformation. To realize this, a skillful developer who is familiar with the convention should implement the transformation. Another advantage of the transformation is that the generated code always has the same structure and, if something has to be changed, then the entry point is easy to find.

5.3.2.2 Q2.M2: Is it possible to assure syntactical correctness of parts or the complete AIS?

In traditional AIS creation projects, syntactical correctness means that configuration for particular artifacts are specified so that they can be executed without errors. For instance in the data warehouse layer, this means a SQL script that creates tables for a ROLAP schema. It cannot be assured that these defined models are correct ROLAP models. This fact, as introduced in section 3.1.1.3, leads to errors that are difficult to find. In some cases, syntactical errors can only be found if the complete AIS is used, for instance, if a missing parent for a category is not found within the ROLAP schema definition. This error can only be located after data integration, because if incorrect computations of a measure is due to the missing relation, the aggregation does not work properly. Finding and fixing this error is costly as it is not always obvious that a syntactical error is the cause of the error. Therefore, syntactical correctness cannot be assured in rational AIS creation projects.

In autoMAIS, this is completely different, as introduced in section 4.7.1. Each language instance is checked for syntactical errors as well as the synchronization of the models. If there is an error, it must be fixed; otherwise, it cannot be used in the further autoMAIS process. If a model instance does not contain any syntactical errors, it can be assured that it can be used in other languages, and transformations based on this instance will be executable. A big advantage of the autoMAIS approach against traditional approaches is that it can ensure syntactical correctness.

This was a big advantage during the CARESS@RKI project from section 5.2.3. It could be assured that the defined models were syntactically-correct and therefore it was assured that they could be generated and that the generation would produce a valid AIS.

5.3.2.3   Q2.M3 Is it possible to assure or detect semantical correctness of parts or the complete AIS?

Semantical correctness means that there are no logical errors within the different model instances. This is part of the validation process. Validation ensures that an AIS corresponds to its requirements. This is something that cannot be automatically tested with the help of tools. This cannot be done in a traditional approach or within the autoMAIS approach. Instead, this has to be done by the target domain expert.

As said, it is not possible to assure semantical correctness in both approaches. However, in some cases there is expert knowledge about possible semantical incorrectness. This knowledge for incorrectness is owned by a skillful AIS design expert. Two examples for possible incorrectness are: Existence of less than three categories within a level, and different physical data layers within a hierarchy. It would help in the verification process if this knowledge could be persistent and automatically executed on different AIS instances.

In the traditional approach, some issues could be detected but a realization of these would be costly because it requires technical knowledge about the platform as well as knowledge about mapping the technical concepts to domain concepts. If the platform changes, those have to be adapted to the new platform. Theoretically this is possible, but in practice, this is not applied. In the Gesundheit NRW project, the semantical correctness was checked by the skillful AIS design expert and the provided suggestions and hints for the other developers.

This is different within autoMAIS. Within the language instances, the AIS domain knowledge is persistent. When considering semantical issues, AIS domain issues can be used instead of their technical representation. These kinds of checks were introduced in section 4.5.1 as one advantage of an integrated meta model. Furthermore, in the process model definition in section 4.3.1, these checks have been considered. In the process model, all checks within the *check plausibility* activity have to be passed; otherwise, it is not possible to execute the transformation because these checks assure syntactical correctness. This is different when applying semantical correctness checks. If a check fails, only a warning would be given. The AIS design expert then has to decide if he wants to fix it or not.

Another issue within autoMAIS to improve semantical correctness are the defined models. The shown model instances can be provided to the target domain expert. As the provided models have a higher level of abstraction, they can be used for discussion, so he can decide if the provided models are semantically-correct. With the help of autoMAIS, it is possible to detect semantical incorrectness.

5.3.2.4 Q2.M4 Can the correctness of integration be assured?

In a traditional approach, this can not be assured, because no connection exists within the different layers, as introduced in section 3.1.1.3 and section 3.1.2.2. This leads to errors within the AIS creation process because of the non-existing integration. For instance, in the PEIS project from section 3.1.2.2, the measure definition was not integrated with the multidimensional schema. It could not be said if a referred dimension or base measure in the measure definition will exist in the multidimensional schema. This can lead to errors during development time.

In the autoMAIS approach, the correctness of integration can be assured because the different model instances are integrated with each other because, as noted in section 4.3, the different language instances depend on each other as they use the same domain concepts. At the end of the autoMAIS creation process, an integrated meta model instance for the complete resulting AIS has been created. Using transformations the AIS is generated. For generating a single component within the AIS reference architecture, different language instances are used, as introduced in section 4.6.1. During transformation, an integration exists, too. For the resulting AIS, this means that the different layers are integrated with each other and integration errors, as they can occur in the traditional approaches, are prevented.

In general, it can be said that autoMAIS improves the verification of AIS creation projects because it provides syntactical correctness on languages as well as on the integrated meta model instances. Additionally, it provides help doing the semantic correctness tests. The approach also provides the possibility to automate test generation. These issues could not be handled within the Gesundheit NRW project.

5.3.3 Q3. Does autoMAIS improve AIS documentation in AIS creation projects?

The documentation of an AIS creation project is also an issue, as introduced in section 3.1.3.3. In the introduced example projects, documentation was not done in depth. However, it would have been helpful to have documentation in these AIS creation projects. This documentation could be used internally when introducing new employees to the teams, or for the customers as introduced in the particular projects. In some projects, documentation exists but it is often outdated. In several AIS projects, the existence of documentation is required by the management or by law.

5.3.3.1   Q3.M1. Can documentation automatically be generated?

Within the AIS creation process, it is possible to generate up-to-date documentation in both approaches. In the traditional approach, the logical schema of the data warehouse can be generated. The logical schema consists of tables and their relations. In the Gesundheit NRW project, the visualization tools of the Microsoft SQL Server were used to generate this documentation. These tools, as shown in figure 5.13, have also been used in the autoMAIS approach to visualize the logical schema of the data warehouse. Next to this, no other documentation could be generated in the traditional approach. This is different within autoMAIS. Here, all language instances could be used as documentation. As there are six hierarchies, two analyses, two data transformations, and one measure definition, this results in 12 documents overall, including the logical schema.

It can be discussed if all the provided languages instances are suitable for the AIS documentation. For instance, the hierarchy language instances are also included within the analysis instances, so perhaps there is no need to present them again. Perhaps these documents, for example, the data transformation language instances, are not suitable for the documentation. At least the analysis schemas and the measures instance provide suitable documentation, as this kind of documentation is also used within traditional approaches. AutoMAIS enables more automatically-generated documentation than in a traditional approach, with no extra effort. For more meaningful documentation, transformations based on the integrated meta model could be defined that generate this documentation. According to [GR09a], and with experience from the CARESS@RKI project, an AIS documentation must consists of the following part: Data staging schemas, data warehouse schemas, deployment schemas, bus and overlapping matrices, logical schemas, and fact schema documentation.

The data staging schema describes how the different data sources are transformed into the integrated schema. The data warehouse schema describes what data sources are used in which computation. So, this is a kind of integrated document for the whole AIS because all layers of the reference architecture are included. The deployment schema describes where the different components of the AIS are physically located. Bus and overlapping matrices describes which hierarchies are used in which analysis and how the data layers overlap. The logical schema describes the tables and relations within the data warehouse component. The fact schema displays the multidimensional model of analysis.

In the autoMAIS approach, all required figures for the documentation can be generated. To do so, an additional transformation that generates the figures are needed. This must be done for the documentation elements data warehouse schema, data staging, and the bus and overlapping matrices, because these elements are different from the concrete syntax of the introduced languages. A sample is shown in figure 5.23. Here, the data warehouse schema for the hospital statistics are displayed and shows which analysis and data sources are used. This figure can be automatically generated by defining a transformation on the integrated meta model. The generated artifact here is a dot-file. To be able to generate the bus and overlapping matrices, all analysis and hierarchy instances would be needed.

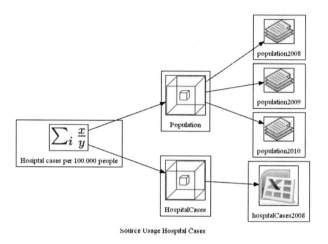

Figure 5.23: Data warehouse schema hospital statistics

For the logical schema, nothing has to be done in either approach because it is identical to the artifact introduced in Q1.M1. For the fact schema definition, the analysis language can be used because these are identical.

The deployment schema cannot be generated by the autoMAIS approach because this aspect is not covered.

To sum it up, it can be said that the bigger part of artifacts can be generated with the autoMAIS approach. As an example, some of them have been presented here. Whether these models are appropriate or not can be discussed. However, only the image or tables can be generated this way. The text has to be written by hand to be useful. This has to be done in both approaches, but with the generated documents with the autoMAIS approach, a helping hand is given for writing the corresponding text.

5.3.3.2   Q3.M2. Recency of documentation

As said before, outdated documentation is an issue in AIS creation. Therefore, this metric deals with recency of documentation. These values are:

With autoMAIS, an MDSD-based approach for AIS creation has been developed. Within an MDSD-based approach, according to [VS06], the role of models within the software creation project changes. They are "'first class citizens'", which means that models play the central role during the creation process. Changes and updates are made

Question	Metric	Traditional	autoMAIS
Schematic work	Q1.M1. Amount of generated code	-	+
	(Q1.M2. Development time	-	+)
Verification	Q2.M1. Coding convention	-	+
	Q2.M2. Syntactical correctness	-	+
	Q2.M3. Semantical correctness	-	0
	Q2.M4. Correctness of integration	-	+
Documentation	Q3.M1. Generation	-	0
	Q3.M2. Recency	0	+

Table 5.8: Evaluation results

on models and, based on these, up-to-date model transformations are executed that generate the artifacts. In other words, if the languages instances act as documentation or are the basis for generated documentation, these are always up-to-date because models are the central elements that can be changed. For instance, if the data layer of analysis is changed, this is done within the analysis instance and, in the same step, the documentation for this is updated as well.

This is different in the traditional approach. Here, documentation is done as an additional task and if the model changes, then the documentation has to be changed as well. So, there is an extra effort required for this. As this is not always done, which was observed in the PEIS project in section 3.1.2.3, this leads to outdated documentation.

5.3.4 Summary of the Estimation

In this section, the estimation of the autoMAIS approach has been done. The results are displayed in table 5.8. The table shows the different questions briefly and the results of the comparision of the measures. In this table, a trivalent scale has been used. Therefore, the values +,- and 0 are available for rating. - stands for negative, 0 for neutral and + for an improvement.

In the field of schematic work, autoMAIS improves the AIS creation process noticeably. It has been shown that 97% of an AIS can be generated in contrast to the tradtional approach, where no generation was done. The development time could be reduced as shown in Metric Q1.M1. The development time could also be reduced with the autoMAIS approach. As this was not the result of an experiment, but an estimation and measurement, this is shown within brackets. However, this measure shows promising results in the reduction of development time. In summary, it can be said that autoMAIS clearly reduces schematic work.

In the field of verification, the autoMAIS approach offers some improvements for the AIS creation process. It has been shown that autoMAIS makes adherence to coding conventions more possible. A big advantage of the autoMAIS approach is the option to show syntactical correctness of the modeled language instances. This is not possible in traditional approaches. This has a great advantage because, if the model instances, their integration, and the transformations are correct, then an AIS can be generated and it is possible to perform the modeled analysis and computations with them. This is particularly advantageous if a project is time-critical, because then there is a certainty that the modeled concepts can be included in an AIS at delivery.

What it is not possible with autoMAIS is the automatic deletion of semantical correctness of the model instances, but this is not possible in a traditional approach either, so this is rated as -. However, the language instances within have a higher level of abstraction. Therefore, the languages instances can be used to discuss with the customer, the target domain expert, detection of semantical incorrectness. Therefore, this aspect has been rated with a 0 for autoMAIS.

The correctness of integration can be assured, as shown in section 4.5, therefore it is rated with a +. As this is impossible in the traditional approach, it is rated with a -. To sum it up, it can be said that autoMAIS improves the verification of an AIS creation project, especially in the field of syntactical correctness and integration.

In the field of documentation, it is possible to generate figures and tables for the documentation of an AIS project. But next to figures and tables, documentation consists of text, and this is something that cannot be automatically generated because the text must be meaningful for the target audience, and this is not possible with generation. So the automatic generation of documents is rated as 0 because it provides criterion for writing it.

It can be said that the autoMAIS approach masters the challenges introduced in section 3.1.3, and made concrete in the requirements section 4.1, are fulfilled. And therefore, autoMAIS benefits the AIS creation process compared to traditional approaches.

5.4   Conclusion

In this section the evaluation of the autoMAIS approach was introduced. Then, the prototype implementation of the languages and the transformations were introduced. The transformations have been realized based on the MUSTANG platform. Using this prototype implementation, the application of the approach has been shown. To do so, two AIS have been realized with the help of autoMAIS. Both application scenarios are based on real world projects. In the first application scenario, Gesundheit NRW, a complete AIS was created, but the overall extent was reduced. In the second application, CARESS@RKI, the complete data warehouse was generated by using autoMAIS. This second scenario shows that autoMAIS can be used in real, time-critical projects and benefits them.

After showing that autoMAIS can be used in real world AIS creation projects, the comparison to traditional AIS creation projects has been done. For this comparison, the

GQM approach has been used. This comparison shows that autoMAIS improves the AIS creation process in the field of schematic work, verification, and documentation.

6 Summary and Outlook

6.1 Classification

In the evaluation, it could be shown that the autoMAIS approach introduced reduces schematic work, and improves verification and documentation. AutoMAIS also provides some improvements in the field of Model-Driven Software Development (MDSD) and Software Language Engineering (SLE) approaches in the field of AIS creation. In table 6.1, the classification matrix from the related work section 3.2 is displayed again. Here, a column for the autoMAIS approach has been added. It can been seen that the autoMAIS approach matches all items except the application issues. It can be discussed whether all checkmarks in the autoMAIS approach are equivalent to those in the particular related work. For instance, the integrated meta model of the CWM is much more complex than the meta model provided in this thesis, but the suggested meta model in this thesis coveres the relevant aspects of AIS creation. Nevertheless, the autoMAIS approach fulfills the requirements as laid out in section 4.1.

The reason why autoMAIS does not cover the aspect of application is that this thesis has a different goal. The goal of autoMAIS is to generate a general AIS. This general AIS is not limited to specific analysis and is able to support all kinds of analysis.

One example of analysis software is MUSTANG. Most of the functionality of the application aspect as introduced in the related work and much more can be covered with MUSTANG [MTA09] or other analysis software. It provides a way of executing complex mathematical procedures like regression and also covers the mapping of cubes to computation as described in section 4.4.1. If MUSTANG did not provide this functionality, the transformations woudl have had to be changed. In this case, mapping measures to MDX cubes could be realized with the help of model-to-model transformations. This model could contain derived cubes, an intersection of the different involved base measures, and cubes. Then measures can be addressed in the same way as base measures. Another functionality of MUSTANG is performing ad hoc analysis. Therefore, no additional transformations have to be made. Also, in this case, the integrated meta model contains all relevant information to do so.

6.2 Outlook

In this section, some additional research ideas and perspectives are introduced. In section 6.2.1, realization alternatives and possibilities are shown. Section 6.2.2 presents some thoughts about modeling hierarchies within a data integration approach. Extension of autoMAIS to ensure data provenance in AIS systems is introduced in section 6.2.3.

	CWM	Trujillo	Rizzi	CAWE	AutoMAIS
Integration					
Process Model		✓		✓	✓
Integrated Meta Model					✓
Software Generation		✓	✓	✓	✓
Language Properties					
Language Development		✓	✓	✓	✓
Usage of Existing Languages				✓	✓
Textual Language	✓		✓		✓
Graphical Language		✓	✓	✓	✓
Aspects					
Application	✓	✓	✓		CARESS
Computation					✓
Multidimensional Model	✓	✓	✓	✓	✓
Data Sources	✓	✓			✓
Data Quality					✓
Data Transformation	✓	✓			✓

Table 6.1: Classification of related work including autoMAIS

6.2.1   Alternatives in Realization

In section 5.1, the realized transformations and languages within the prototype have been introduced. To support other alternative components, different transformations have to be realized and be a part of the approach. Then the generation of a star- or MADEIRA schema, or a MOLAP data warehouse, would be possible. Similarly, by changing the transformation, different external mathematical components, like MDX, can be used. This would have the advantage that all functionality can be directly realized within the OLAP server. Then no additional analysis application would be required. This approach makes sense when using, for example, Microsoft Analysis Services, because then the OLAP server could be accessed by using Excel. In this case, the users have a known analysis environment and do not need to learn a new software. This is mentioned here because in the example projects in section 3.1, this was an important requirement.

As shown in section 2.1.2, it is possible to exchange the concrete syntax of a language. In some cases, this might be useful to support other requirements. Therefore, it would be conceivable to have a textual analysis of the hierarchy language. This would enable faster creation of instances. In this case, the meta model would not have to be changed because, with the way it has been developed, it should cover all relevant aspects. Changes in the meta model would also be possible as the different meta models are technically separated. However, it would get more complicated if common elements have to be changed.

These introduced aspects show some of the flexibility of the autoMAIS approach. The approach is not fixed, but can be tailored to personal needs.

6.2.2 Data Integration View on Hierarchies

Also in the field of hierarchy modeling, the following ideas can be used for further research. In the evaluation, it could be seen that a hierarchy can be divided into two types: the data sources, and the generated ones. The data source-based hierarchies were ICD and region. For this hierarchy, data sources were given based on which the category definition was built on. In the case of generated ones, the category definition can be generated by rules. Examples for those kinds of hierarchies were time and age. The suggested autoMAIS approach does not differ between those kinds of dimensions. The source of the category definition is not considered. It could be possible to introduce production rules for category definition. This could be helpful, for example, when defining a time hierarchy that contains categories for each day of the year for 20 years. In this case, an automatic generation of the complete hierarchy could be possible, with almost no modeling needed. Also, it would be possible to generate new categories when new data is integrated. In the case of hierarchies based on data sources, an integration process similar to those introduced in this thesis is imaginable. With these approaches, it would be possible to enable traceability of hierarchies as well. So, for each analysis, it can be determined what the source of the used categories were. For instance, in the field of diagnoses, there are different versions and with the introduced approach, it can be said which version has been used. It also would reduce the overall hierarchy modeling effort, which was the most extensive aspect of the evaluation.

6.2.3 Empowering Data Provenance

Data provenance in an AIS is a general challenge, although some approaches, like [CW01], exist. With a little modification of the meta model, autoMAIS can be used for data provenance. When all information of an AIS, including cells and data sources, is stored in the meta model, concrete analysis can be mapped back to the sources. The procedure would be similar to the AIS schema documentation from section 5.3.3.1, but a little bit more complex. For results of particular analyses, or to show the provenance, the corresponding meta model element has to be identified. If the corresponding element is found, the path in the meta model can be followed and the source can be identified. To do so, the data sources and their content have to be introduced into the autoMAIS meta model. Then additional global AIS checks could perform this task. For identifying the corresponding meta model element of an analysis, some logging and tracing mechanisms also have to be provided. Conceptually, this is not a big challenge but technically it is. In this thesis, only describing parts of the AIS were modeled and not the complete AIS. Holding a complete AIS with all cells and all sources in a meta model would make these models rather large. This would lead to challenges in handling these models, so in this field, more research would be needed to realize this approach.

6.3 Results

In this thesis, it has been shown how an MDSD and SLE approach for the creation of AIS can be used. It has been shown that different existing languages can be used and extended for this purpose. It has also been shown that it is possible to cover the complete AIS creation process and provide an integrated meta model. In the evaluation, it shows that autoMAIS improves the AIS creation process. The autoMAIS approach has extended the existing research in this particular research area.

In this thesis, the autoMAIS approach was introduced and applied. With the developed artifacts, it is possible to fulfill the requirements from section 4.1. The autoMAIS approach enables automatic generation of an AIS configuration based on models. The autoMAIS approach consists of the following contributions.:

- **Process model:** The autoMAIS process model defines in which order the different languages instances should be created to ensure that the generation of the AIS will succeed. It has also been shown how this process model can be integrated into a software development process. Finally, the overall autoMAIS process and the elements connections are given.

- **autoMAIS languages:** The autoMAIS approach is an MDSD approach which provides different languages to describe the different aspects of AIS creation. For each language, the decision to use an existing, well-engineered language, or to develop a new one, was considered. In most cases, an existing language could be used, but in some cases, the existing language had to be extended. All languages in autoMAIS come with an abstract and concrete syntax. The languages included in autoMAIS are the following:

  - **Measures:** The measure language is used to describe computation within the resulting AIS. The measure language was mainly self-defined. It describes computation of measures and the definition of measures within an AIS creation project. The measures themselves are defined by using mathematical expressions. External calls can also be defined. This language is used to configure a project and define relationships.

  - **Analysis:** The analysis language is used to describe multidimensional structures for the resulting AIS. The instances of this languages can be used as documentation and can also be used to interact with the target domain expert, as shown in [TRA10].

- **Hierarchies:** For the logical modeling of analysis, the hierarchies language was introduced. In this language, textual and graphical elements were included to enable the conceptual and logical modeling of hierarchies.

- **Data sources:** The data source language is used to described data sources for the resulting AIS. The data source language includes elements for the technical access, the structural description, and information about the content.

- **Data transformation:** The data transformation language describes how data sources can be mapped and transformed to the format of the integrated schema. Similar to the hierarchy languages, the data transformation language consists of a graphical and a textual language. In the evaluation, it has been shown that it is possible to perform data integration with this language, but it has also been shown that the process is different from the data integration process that was shown in the example projects.

- **Data quality:** Data quality is integrated into the ETL process. As data quality is a broad aspect, it could only be considered as a small aspect in this thesis. Therefore, only one example data quality problem has been covered. The language is interesting to the field of SLE, because it is a language that has been developed for the use of real users.

• **Integrated meta model:** The different languages or their meta models are integrated into one meta model. This meta model describes the complete resulting AIS. It can be used to generated the AIS instances, and for verification and testing. As this meta model describes the complete resulting AIS, it covers the different aspects and levels of detail. The integrated meta model is also used for the synchronization of model instances. With this integrated meta model, verification is improved.

• **Generation:** One goal of the autoMAIS approach is to enable code generation for a complete AIS creation process. As shown in the evaluation, this generation reduces schematic work. It has also been shown that the transformations are specific to the chosen standard component.

Therefore, autoMAIS enables an MDSD and SLE approach for AIS creation, and improves traditional approaches in the fields of schematic work, verification, and documentation.

A Appendix

Now in this section additional content is provided. In section A.1 additional content from section 2.1.2.2 is provided. Here the description of data sources and dimension are presented in their original German language description form the Gesundheit NRW project. For the PEIS project the definition of measures a complete example is presented.

In section A.2 the relevant grammar elements from the R$_2$O languages is given. This language used to realize the transformation in the data transformation language in section 4.4.5.

In section A.3 the model instances from the evaluation chapter 5 in their original German languages form a presented.

A.1 Original Data Description and Code Fragments from the Example Projects

A.2 R$_2$O Grammar

```
1  conceptmapping-definition ::= conceptmap-def name documentation?
2          identified-by+ (uri-as transformation)?
3          described-by propertymap-def)*
4          (applies-if cond-expr)? (joins-via join-list)?
5  identified-by ::= identified-by literal
6  join-list ::= documentation? (hasjoin joindesc)+ (overwrites literal)?
7  joindesc ::= (hasCol literal)+
```

Listing A.3: General mapping definition taken from [BsCGp04] and transformed to the xtext syntax

```
1  cond-expr::= orcond-expr | AND andcond-expr orcond-expr
2  orcond-expr::= notcond-expr | OR orcond-expr notcond-expr
3  notcond-expr::= condition | NOT condition
4  condition::= primitive-condition (arg-restriction arg-restriction)*
5  primitive-condition::= lo_than | loorequal_than | lo_than_str |
6      loorequal_than_str | hi_than | hiorequal_than |
7      hi_than_str | hiorequal_than_str | equals |
8      equals_str | in_keyword | in_set | in_set_str |
9      between | between_str | date_before | date_after |
10     date_equal
11  arg-restriction::= parameter-selector restriction
12  parameter-selector::= on-param literal
13  restriction::= has-value constant-value | has-column literal |
14      has-transform transformation
15  constant-value::= datatype literal
```

Listing A.4: Conditional expressions in R$_2$O

German dimension Name	Translated name
ICD	ICD
Alter	Age
Geschlecht	Gender
Zeit	Time
Gebiete	Region
Nationalität	Nationality
(mögl.)Infektionsort	Location of infection
Bezugsraum (Std.bev.)	Point of reference
Meldekategorie	Reporting category
Hospitalisiert	Hospitalizes
epidemiologischer Zusammenhang	Epidemiological link
Erregernachweis	Pathogen-proof
Erkrankt Status	Disease status
Status Verstorben	Death status
Falldefinitionskategorie	Case definition category
Referenzdefinition (RKI)	Reference definition (RKI)
Historische Zeit	Historical time
Pflegeart	Type of care
Pflegestufe	Level of care
Operation	Surgery
Art der Unterbringung (PsychKG)	Type of placement
Dienstzeit (PsychKG)	Period of service
Gewöhnlicher Aufenthaltsort (PsychKG)	Habitual place of residence
Arztgruppe (PsychKG)	Physician group
Krankheitsbild (PsychKG)	Disease
Unterbringung durch Betreuer (Btr)	Accommodation provided by carers
Aufenthaltsort vor Unterbringung (Btr)	Whereabouts prior
Art der Vorführung (Btr)	Type of performance

Table A.1: Original and translated name from table 3.1

Source name	Source name translated
Einwohner (Jahresmittel)	Population
Infektionskrankheiten	Infectious diseases
Infektionskrankheiten (Jahresbericht)	Infectious diseases (Annual Report)
Standardbevölkerungsdatenbasis	Standard population
Patiententage	Patient-days
nfektionskrankheiten historisch	Historical infectious diseases
Einwohnerdaten historisch	Historical population
Einwohner (31.12.)	Inhabitants (31.12.)
amtl. mittl. Bevölkerung	Official median population
Todesursachenstatistik	Reason of deaths
Sterbefälle	Deaths
Tod durch häuslichen Unfall	Death by accident at home
Krankenhausfälle	Hospital statisctics
Rehafälle	Rehabilitation cases
krebsregister	Cancer Registry
pflegebegutachtung	Assement of care
PflegeStatistik	Care statistics
Schwerbehinderte	Severely disabled
Rentenzugaenge	New pensions
VDR Rehabilitation	Rehabilitation
Aktiv Versicherte (VDR)	Active insured
Rentenbestand (VDR)	Pension population
BKK Mitglieder	Health Insurance Fund members
BKK Arbeitsunfähigkeit Fälle	Cases of inability to work
BKK Arbeitsunfähigkeit Tage	Days of inability to work
PsychKG Fälle nach Art der Unterbringung	Mental health law kind of placement
PsychKG Fälle nach Dienstzeit	Mental health law cases in period of service
PsychKG Fälle nach Aufenthaltsort	Mental health law cases by habitual place of residence
PsychKG Fälle nach Alter und Geschlecht	Mental health law cases by age and gender
PsychKG Fälle nach Arztgruppe	Mental health law cases by physician group
PsychKG Fälle nach Krankheitsbild	Mental health law cases by disease
Btr Zahl aller Betreuten	Law of Care number of supervised
Btr Fälle nach Art der Unterbringung	Law of Care cases by kind of placement
Btr Fälle nach Aufenthaltsort	Law of Care cases by habitual place of residence
Btr Fälle nach Alter und Geschlecht	Law of Care cases by age and gender
Btr Zahl der Vorführungen	Number of displays

Table A.2: List of data sources for the Gesundheit NRW project

```
 1  private SummaryAttributeVO HandleGetSummaryDPIPerAsset() {
 2      // Basiswürfel:
 3      // ------------
 4      SummaryAttributeVO summaryKapitalabrufe = ServiceFactory.Instance.
            FamilyOfficeBaseSummaryAttributeService.
            GetBaseSummaryKapitalabrufeKumuliert(null);
 5      RestrictingDimensionSetVO
            rueckzahlungOKostenKummuliertRestrictingDimensionSetVo = new
            RestrictingDimensionSetVO();
 6      rueckzahlungOKostenKummuliertRestrictingDimensionSetVo[ServiceFactory.
            Instance.FamilyOfficeDimensionService.GetDimensionRueckzahlungsart()]
            = true;
 7      SummaryAttributeVO summaryKapitalrueckfluesse = ServiceFactory.Instance.
            FamilyOfficeBaseSummaryAttributeService.
            GetBaseSummaryRueckzahlungOhneKostenKumuliert(
            rueckzahlungOKostenKummuliertRestrictingDimensionSetVo);
 8
 9      // Zielwürfel:
10      // -----------
11      SummaryAttributeVO summaryDPI = new SummaryAttributeVO() {
12          IsAdhoc = false,
13          ShortName = "DPI",
14          LongName = "DPI",
15          Description = "DPI",
16          IsVisible = true,
17          IsBase = false,
18          DerivedDetails = new MeasureDerivedVO()
19      };
20
21      // Berechnungsfunktion des Zielwürfels:
22      // ------------------------------------
23      summaryDPI.DerivedDetails.Function = new StatisticalFunctionVO() {
24          ShortName = "DPI",
25          LongName = "DPI",
26          Library = String.Empty,
27          Instructions = new List<String>(),
28          Operands = new List<String>()
29      };
30      summaryDPI.DerivedDetails.Function.Operands.Add("abrufe");
31      summaryDPI.DerivedDetails.Function.Operands.Add("rueckfluesse");
32
33      summaryDPI.DerivedDetails.Function.Instructions.Add("rueckfluesse/abrufe")
            ;
34
35      // Zuordnung der Basiswürfel zu den Operanden:
36      // ------------------------------------------
37      summaryDPI.DerivedDetails.SummaryOperandMapping = new SummaryMappingVO();
38      summaryDPI.DerivedDetails.SummaryOperandMapping[summaryKapitalabrufe] = "
            abrufe";
39      summaryDPI.DerivedDetails.SummaryOperandMapping[summaryKapitalrueckfluesse
            ] = "rueckfluesse";
40
41      return summaryDPI;
42
43  }
```

Listing A.1: Complete definition of DPI from the PEIS project

```
1  private SummaryAttributeVO HandleGetSummaryNetCashFlowPerAsset() {
2       // Basiswürfel:
3       // -------------
4       SummaryAttributeVO summaryEinzahlung = ServiceFactory.Instance.
           FamilyOfficeBaseSummaryAttributeService.
           GetBaseSummaryEinzahlungGesamtVerteilt(null);
5       SummaryAttributeVO summaryRueckzahlung = ServiceFactory.Instance.
           FamilyOfficeBaseSummaryAttributeService.
           GetBaseSummaryRueckzahlungGesamtVerteilt(null);
6
7       // Zielwürfel:
8       // -----------
9       SummaryAttributeVO summaryNetCashFlow = new SummaryAttributeVO() {
10        IsAdhoc = false,
11        ShortName = "Net Cash Flow",
12        LongName = "Net Cash Flow",
13        Description = "Net Cash Flow",
14        IsVisible = true,
15        IsBase = false,
16        DerivedDetails = new MeasureDerivedVO()
17      };
18
19      // Berechnungsfunktion des Zielwürfels:
20      // ------------------------------------
21      summaryNetCashFlow.DerivedDetails.Function = new StatisticalFunctionVO() {
22        ShortName = "Net Cash Flow",
23        LongName = "Net Cash Flow",
24        Library = String.Empty,
25        Instructions = new List<String>(),
26        Operands = new List<String>()
27      };
28      summaryNetCashFlow.DerivedDetails.Function.Operands.Add("einzahlung");
29      summaryNetCashFlow.DerivedDetails.Function.Operands.Add("rueckzahlung");
30
31      summaryNetCashFlow.DerivedDetails.Function.Instructions.Add("rueckzahlung-
           einzahlung");
32
33      // Zuordnung der Basiswürfel zu den Operanden:
34      // -------------------------------------------
35      summaryNetCashFlow.DerivedDetails.SummaryOperandMapping = new
           SummaryMappingVO();
36      summaryNetCashFlow.DerivedDetails.SummaryOperandMapping[summaryEinzahlung]
           = "einzahlung";
37      summaryNetCashFlow.DerivedDetails.SummaryOperandMapping[
           summaryRueckzahlung] = "rueckzahlung";
38
39      return summaryNetCashFlow;
40    }
```

Listing A.2: Complete definition of netto cashflow from the PEIS project

```
1  transformation::= primitive-transformation (arg-restriction arg-restriction)*
2  primitive-transformation::= get_nth_char | get _delimited | get_substring |
3     concat | add_type | subtract_type |
4     multiply_type | divide_type | constant
```

Listing A.5: Transformation expressions in R$_2$O taken from [BsCGp04] and transformed to the xtext syntax

Dimension
Zeitpunkt
Stichtag
Vermögensinhaber
Asset
Investor
Währung
Einzelinvestment
Kostenart
Rückzahlungsart
Stammdatentyp
Kalendertyp
Notizart
Stichmonat
Zeichnungsjahr
Region
Fokus

Table A.3: Dimension list for PEIS

```
1  propertymap-def::= attributemap-def | relfromatt-def | relationmap-def
2  attributemap-def::= attributemap-def name use-dbcol* selector* documentation
3  relfromatt-def::= relfromatt-def name use-dbcol* selector* newobj-type?
      documentation?
4  relationmap-def::= relationmap-def to-concept
5  use-dbcol::= use-dbcol literal
6  selector::= selector (applies-if cond-expr)? (aftertransform transformation)?
7  newobj-type::= newobject-type literal
8  to-concept::= to-concept literal
```

Listing A.6: Property expressions in R₂O taken from [BsCGp04] and transformed to the xtext syntax

A.3   Model Instances from the Evaluation in German Language

```
Parameter is MeasureType has Name bev;
Parameter is MeasureType has Name fallzahl;
Parameter is DimensionType has Name iterativeDimension;
Parameter is DimensionType has Name altersDimension;
Parameter is MeasureType has Name studienbevoelkerung;


        Measure { Name: CrudeRate,
            uses Parameter: fallzahl ,bev;
            Computation: (Fallzahl / bev)  * 1000000;
            Description: "Describes crude rate";
        }
        Measure { Name: Percentage ,
            uses Parameter: fallzahl,iterativeDimension;
            Computation: External Call: Package: "OLAP" ,Instruction: "Percentage";
            Description: "Berechnet den prozentualen Anteil für eine Dimension";

        }


        Measure { Name: AgeSandardizedRate ,
            uses Parameter: Rate,bev,iterativeDimension ;
            Computation: External Call: Package: "ekn" ,Instruction:"FunctionDmdr";
            Description: "Berechnung DMDR";

        }


Project Measure Definition {
    Project Name: GesundheitNRW Description: "Gesundheit NRW Liga"

    Base Measure id=KrankenhausFaelle , Longname="Krankenhaus Fälle"
    Base Measure id=Bevoelkerung , Longname="Bevöelkerung"
    Dimension =Alter
    Dimension =Geschlecht
    Dimension =Region

    Measure CasesCrudeRate has type Rate
        { Longname: "Crude rate hospital cases" Description "cases per 100.000 people"
            Operator Mapping:
            Bevoelkerung  has role bev
            KrankenhausFaelle has role fallzahl;
        }

    Measure PercentageAge has type Percentage
        { Longname: "Age percentages" Description "percentages for Ages"
            Operator Mapping:
            CasesCrudeRate has role fallzahl
            Alter has role iterativeDimension;
        }

    Measure PercentageGender has type Percentage
        { Longname: "Gender percentages" Description "percentages for Gender"
            Operator Mapping:
            CasesCrudeRate has role fallzahl
            Geschlecht has role iterativeDimension;
        }

    Measure AgeStanHospital has type AgeSandardizedRate
        { Longname: "Standardized Rate" Description"Age Standardized Rate "
            Operator Mapping:
            CasesCrudeRate has role fallzahl
            Alter has role altersDimension;
        }
}
```

Figure A.1: Instance of Measure Language in German

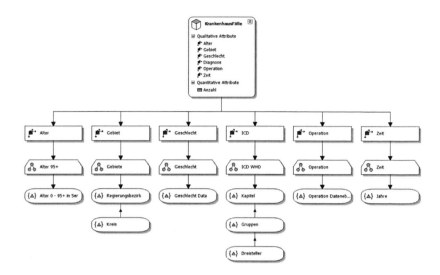

Figure A.2: Analysis schema instance for hospital case in German

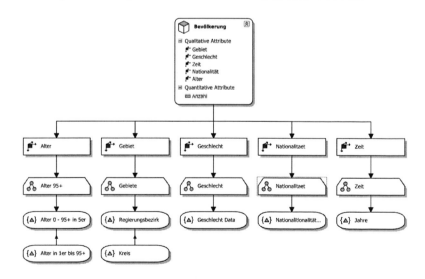

Figure A.3: Analysis schema instance for population in German

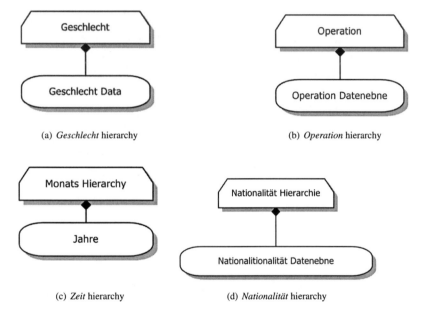

(a) *Geschlecht* hierarchy

(b) *Operation* hierarchy

(c) *Zeit* hierarchy

(d) *Nationalität* hierarchy

Figure A.4: Simple hierarchies in the evaluation

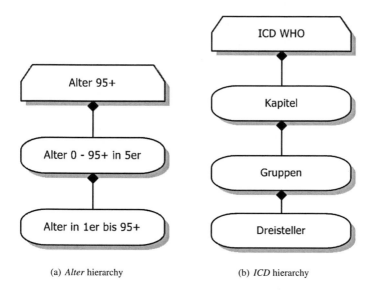

(a) *Alter* hierarchy   (b) *ICD* hierarchy

Figure A.5: *More complex hierarchies in the evaluation*

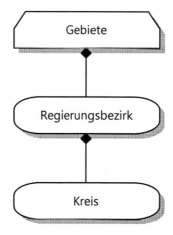

Figure A.6: *Region hierarchy in the Gesundheit NRW project in German*

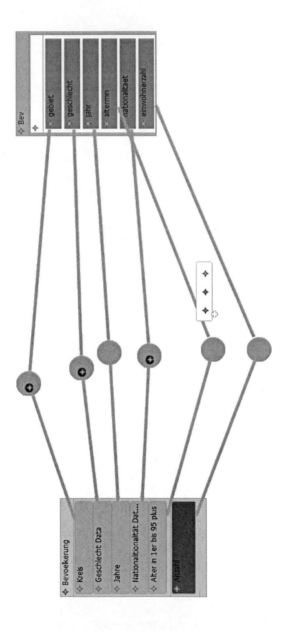

Figure A.7: Complete schema matching for population in German

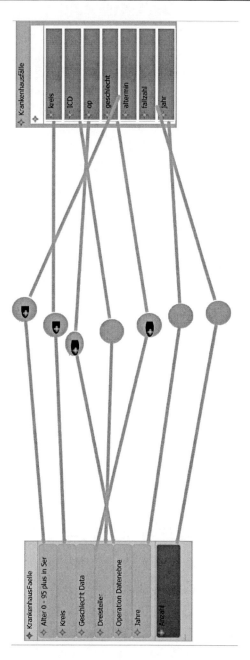

Figure A.8: Complete defined schema matching for the hospital cases

```
'arameter is MeasureType has Name bevoelkerung;
'arameter is MeasureType has Name fallzahlen;
'arameter is MeasureType has Name standardbevoelkerung;
'arameter is DimensionType has Name Alter;

leasure { Name:Personyears,
    uses Parameter: bevoelkerung;
    Computation: External Call: Package: "ekn",Instruction:"Pop";
    Description: "Definition of person years";
    }

    Measure { Name: CrudeRate,
        uses Parameter: fallzahlen ,bevoelkerung;
        Computation: fallzahlen /bevoelkerung * 100000;
        Description: "Rohe Rate Fallzahl";
    }

    Measure { Name:CumulativeRate,
        uses Parameter: fallzahlen,Alter;
        Computation: External Call: Package: "ekn",Instruction:"CUMULATIVERATE";
        Description: "Describes the comulative rate";
    }

    Measure { Name:ConfidenceIntervall,
        uses Parameter: fallzahlen,bevoelkerung;
        Computation: External Call: Package: "ekn",Instruction:"ci_crude_rate";
        Description: "confidence interval";
    }

    Measure { Name:DMDR,
        uses Parameter: bevoelkerung,fallzahlen,Alter;
        Computation: External Call: Package: "ekn",Instruction:"direct_std";
        Description: "direct standarized rate based on standard population";
    }
```

Figure A.9: Measure definition for the CARESS@RKI project in German

```
'roject Measure Definition {
    Project Name: CaressRKI Description: "Definitionen der Kennzahlen für den ersten Meilenstein"

    Base Measure id=bevoelkerung , Longname="Bevölkerung"
    Base Measure id=inzidenz    , Longname="Tumor inforamtion der 15 landeskrebsregister"
    Base Measure id=standardbevoelkerung , Longname="Standard Bevölkerung"
    Dimension =Alter

    Measure Personenjahre has type Personyears
    { Longname: "Personenjahre" Description"Personenjahre"
        Operator Mapping: bevoelkerung has role bevoelkerung;
    }

    Measure RoheRateInzidenz has type CrudeRate
    { Longname: "Rohe Rate Inzidenz" Description"Rohe Rate für die Inzidenz"
        Operator Mapping:
          bevoelkerung has role bevoelkerung
          inzidenz has role fallzahlen;
    }

    Measure RoheRateInzidenzStandardBevoelkerung has type CrudeRate
    { Longname: "Rohe Rate Inzidenz Standardbevölkerung" Description"Rohe Rate Inzidenz für Standardbevölkerung"
        Operator Mapping:
          standardbevoelkerung has role bevoelkerung
          inzidenz has role standardbevoelkerung;
    }

    Measure KomulativeRateInzidenz has type CumulativeRate
    { Longname: "Komulative Rate Inzidenz" Description"Komulative Rate für die Inzidenz"
        Operator Mapping:
          RoheRateInzidenz  has role fallzahlen
          Alter has role Alter;
    }

    Measure RoheRateInzidenzKI has type ConfidenceIntervall
    { Longname: "Rohe Rate (KI) Inzidenz" Description"Konfidenzintervall für Rohe Rate Inzidenz"
        Operator Mapping:
          RoheRateInzidenz has role fallzahlen
          bevoelkerung has role bevoelkerung;
    }

    Measure KI has type ConfidenceIntervall
    { Longname: "Konfidenzontervall" Description"Konfidenzontervall Inzidenz"
        Operator Mapping:
          inzidenz has role fallzahlen
          bevoelkerung has role bevoelkerung;
    }

    Measure DmdrInzidenz has type DMDR
    { Longname: "DMDR Inzidenz " Description""
        Operator Mapping:
          bevoelkerung has role bevoelkerung
          RoheRateInzidenz has role fallzahlen;
    }

    Measure DmdrStudyIncidence has type DMDR
    { Longname: "DMDR Inzidenz Studienpopulation" Description""
        Operator Mapping:
          standardbevoelkerung has role bevoelkerung
          RoheRateInzidenz has role fallzahlen;
    }
```

Figure A.10: Project measure definition for the CARESS@RKI project in German

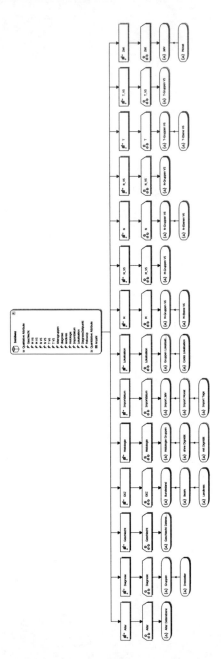

Figure A.11: Cases CARESS@RKI in German

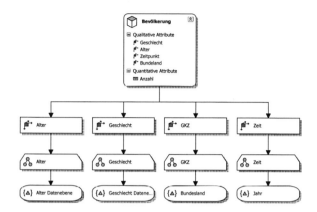

Figure A.12: Population in CARESS@RKI in German

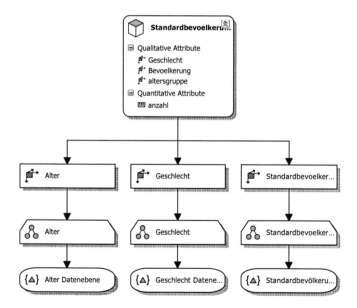

Figure A.13: Standard Population in CARESS@RKI

Glossary

The following glossary summarizes, in alphabetical order, the essential definitions and terms of this thesis. The symbol ∼ is used as a placeholder for the term that is explained in the entry. A vertical ↑ in front of a term references another glossary entry.

Abstract syntax The ∼ describes the structure and the grammatical rules of a language. In most cases the ∼ is represented by a ↑meta model. A meta model describes the internal structure and relation of a model. For the definition of a meta model, UML or ↑MOF is used.

ADAPT (Application Design for Analytical Processing Technologies) ∼ is a ↑graphical language that is used to describe multidimensional structures.

Age-specific rate An ∼ is measure that is used in the ↑target domain of health reporting. It computes the rate for a specific age group.

Aggregation function An ∼ is a computation within the ↑multidimensional model. ∼ describes, how cells are grouped together on higher ↑levels. Common aggregations are sum or count.

Aggregation path A ∼ is an element of the ↑multidimensional model. It shows the path form the root node, to one of the leafs in a ↑hierarchy.

AIS design expert ∼ is a role in the ↑autoMAIS process model. He is an expert for creating AIS systems. He has already developed different AIS for different target domains. He knows about hierarchy, cube, and measure modeling.

Analytical information system (AIS) In a ∼ information is used for analysis, and to support operational professionals and managers. The term is used as a conceptual clip for approaches such as data warehouse, OLAP, and Data Mining.

ATL (Atlas Transformation Language) ∼ is a model-to-model transformation language that provides an implementation based on the Eclipse platform.

AutoMAIS Name of the approach developed in this thesis. It stands for **Auto**matic **A**nalytical **I**nformation **S**ystems.

base measure ∼ describes a target analysis in the resulting AIS. A ∼ is atomic, and cannot be computed. Based on a measure analysis are defined. The concrete values of a ∼ is integrated from data source.

Category A ∼ is an element of the ↑multidimensional model. A ∼ describes concrete items within a ↑level. It is the smallest element within the ↑multidimensional model. In a time hierarchy, ∼ could be, for example, a concrete year oder date.

CAWE ∼ is an approach that combines ↑MDA and Architecture-Driven Modernization for data warehousing. The goal of ∼ is the creation of a model-driven framework that enables model-driven forward-, reverse- and re-engineering for AIS.

Cell A ∼ is an element of the ↑multidimensional model. A ↑cube consists of cells. The number of cells is the product of all categories for all cube dimensions. Each cell has a coordinate, one category for each dimension. Each cell has a value, in most cases a numerical one.

Cell-by-cell computation A ∼ is a special computation for multidimensional structures. In a ∼ cells the cubes are iterated and the results are computed for each cell.

Computation-Independent Model (CIM) ∼ is a model of ↑MDA. The ∼ describes the domain concepts of an application. It is independent from a realization or platform.

Component-and-connector style A ∼ is a special way to describe a software architecture at runtime.

Conceptual modeling of ETL ∼ is the mapping and transformation between data sources and targets.

Conceptual modeling of hierarchies ∼ is the modeling of levels and their connections to each other.

Concrete syntax A ∼ describes the symbols and notations the language user works with.

Common Warehouse Metamodel (CWM) The ∼ is a ↑OMG Standard that describes an integrated meta model for DWH. It consists of different packages, and they describe all relevant aspects of a data warehouses.

Consistency demand check In the ∼ the segment definition is reviewed. It checks if the segment has been transformed into a real modeling instance.

Crude rate A ∼ is a statistical function that it used in health reporting. It is used, to make region with different numbers of inhabitants, comparable by eliminating the amount of population.

Cube A ∼ is an element of the multidimensional model. A ∼ describes the data structure that actually stores the data in the model.

Data cleansing ∼ is a task during the ↑ETL process. Here, wrong or poor quality data is tried to be eliminated.

Data level A ∼ describes, on which ↑level of detail, information can be found. In a ↑analysis the ∼ has the highest level of detail.

Data source $\sim$ are operational systems or external data which content is integrated in the ↑data warehouse.

Data warehouse A $\sim$ is a central component of an AIS. It is the technical integrated dataset.

Dimensional Fact Modeling (DFM) $\sim$ is a ↑graphical language that is used to describe multidimensional structures.

Distributions to Paid (DPI) $\sim$ is a measure in the target domain of family offices. It describes the relative return from called capital. It is an performance indicator for enhancement in values.

Domain-Specific Language Tools $\sim$ a framework from Microsoft for the definition of graphical DSLs within Visual Studio.

Domain-Specific Language (DSL) A $\sim$ is a formal language that has been developed for a certain problem domain. A $\sim$ is used by domain experts. The opposite of a $\sim$ is a ↑GPL. There are two kinds of $\sim$: ↑textual and ↑graphical. A $\sim$ has two main parts: the ↑abstract syntax and the ↑concrete syntax.

Ecore In ↑EMF $\sim$ is used to represent models.

Eclipse Modeling Framework (EMF) The $\sim$ is a modeling framework based on Eclipse.

Engineering part The $\sim$ describes the needed steps and tasks for realizing an AIS, based on the reference architecture.

ETL The $\sim$ is a process. It stands for Extract, Transform, and Load (ETL), and refers to a process to combine data from multiple data sources with different structures in a target database. This process is accomplished in three steps:

1. Extract data from different data sources.
2. Transform data from the source schemas into the target schema.
3. Load transformed data into the target database.

Extended Backus-Naur Form (EBNF) A $\sim$ is a notation used for describing grammars.

Generic code In terms of MDSD, $\sim$ is that code which is identical for all kind of applications.

Gesundheit NRW $\sim$ is a project which was developed for LIGA. It deals with the ↑target domain of health reporting. It is used to describe real world AIS creation projects.

Global AIS check ∼ exist for the improvement of the AIS creation process. They provide information that would be difficult to get without autoMAIS. They combine different levels of abstraction and technical heterogeneity.

Global dimension A ∼ is a ↑dimension valid for the whole resulting AIS. It contains all used hierarchies, levels, and categories. All these dimension elements are defined in the ∼ . They are identified by name.

Graphical modeling framework (GMF) ∼ is an Eclipse project for the development of ↑graphical languages.

Graphical language A ∼ is specific kind of language. In a ∼ the ↑concrete syntax consists of graphical elements and their connections. The elements a represented by boxes, shapes, or icons.

InDaQu ∼ is the name of a language introduced in this thesis. ∼ was originally developed for the domain of public health care systems, and deals with the identification of inconsistencies.

Individual code In terms of MDSD, ∼ is specific for the particular project.

Information integration ∼ deals with all aspects of integrating different sources, or systems into one integrated, central database.

LIGA ∼ is the federal institute for health and work in North Rhine-Westphalia. The general task of ∼ is to provide health information to the local government and interested citizens.

Lines of Code (LOC) ∼ is a software metric. It is defined by counting the number of lines in the source code of a program or artifact.

Local dimension A ∼ is used in aa analysis, or cube description. The ∼ refer to the global dimension, but in most cases, only a subset is referred.

Logical modeling of hierarchies ∼ is a more detailed modeling process of hierarchies. Here, the elements within the levels (categories) are defined and connected.

Logical modeling of ETL ∼ describes the data flow during the ↑ETL process.

MADEIRA ∼ is concept of mapping multidimensional structures in a relational way. This schema was developed by OFFIS.

Measure A ∼ is the result of a computation of ↑base measures .

Meta Object Facility (MOF) ∼ is a language for defining meta models by the OMG.

MDX ∼ is a query language for multidimensional models.

Model Driven Architecture (MDA) ∼ is an OMG standard [OMG11b] that focuses on certain aspects of MDSD. The models in ∼ are based on UML. MDA provides three main models: ↑CIM, ↑PIM, and ↑PSM.

Model-Driven Software Development (MDSD) ∼ is a specific approach in software development. The general idea is to generate a large part of software, based on models and their transformations.

Model-to-model transformation A ∼ is used in ↑MDSD. In a ∼ meta models are transformed to other meta models.

Model-to-text transformation A ∼ is used in MDSD. In a ∼ models is transformed to text. This text can be source code, such as Java, SQL, or some documents.

MOLAP ∼ stands for multidimensional ↑OLAP and it is a technical OLAP alternative. In this alternative, cubes and dimensions are stored directly as multidimensional entities on the hard drive.

Multidimensional Entity Relationship-Model (MERM) ∼ is a ↑graphical language that is used to describe multidimensional structures. It is based on entity relationship-model.

Multidimensional model The ∼ is a conceptual model, or paradigm, to describe analysis models for an AIS. It enables ↑OLAP, and helps to navigate through data efficiently. The main concepts of the ∼ are: ↑dimension, ↑level, and ↑category.

MUSTANG ∼ is a data analysis platform developed at OFFIS. It is used as ↑AIS.

Online Analytical Processing (OLAP) ∼ is a usage paradigm for data analysis. It describes, how users can interact with massive data. ∼ is based on the ↑multidimensional model.

PEIS ∼ is a project describes in the example projects. ∼ was a project for a family office. It was an InfoAnalytics project with OFFIS as the sub-contractor.

Platform-independent model (PIM) A ∼ is a specific kind of model used on ↑MDA. The ∼ describes the model for the resulting software without providing any detail on the specific implementation.

Platform-specific model (PSM) A ∼ is a specific kind of model used on ↑MDA. ∼ contains the specific technical implementation details that the ↑PIM does not provide.

QVT ∼ stands for Query/View/Transformation and provides standard languages for model transformations. It has been provided by the OMG.

R Project ∼ is an software tool for statistical calculations.

R₂O $\sim$ stands for Relational to Ontology and is a mapping language. This language has been developed, to map relational databases to ontologies. In this thesis, it used to describe data transformations.

ROLAP $\sim$ stands for relational OLAP and it is a technical OLAP alternative. In this alternative cubes and dimensions are stored in a relational database.

Schematic work $\sim$ is a term, describing the schematic part of an application by [SVE07]. Schematic describes that kind of work in a project that follows a certain template or principle. When writing code, schematic work is: Copy&Paste with adaption ti the specific case.

Snowflake schema $\sim$ is a concept of mapping multidimensional structures in a relational way.

SQL $\sim$ is a language for querying relational databases.

Standard software A $\sim$ is a kind of software that has a well-defined application scope. It has not been developed for a particular customer, but for a range of costumers. An example of a $\sim$ for writing documents, is Microsoft Word.

Standardized incidence rate A $\sim$ is a measures, used in the ↑target domain of health reporting.

Standardized population A $\sim$ is term that is used in the ↑target domain of health reporting. It describes how many persons are normally in specific age groups.

Star schema $\sim$ is a concept of mapping multidimensional structures in a relational way.

System administrator A $\sim$ is a role in the autoMAIS process model. It represents is a technical expert for the operational systems. This also includes database administration. He is familiar with the accessibility, and knows the functional contact person.

Target domain $\sim$ is the domain of the resulting AIS. In the case of Gesundheit NRW, this is public health reporting.

Target domain expert A $\sim$ is a role in the autoMAIS process model. A $\sim$ is an expert of the target domain and, in most cases, also the orderer of the AIS. The resulting AIS will help him in his daily work. He knows about useful analysis, and knows the relevant target domain measures.

Textual language In a $\sim$ all elements are represented by text. The definition of a textual language is done, in most cases, with a grammar. An example of a textual language is SQL.

User-driven $\sim$ is a developing methodology for AIS. This approach focuses more on the business user, than on the top-management. The needed information is gathered from different users, and then transformed into a common multidimensional schema.

Verification ∼ is a process to ensure that a software meets its specification.

Xpand ∼ is a model-to-text transformation languages that uses ↑Ecore.

Xtext ∼ is an Eclipse project for modeling textual languages. The definition of ∼ is done with the definition of an ↑EBNF.

Abbreviations

AIS	Analytical Information System
APM	Agile Project Management
BI	Business Intelligence
CIM	Computation Independent Model
CRM	Customer-Relationship-Management
CWM	Common Warehouse Metamodel
DDI	Data Documentation Initiative
DPI	Distributions to Paid In
DSL	Domain-Specific Language
DSM	Domain-Specific Modeling
DWH	Data Warehouse
ECB	European Central Bank
ERP	Enterprise Resource Planning
ETL	Extract, Transform, Load
ICD	International Statistical Classification of Diseases and Related Health Problems
IDE	Integrated development environment
MDA	Model Driven Architecture
MDSD	Model-Driven Software Development
NAV	Net Asset Value
ODBC	Open Database Connectivity
OLAP	Online Analytical Processing
OLTP	Online transaction processing
PIM	Platform-Independent Model
PSM	Platform-Specific Model
SQL	Structured Query Language
SLE	Software Language Engineering
UBL	Universal Business Language

Figures

References

[Abe02]   Alberto Abelló. *YAM2: a multidimensional conceptual model extending UML*. PhD thesis, YAM2: a multidimensional conceptual model extending UML, 2002.

[AN09]   Alexander Albrecht and Felix Naumann. Metl: Managing and integrating etl processes. In Philippe Rigaux and Pierre Senellart, editors, *VLDB PhD Workshop*. VLDB Endowment, 2009.

[Bai03]   Lynn Bailey.   Health care corner: The costs of poor quality health care.   *Publications of the Institute of Applied Research*, 49, 2003. http://mooreschool.sc.edu/moore/research/Publications/BandE/bande49/49n2/health.html, last accessed on: Friday 24th Feburary, 2012.

[Bal00]   Helmut Balzert. *Lehrbuch der Software-Technik - Software-Entwicklung*. Spektrum-Akademischer Vlg, 2000.

[Ban10]   Carsten Bange. *Analytische Informationssysteme: Business Intelligence-Technologien und -Anwendungen*, chapter Werkzeuge für analytische informationssysteme, pages 132–155. Springer Berlin Heidelberg, 2010.

[BCR94]   Victor R. Basili, Gianluigi Caldiera, and H. Dieter Rombach. The goal question metric approach. In *Encyclopedia of Software Engineering*. Wiley, 1994.

[BF06]   Dan Bulos and Sarah Forsman. Getting started with adapt. Internet, 2006. http://www.symcorp.com/downloads/ADAPT_white_paper.pdf, last accessed on: Friday 24th Feburary, 2012.

[BG09]   Andreas Bauer and Holger Günzel. *Data-Warehouse-Systeme. Architektur, Entwicklung, Anwendung*. Dpunkt Verlag, 2009.

[Biz03]   Christian Bizer. D2r map - a database to rdf mapping language. *WWW Posters*, pages 2–3, 2003.

[Boe88]   B. W. Boehm. A spiral model of software development and enhancement. *Computer*, 21(5):61 –72, may 1988.

[BsCGp04] Jesús Barrasa, Óscar Corcho, and Asunción Gómez-pérez.   R2o, an extensible and semantically based database-to-ontology mapping language. In *in In Proceedings of the 2nd Workshop on Semantic Web and Databases(SWDB2004*, pages 1069–1070. Springer, 2004.

[BTA10]   Stefan Brüggemann, Yvette Teiken, and Hans-Jürgen Appelrath. Indaqu:
            Enabling user-centered definition and exchange of consistency constraints
            for data cleaning. In *6th Workshop on Semantic Web Applications and
            Perspectives (SWAP 2010)*, 9 2010.

[Bul96]   Dan Bulos. Olap database design: A new dimension. *Database Program-
            ming&Design*, Vol. 9(6), 1996.

[Bur08]   Christian Burmeister.   Modellgetriebene bereitstellung von daten-
            integrations-services im analytischen performance management. Diplo-
            marbeit, Carl von Ossietzky the University of Oldenburg, June 2008.

[CBB⁺10]   Paul Clements, Felix Bachmann, Len Bass, David Garlan, James Ivers,
            Reed Little, Paulo Merson, and Robert L. Nord. *Documenting Software
            Architectures: Views and Beyond*. Addison Wesley, 2010.

[CBvD10]   Matt Casters, Roland Bouman, and Jos van Dongen. *Pentaho Kettle Solu-
            tions: Building Open Source ETL Solutions with Pentaho Data Integration*.
            John Wiley & Sons, 2010.

[CCS93]   Edgar F. Codd, Sharon B. Codd, and Clynch T. Salley. Providing olap to
            user-analysts : An it mandate. White paper, E.F. Codd Associates, 1993.

[CG09]   Peter Chamoni and Peter Gluchowski.   *Analytische Informationssys-
            teme. Business Intelligence-Technologien und -Anwendungen: Business
            Intelligence-Technologien Und -Anwendungen*. Springer, Berlin, 2009.

[Che76]   Peter Pin-Shan Chen. The entity-relationship model - toward a unified view
            of data. *ACM Trans. Database Syst.*, 1:9–36, March 1976.

[CJK07]   Steve Cook, Gareth Jones, and Stuart Kent. *Domain Specific Develop-
            ment with Visual Studio DSL Tools (Microsoft .net Development)*. Addison-
            Wesley Longman, Amsterdam, 2007.

[CMPT10]   Jordi Cabot, Jose-Norberto Mazón, Jesús Pardillo, and Juan Trujillo. Spec-
            ifying aggregation functions in multidimensional models with ocl. In Par-
            sons et al. [PSS⁺10], pages 419–432.

[CMR10]   Andrea Carmè, Jose-Norberto Mazón, and Stefano Rizzi. A model-driven
            heuristic approach for detecting multidimensional facts in relational data
            sources. In Torben Bach Pedersen, Mukesh K. Mohania, and A Min Tjoa,
            editors, *DaWak*, volume 6263 of *Lecture Notes in Computer Science*, pages
            13–24. Springer, 2010.

[CW01]   Yingwei Cui and Jennifer Widom. Lineage tracing for general data ware-
            house transformations. In *27th International Conference on Very Large
            Data Bases (VLDB 2001)*, 2001.

[Dat09]   Data Documentation Initiative. Data documentation initiative (ddi) technical specification part i: Overview version 3.1. Internet, 10 2009. last accessed on: Friday 24th Feburary, 2012.

[Dat11]   Data Documentation Initiative. What is ddi? Internet, 05 2011. Webseite about DDI, last accessed on: Friday 24th Feburary, 2012.

[Dav09]   James Davenport. On writing openmath content dictionaries. Technical report, The OpenMath Consortium, 2009. last accessed on: Friday 24th Feburary, 2012.

[DIM11]   DIMDI. Icd-10 internationale klassifikation der krankheiten. Internet, 8 2011. last accessed on: Friday 24th Feburary, 2012.

[EN10]   Ramez Elmasri and Shamkrant Navathe. *Fundamentals of Database Systems*. Prentice Hall International, 2010.

[ES05]   Horst Entorf and Hannes Spengler. Research notes 2005: Die abschreckungswirkung der deutschen strafverfolgung. neue evidenz durch verknüpfung amtlicher statistiken. Technical report, Deutsches Institut für Wirtschaftsforschung, 2005. ISSN 1860-2185.

[FF10]   Klaus-Peter Fähnrich and Bogdan Franczyk, editors. *Informatik 2010: Service Science - Neue Perspektiven für die Informatik, Beiträge der 40. Jahrestagung der Gesellschaft für Informatik e.V. (GI), Band 1, 27.09. - 1.10.2010, Leipzig*, volume 175 of *LNI*. GI, 2010.

[FGLW08]   Jean-Marie Favre, Dragan Gasevic, Ralf Lämmel, and Andreas Winter. Editorial - software language engineering. *IEE Software Engineering*, 2(3):161–164, 2008.

[FH76]   I P Fellegi and D Holt. A systematic approach to automatic edit and imputation. *Journal of the American Statistical Association*, 71(353):17–35, 1976.

[FHTA09]   Stefan Flöring, Tobias Hesselmann, Yvette Teiken, and Hans-Jürgen Appelrath. Kollaborative visuelle analyse multidimensionaler daten auf surface computern (collaborative visual analysis of multidimensional data on surface computers). *Datenbank Spektrum - Zeitschrift für Datenbanktechnologie und Information Retrieval*, 31:17–25, 2009.

[Fri11]   Jeroen Frijters. Ikvm.net home page. Internet, 05 2011. Hompeage of the software product IKVM, http://www.ikvm.net/ ,last accessed on: Friday 24th Feburary, 2012.

[GDCZ10]   Oksana Grabova, Jerome Darmont, Jean-Hugues Chauchat, and Iryna Zolotaryova. Business intelligence for small and middle-sized entreprises. *SIGMOD Rec.*, 39:39–50, December 2010.

[GGD08]   Peter Gluchowski, Roland Gabriel, and Carsten Dittmar. *Management Sup-port Systeme und Business Intelligence. Computergestützte Information-ssysteme für Fach- und Führungskräfte*. Springer Berlin Heidelberg, 2008.

[GHJV94] Erich Gamma, Richard Helm, Ralph E. Johnson, and John Vlissides. *De-sign Patterns. Elements of Reusable Object-Oriented Software*. Addison-Wesley Longman, 1994.

[GKS09]   Peter Gluchowski, Christian Kurze, and Christian Schieder. A modeling tool for multidimensional data using the adapt notation. In *Proceedings of the 42nd Hawaii International Conference on System Sciences (HICSS-42), IEEE, Waikoloa, Big Island, Hawaii, 05.-08. Januar*, 2009.

[GMR98]   Matteo Golfarelli, Dario Maio, and Stefano Rizzi. The dimensional fact model: A conceptual model for data warehouses. *International Journal of Cooperative Information Systems*, 7:215–247, 1998.

[GMT10]   Octavio Glorio, Jose-Norberto Mazón, and Juan Trujillo. A model driven process for spatial data sources and spatial data warehouses reconcilation. In David Taniar, Osvaldo Gervasi, Beniamino Murgante, Eric Pardede, and Bernady O. Apduhan, editors, *ICCSA (1)*, volume 6016 of *Lecture Notes in Computer Science*, pages 461–475. Springer, 2010.

[Gol09]   Matteo Golfarelli. *Data Warehousing Design and Advanced Engineering Applications: Methods for Complex Construction*, chapter From User Re-quirements to Conceptual Design in Data Warehouse Design - a Survey. Information Science Reference, 2009.

[GR08]   Matteo Golfarelli and Stefano Rizzi. Uml-based modeling for what-if analysis. In Il-Yeol Song, Johann Eder, and Tho Manh Nguyen, editors, *DaWaK*, volume 5182 of *Lecture Notes in Computer Science*, pages 1–12. Springer, 2008.

[GR09a]   Matteo Golfarelli and Stefano Rizzi. *Data Warehouse Design: Modern Principles and Methodologies*. Mcgraw-Hill Professional, 2009.

[GR09b]   Matteo Golfarelli and Stefano Rizzi. Expressing olap preferences. In Mari-anne Winslett, editor, *SSDBM*, volume 5566 of *Lecture Notes in Computer Science*, pages 83–91. Springer, 2009.

[Gro09]   Richard C. Gronback. *Eclipse Modeling Project: A Domain-Specific Lan-guage (DSL) Toolkit*. Addison-Wesley Professional, 2009.

[GTTY06] Yuhong Guo, Shiwei Tang, Yunhai Tong, and Dongqing Yang. Triple-driven data modeling methodology in data warehousing: a case study. In *Proceedings of the 9th ACM international workshop on Data warehousing and OLAP*, DOLAP '06, pages 59–66, New York, NY, USA, 2006. ACM.

[GWS07]   Marci Frohock Garcia, Edward Whalen, and Mitchell Schroeter. *Microsoft SQL Server 2005 - Das Handbuch*. Microsoft Press Deutschland, 2007.

[Hin02]   Holger Hinrichs. *Datenqualitätsmanagement in Data Warehouse-Systemen*. PhD thesis, Carl von Ossietzky Universität Oldenburg, 2002.

[HKK⁺10]   Gabriele Husmann, Peter Kaatsch, Alexander Katalinic, Joachim Bertz, Jörg Haberland, Klaus Kraywinkel, and Ute Wolf. Cancer in germany 2005/2006 incidence and trends. Internet, 2010. `http://www.rki.de/cln_160/nn_1219822/EN/Content/Health_ _Reporting/GBEDownloadsB/KID2010,templateId=raw, property=publicationFile.pdf/KID2010.pdf`, last accessed on: Friday 24th Feburary, 2012.

[Hol02]   Ric Holt. TA: The Tuple Attribute Language, 07 2002. `http://plg.uwaterloo.ca/~holt/papers/ta-intro.htm`, last accessed on: Friday 24th Feburary, 2012.

[HPN03]   Dora Hettler, Peter Preuss, and Joachim Niedereichholz. Vergleich ausgewählter ansätze zur semantischen modellierung von data-warehouse-systemen. *HMD - Praxis Wirtschaftsinform.*, 231, 2003.

[IBM11]   IBM. Spss software und lösungen für predictive analytics. Internet, 2011. Website of the software product SPSS, `http://www-01.ibm. com/software/de/analytics/spss/` last accessed on: Friday 24th Feburary, 2012.

[Inm96]   William H. Inmon. *Building the Data Warehouse*. Wiley & Sons, 1996.

[Int01]   International Union Against Cancer (UICC). *TNM Classification of Malignant Tumours, 6th edition*. John Wiley & Sons, Hoboken, New Jersey, 2001.

[JABK08]   Frédéric Jouault, Freddy Allilaire, Jean Bézivin, and Ivan Kurtev. Atl: A model transformation tool. *Science of Computer Programming*, 72(1-2):31 – 39, 2008. Special Issue on Second issue of experimental software and toolkits (EST).

[JD09]   Thomas Jörg and Stefan Deßloch. Formalizing etl jobs for incremental loading of data warehouses. In Johann Christoph Freytag, Thomas Ruf, Wolfgang Lehner, and Gottfried Vossen, editors, *BTW*, volume 144 of *LNI*, pages 327–346. GI, 2009.

[Jed11]   Jedox AG. Palo for excel. Internet, 2011. Website for Palo for Excel, `http://www.palo.net/de/`, last accessed on: Friday 24th Feburary, 2012.

[JVVL10]   Matthias Jarke, Panos Vassiliadis, Panos Vassiliadis, and Maurizio Lenz-erini. *Fundamentals of Data Warehouses*. Springer Berlin Heidelberg, 2010.

[JW00]   Reinhard Jung and Robert Winter, editors. *Data Warehousing Strategie*. Springer, Heidelberg, 2000.

[KBM10]   Hans-Georg Kemper, Henning Baars, and Walid Mehanna. *Business Intelligence - Grundlagen und praktische Anwendungen: Eine Einführung in die IT-basierte Managementunterstützung*. Vieweg+Teubner, 2010.

[KG10a]   Christian Kurze and Peter Gluchowski. Computer-aided warehouse engineering (cawe): Leveraging mda and adm for the development of data warehouses. In *Proceedings of the Sixeenth Americas Conference on Information Systems, Lima, Peru, August 12-15*, 2010.

[KG10b]   Christian Kurze and Peter Gluchowski. Model driven architecture für data warehouses: Computer aided warehouse engineering - cawe. In *Tagungsband der Multikonferenz Wirtschaftsinformatik, 23.-25.02.2010, Göttingen*, pages 1077–1088, 2010.

[Koc01]   Sascha Koch. Anwendbarkeit statistischer verfahren auf multidimensionalen daten in der explorativen datenanalyse. Diplomarbeit, university of oldenburg, 2001.

[KP09]   Steven Kelly and Risto Pohjonen. Worst practices for domain-specific modeling. *IEEE Software*, 26(4):22–29, 2009.

[KR02]   Ralph Kimball and Margy Ross. *The Data Warehouse Toolkit: The Complete Guide to Dimensional Modeling*. John Wiley & Sons, 2002.

[KT08a]   Steven Kelly and Juha-Pekka Tolvanen. *Domain-Specific Modeling: Enabling Full Code Generation*. John Wiley & Sons, 2008.

[KT08b]   Sascha Koch and Yvette Teiken. Semi-automatische überwachung von zielsystemen. In *Multikonferenz Wirtschaftsinformatik*, 2008.

[Kur11]   Christian Kurze. *Computer Aided Warehouse Engineering (CAWE): Anwendung modellgetriebener Entwicklungsparadigmen auf Data-Warehouse-Systeme*. PhD thesis, Technische Universität Chemnitz, 2011.

[Lan05]   Landesinstitut für den Öffentlichen Gesundheitsdienst des Landes NRW. Indikatorensatz für die gesundheitsberichterstattung in nordrhein-westfalen - band 3: Themenfelder 9 - 11. Internet, 2005. http://www.loegd.nrw.de/_media/pdf/gesundheitberichtedaten/indikatoren/indikatoren_nrw_bd_3.pdf, last accessed on: Friday 24th Feburary, 2012.

[Lan08a]   Landesinstitut für Gesundheit und Arbeit des Landes Nordrhein-Westfalen (LIGA.NRW). Data delivery and description for the gesundheit nrw project provided by liga for offis. 2008.

[Lan08b]   Landesinstitut für Gesundheit und Arbeit des Landes Nordrhein-Westfalen (LIGA.NRW). Meldepflichtige infektionskrankheiten in nordrhein-westfalen - jahresbericht 2007, 2008.

[Lan11]   Landeszentrum Gesundheit Nordrhein-Westfalen. Infektionsjahresbericht 2010. Internet, 10 2011. http://www.lzg.gc.nrw.de/themen/ gesundheit_berichte_daten/infektionsberichte/ jahresbericht2010/index.html, last accessed on: Friday 24th Feburary, 2012.

[LBMS02]   Beate List, Robert M. Bruckner, Karl Machaczek, and Josef Schiefer. A comparison of data warehouse development methodologies case study of the process warehouse. In *DEXA '02: Proceedings of the 13th International Conference on Database and Expert Systems Applications*, pages 203–215, London, UK, 2002. Springer-Verlag.

[Leh03]   Wolfgang Lehner. *Datenbanktechnologie für Data-Warehouse-Systeme. Konzepte und Methoden.* Dpunkt Verlag, 2003.

[Lin11]   Linking Open Data Project . Linked data - connect distributed data across the web. Internet, 2011. Webseite of the Linking Open Data Project, http://linkeddata.org/, last accessed on: Friday 24th Feburary, 2012.

[LMT06]   Sergio Luján-Mora and Juan Trujillo. Physical modeling of data warehouses using uml component and deployment diagrams: Design and implementation issues. *J. Database Manag.*, 17(2):12–42, 2006.

[LMTS02a]   Sergio Luján-Mora, Juan Trujillo, and Il-Yeol Song. Extending the uml for multidimensional modeling. In Jean-Marc Jézéquel, Heinrich Hußmann, and Stephen Cook, editors, *UML*, volume 2460 of *Lecture Notes in Computer Science*, pages 290–304. Springer, 2002.

[LMTS02b]   Sergio Luján-Mora, Juan Trujillo, and Il-Yeol Song. Multidimensional modeling with uml package diagrams. In Stefano Spaccapietra, Salvatore T. March, and Yahiko Kambayashi, editors, *ER*, volume 2503 of *Lecture Notes in Computer Science*, pages 199–213. Springer, 2002.

[LMVT04]   Sergio Luján-Mora, Panos Vassiliadis, and Juan Trujillo. Data mapping diagrams for data warehouse design with uml. In Paolo Atzeni, Wesley W. Chu, Hongjun Lu, Shuigeng Zhou, and Tok Wang Ling, editors, *ER*, volume 3288 of *Lecture Notes in Computer Science*, pages 191–204. Springer, 2004.

[LN05]   Ulf Leser and Felix Naumann. *Informationsintegration: Architekturen und Methoden zur Integration verteilter und heterogener Datenquellen.* Dpunkt Verlag, 2005.

[Mas11]   Kai Maschke. Saint metais: Semi-automatische integration von daten-quellen über metamodelle in analytische informationssysteme. Diplomar-beit, Carl von Ossietzky the University of Oldenburg, December 2011.

[Mic11a]   Microsoft Corporation. Code metrics values in visual studio 2010. Internet, 2011. Website for the code metrics computation for Vi-sual Studio, http://msdn.microsoft.com/en-us/library/bb385914.aspx, last accessed on: Friday 24th Feburary, 2012.

[Mic11b]   Microsoft Corporation. Excel 2010, 2011. Website for the Soft-ware product excel, http://office.microsoft.com/en-us/excel/, last accessed on: Friday 24th Feburary, 2012.

[Mic11c]   Microsoft Corporation. Introducing business intelligence development studio. Internet, 2011. Website of the software priduct Business Intelligence Development Studio, http://msdn.microsoft.com/en-us/library/ms173767.aspx, last accessed on: Friday 24th Feburary, 2012.

[Mic11d]   Microsoft Corporation. Microsoft sql server. Internet, 2011. Website for the the database Server MS SQL Server, http://www.microsoft.com/germany/sql/2008/default.mspx, last accessed on: Friday 24th Feburary, 2012.

[Mic11e]   Microsoft Corporation. Sql server integration services. Internet, 6 2011. Webseite for the software Product Integration Services, http://msdn.microsoft.com/en-us/library/ms141026.aspx, last accessed on: Friday 24th Feburary, 2012.

[Mic12a]   Microsoft Corporation. C# coding conventions (c# programming guide). Internet, 2012. http://msdn.microsoft.com/en-us/library/ff926074.aspx, last accessed on: Friday 24th Feburary, 2012.

[Mic12b]   Microsoft Corporation. Sql server analysis services. In-ternet, 2012. Webside for the Microsoft Analysis Services, http://msdn.microsoft.com/de-de/library/ms175609%28v=sql.90%29.aspx?ppud=4, , last accessed on: Friday 24th Feburary, 2012.

[ML03]   Murali Mani and Dongwon Lee. Xml to relational conversion using theory of regular tree grammars. In *Proceedings of the VLDB 2002 Workshop*

EEXTT and CAiSE 2002 Workshop DTWeb on Efficiency and Effectiveness of XML Tools and Techniques and Data Integration over the Web-Revised Papers, pages 81–103, London, UK, 2003. Springer-Verlag.

[MNSV09]   Mukesh K. Mohania, Ullas Nambiar, Michael Schrefl, and Millist W. Vincent. Active and real-time data warehousing. In Ling Liu and M. Tamer Özsu, editors, *Encyclopedia of Database Systems*, pages 21–26. Springer US, 2009.

[MSH03]   Florian Melchert, Alexander Schwinn, and Clemens Herrmann. Das common warehouse metamodel - ein referenzmodell für data-warehouse-metadaten. In Klaus R. Dittrich, Wolfgang König, Andreas Oberweis, Kai Rannenberg, and Wolfgang Wahlster, editors, *GI Jahrestagung (1)*, volume 34 of *LNI*, pages 254–258. GI, 2003.

[MT02]   Enrique Medina and Juan Trujillo. A standard for representing multidimensional properties: The common warehouse metamodel (cwm). In Yannis Manolopoulos and Pavol Návrat, editors, *ADBIS*, volume 2435 of *Lecture Notes in Computer Science*, pages 232–247. Springer, 2002.

[MT08]   Jose-Norberto Mazón and Juan Trujillo. An mda approach for the development of data warehouses. *Decision Support Systems*, 45(1):41–58, 2008.

[MTA09]   Matthias Mertens, Yvette Teiken, and Hans-Jürgen Appelrath. Semantische anreicherung von strukturierten daten und prozessen in analytischen informationssystemen am beispiel von mustang. In Henning Baars and Bodo Rieger, editors, *Forschungskolloquium Business Intelligence 2009 der GI Fachgruppe 5.8 - Perspektiven der betrieblichen Management-und Entscheidungsunterstützung*, 2009.

[MTSP05]   Jose-Norberto Mazon, Juan Trujillo, Manuel Serrano, and Mario Piattini. Applying mda to the development of data warehouses. In *DOLAP '05: Proceedings of the 8th ACM international workshop on Data warehousing and OLAP*, pages 57–66, New York, NY, USA, 2005. ACM.

[OAS10]   OASIS. Universal business language v2.1 public review draft 01. Internet, 09 2010. http://docs.oasis-open.org/ubl/prd1-UBL-2.1/UBL-2.1.html, last accessed on: Friday 24th Feburary, 2012.

[Obj00]   Object Management Group. Omg unified modeling language specification version 1.3. Internet, March 2000. http://www.omg.org/spec/UML/1.3/PDF/index.htm, last accessed on: Friday 24th Feburary, 2012.

[Obj03]   Object Management Group. Common warehouse metamodel (cwm) specification. Internet, Februar 2003. http://www.omg.org/technology/cwm/, last accessed on: Friday 24th Feburary, 2012.

[Obj04]   Object Management Group. Meta object facility(mof) specification version 1.4. Internet, April 2004. `http://www.omg.org/spec/MOF/1.4/PDF/`, last accessed on: Friday 24th Feburary, 2012.

[Obj06]   Object Management Group. Meta object facility (mof) core specification (version 2.0). Internet, January 2006. `http://www.omg.org/spec/MOF/2.0/PDF/`, last accessed on: Friday 24th Feburary, 2012.

[Obj11a]   Object Management Group. Meta object facility (mof) 2.0 query/view/transformation specification. Internet, January 2011. `http://www.omg.org/spec/MOF/2.0/`, last accessed on: Friday 24th Feburary, 2012.

[Obj11b]   Object Management Group. Object constraint language version 2.3.1. Internet, 08 2011. `http://www.omg.org/spec/OCL/2.3.1/PDF`, last accessed on: Friday 24th Feburary, 2012.

[Obj11c]   Object Management Group. Omg model driven architecture. Internet, May 2011. OMG entry page for MDA, `http://www.omg.org/mda/`, last accessed on: Friday 24th Feburary, 2012.

[OFF11]   OFFIS. *Benutzerdokumentation CARESS Version 8.0*. Escherweg 2, 8.0 edition, 2011 11.

[OW07]   Bernd Oestereich and Christian Weiss. *APM - Agiles Projektmanagement: Erfolgreiches Timeboxing für IT-Projekte*. dpunkt.verlag, 2007.

[Pen05]   Nigel Pendse. The olap report: What is olap? Research resource, Business Application Research Center, 2005. `http://www.olapreport.com/fasmi.htm`, last accessed on: Friday 24th Feburary, 2012.

[Pen11]   Pentaho Corporation. Pentaho analysis services (mondrian). Internet, 2011. Website of the software product Mondrain, `http://mondrian.pentaho.com/`, last accessed on: Friday 24th Feburary, 2012.

[Pio09]   Torsten Piotraschke. Konzeption und entwicklung eines systems zur regelbasierten modellierung von konsistenzbedingungen zur datenqualitätssicherung im epidemiologischen krebsregister niedersachsen. Bachelorarbeit, Jade Hochschule Wilhelmshafen Oldenburg Elsfleth, 2009.

[PMT08]   Jesús Pardillo, Jose-Norberto Mazón, and Juan Trujillo. Bridging the semantic gap in olap models: platform-independent queries. In *DOLAP '08: Proceeding of the ACM 11th international workshop on Data warehousing and OLAP*, pages 89–96, New York, NY, USA, 2008. ACM.

[PSS+10]   Jeffrey Parsons, Motoshi Saeki, Peretz Shoval, Carson C. Woo, and Yair Wand, editors. *Conceptual Modeling - ER 2010, 29th International Conference on Conceptual Modeling, Vancouver, BC, Canada, November 1-4,*

2010. Proceedings, volume 6412 of *Lecture Notes in Computer Science*. Springer, 2010.

[PT08]   Jesús Pardillo and Juan Trujillo. Integrated model-driven development of goal-oriented data warehouses and data marts. In Qing Li, Stefano Spaccapietra, Eric S. K. Yu, and Antoni Olivé, editors, *ER*, volume 5231 of *Lecture Notes in Computer Science*, pages 426–439. Springer, 2008.

[RB01]   Erhard Rahm and Philip A. Bernstein. A survey of approaches to automatic schema matching. *The VLDB Journal*, 10:334–350, December 2001.

[Reg10]   Registerstelle des EKN. Krebs in niedersachsen 2006/2007, May 2010.

[RMK04]   Martin Rohde, Jürgen Meister, and Sascha Koch. *Benutzerdokumentation CARESS Version 6.0*. OFFIS, 09 2004.

[Rob04]   Robert Koch-Institut. The robert koch institute - tasks and aims of the robert koch institute. Internet, 11 2004. `http://www.rki.de/cln_178/nn_216264/EN/Content/Institute/General/general__node__en.html?__nnn=true`, last accessed on: Friday 24th Feburary, 2012.

[Roy70]   Walker W. Royce. Managing the development of large software systems: concepts and techniques. *Proc. IEEE WESTCON, Los Angeles*, pages 1–9, August 1970. Reprinted in *Proceedings* of the Ninth International Conference on Software Engineering, March 1987, pp. 328–338.

[RPr11]   The r project for statistical computing. Internet, 2011. Website for the statics software R, `http://www.r-project.org/index.html`, last accessed on: Friday 24th Feburary, 2012.

[SA10]   Ralph Stuber and Hans-Jürgen Appelrath. Integrationsnachgelagertes datenmanagement am beispiel des gesundheitswesens. In Fähnrich and Franczyk [FF10], pages 247–252.

[SAP11]   SAP AG. Sap crystal reports. Internet, 2011. Website for the software product Crystal Reports, `http://crystalreports.com/`, last accessed on: Friday 24th Feburary, 2012.

[SBHD99]   Carsten Sapia, Markus Blaschka, Gabriele Höfling, and Barbara Dinter. Extending the e/r model for the multidimensional paradigm. In Yahiko Kambayashi, Dik-Lun Lee, Ee-peng Lim, Mukesh Mohania, and Yoshifumi Masunaga, editors, *Advances in Database Technologies*, volume 1552 of *Lecture Notes in Computer Science*, pages 1947–1947. Springer Berlin / Heidelberg, 1999. 10.1007/978-3-540-49121-7-9.

[Sch04]   Evan Schuman. At wal-mart, worlds largest retail data warehouse gets even
            larger. Internet, 10 2004. http://tiny.cc/g72rc, last accessed on:
            Friday 24th Feburary, 2012.

[SHW⁺06]   George Spofford, Sivakumar Harinath, Christopher Webb, Dylan Hai
            Huang, and Francesco Civardi. *MDX Solutions: With Microsoft SQL
            Server Analysis Services 2005 and Hyperion Essbase*. John Wiley & Sons,
            2006.

[Sim04]   Alkis Simitsis. *Modeling and Optimization of Extraction-Transformation-
            Loading (ETL) Processes in Data Warehouse Environments*. PhD thesis,
            National Technical Universuty of Athens, 2004.

[Sim05]   Alkis Simitsis. Mapping conceptual to logical models for etl processes. In
            Il-Yeol Song and Juan Trujillo, editors, *DOLAP*, pages 67–76. ACM, 2005.

[Som10]   Ian Sommerville. *Software Engineering*. Addison-Wesley Longman, 2010.

[Spe06]   Robert Spence. *Information Visualization: Design for Interaction*. Prentice
            Hall, 2006.

[Sta08]   Werner Stahel.   Lineare regression.   Internet, 5 2008.   http:
            //stat.ethz.ch/~stahel/courses/regression/
            reg1-script.pdf, last accessed on: Friday 24th Feburary, 2012.

[Ste10]   Stern.de. Kritik an krankenhäusern: 40 prozent aller rechnungen sind
            falsch. Internet, 12 2010. http://www.stern.de/gesundheit/
            kritik-an-krankenhaeusern-40-prozent-aller-re\
            chnungen-sind-falsch-1638177.html,   last   accessed   on:
            Friday 24th Feburary, 2012.

[SVE07]   Thomas Stahl, Markus Völter, and Sven Efftinge. *Modellgetriebene Soft-
            wareentwicklung. Techniken, Engineering, Management*. Dpunkt Verlag,
            2007.

[TBA10]   Yvette Teiken, Stefan Brüggemann, and Hans-Jürgen Appelrath. Inter-
            changeable consistency constraints for public health care systems. In
            Sung Y. Shin, Sascha Ossowski, Michael Schumacher, Mathew J. Palakal,
            and Chih-Cheng Hung, editors, *SAC*, pages 1411–1416. ACM, 2010.

[Tei09]   Yvette Teiken. Modellgetriebene semi-automatische bereitstellung von an-
            alytischen informationssystemen. In Matthias Virgin, André Peters, and
            Dagmar Köhn, editors, *Grundlagen von Datenbanken*, volume CS-02-09
            of *Preprints aus dem Institut für Informatik*, pages 99–103. Universität Ro-
            stock, 2009.

[Tei10]   Yvette Teiken. Using sle for creation of data warehouses. In *Proc. of 1st Doctoral Symposium at SLE*, pages 43–47, Eindhoven, The Netherlands, 2010.

[TF08]   Yvette Teiken and Stefan Flöring. A common meta-model for data analysis based on dsm. In Jeff Gray, Jonathan Sprinkle, Juha-Pekka Tolvanen, and Matti Rossi, editors, *8th DSM workshop at OOPSLA 2008 (DSM'08)*, pages 35–38. UAB Printing Solutions, Birmingham, Alabama, 9 2008.

[The10]   The Eclipse Foundation. Xpand. Internet, December 2010. Webseite of the eclipse project xpand http://wiki.eclipse.org/Xpand, last accessed on: Friday 24th Feburary, 2012.

[The11]   The Eclipse Foundation. xtext overview. Internet, 2011. Entry page of the ducumentation of the software project, xtext, http://www.eclipse.org/Xtext/documentation/2_0_0/000-introduction.php, last accessed on: Friday 24th Feburary, 2012.

[TJ98]   Andreas Totok and Ramon Jaworski. Modellierung von multidimensionalen datenstrukturen mit adapt - ein fallbeispiel, 1998. ISBN: 3-930166-92-5.

[TLM03]   Juan Trujillo and Sergio Luján-Mora. A uml based approach for modeling etl processes in data warehouses. In Il-Yeol Song, Stephen W. Liddle, Tok Wang Ling, and Peter Scheuermann, editors, *ER*, volume 2813 of *Lecture Notes in Computer Science*, pages 307–320. Springer, 2003.

[TRA10]   Yvette Teiken, Martin Rohde, and Hans-Jürgen Appelrath. Model-driven ad hoc data integration in the context of a population-based cancer registry. In *ICSOFT 2010 International Conference on Software and Data Technologies*, 8 2010.

[TRK+10]   Wilfried Thoben, Martin Rohde, Sascha Koch, Hans-Jürgen Appelrath, and Ralph Stuber. Konzepte und technologien für die strategische planung im krankenhausmarkt. *In: Krankenhaus-IT*, 5:26–27, 2010.

[TRM10]   Yvette Teiken, Martin Rohde, and Matthias Mertens. Mustang: Realisierung eines analytischen informationssystems im kontext der gesundheitsberichterstattung. In Fähnrich and Franczyk [FF10], pages 253–258.

[Ulr07]   William Ulrich. Architecture-driven modernization: Transforming the enterprise. Technical report, OMG, 2007.

[Völ11]   Markus Völter. MD*/DSL best practices (version 2.0), April 2011.

[VS06]   Markus Völter and Thomas Stahl. *Model-Driven Software Development.*
            Wiley & Sons, 2006.

[VSG⁺05]   Panos Vassiliadis, Alkis Simitsis, Panos Georgantas, Manolis Terrovitis,
            and Spiros Skiadopoulos. A generic and customizable framework for the
            design of etl scenarios. *Inf. Syst.*, 30:492–525, November 2005.

[VSS02]   Panos Vassiliadis, Alkis Simitsis, and Spiros Skiadopoulos. Conceptual
            modeling for etl processes. In *Proceedings of the 5th ACM international
            workshop on Data Warehousing and OLAP*, DOLAP '02, pages 14–21,
            New York, NY, USA, 2002. ACM.

[WA05]   H.J. Watson and T. Ariyachandra. Data warehouse architectures: Factors
            in the selection decision and the success of the architectures. Technical
            report, Terry College of Business, University of Georgia, July 2005.

[Whi10]   Jim Whitehead. Welcome to webdav resources. Internet, 04 2010. Start-
            page for the WebDAV protocol,http://www.webdav.org/, last ac-
            cessed on: Friday 24th Feburary, 2012.

[Wie00]   Frank Wietek.   *Intelligente Analyse multidimensionaler Daten in
            einer visuellen Programmierumgebung und deren Anwendung in der
            Krebsepidemiologie.* Dissertation, Carl von Ossietzky Universität Old-
            enburg,   2000.   http://docserver.bis.uni-oldenburg.
            de/publikationen/dissertation/2000/wieint00/
            wieint00.html, last accessed on: Friday 24th Feburary, 2012.

[Wik07]   Wikimedia Foundation. Welcome to mediawiki.org. Internet, January
            2007,. website of the MediaWiki software, http://www.mediawiki.
            org/wiki/MediaWiki, last accessed on: Friday 24th Feburary, 2012.

[WSCD10]   Kevin Wilkinson, Alkis Simitsis, Malú Castellanos, and Umeshwar Dayal.
            Leveraging business process models for etl design.   In Parsons et al.
            [PSS⁺10], pages 15–30.

[Zeh03]   Thomas Zeh. Data warehousing als organisationskonzept des datenman-
            agements: Eine kritische betrachtung der data-warehouse-definition von
            inmon. *Inform., Forsch. Entwickl.*, 18(1):32–38, 2003.

[Zen08]   Zentralstelle für die Überwachung von Infektionskrankheiten NRW.
            Meldepflichtige infektionskrankheiten in nordrhein-westfalen - jahres-
            bericht 2007, 2008.

[ZW05]   Klaus Zeppenfeld and Regine Wolters. *Generative Software-Entwicklung
            mit der MDA.* Spektrum Akademischer Verlag, 2005.

Index